The Political System

AN INQUIRY INTO THE STATE OF POLITICAL SCIENCE

The Political System

AN INQUIRY INTO THE STATE OF POLITICAL SCIENCE
SECOND EDITION

David Easton

THE UNIVERSITY OF CHICAGO

Alfred A. Knopf **NEW YORK**

This is a BORZOI BOOK
Published by ALFRED A. KNOPF, INC.

Copyright 1953, © 1971 by ALFRED A. KNOPF, INC. *All
rights reserved under International and Pan-American Copy-
right Conventions. Published in the United States by Alfred
A. Knopf, Inc., New York, and simultaneously in Canada by
Random House of Canada Limited, Toronto. Distributed by
Random House, Inc., New York.*
ISBN: 0–394–31536–7

Library of Congress Catalog Card Number: 78–137991

Manufactured in the United States.
Published January 16, 1953. Reprinted ten times.

Second Edition

9 8 7 6 5 4 3 2 1

To MERVIN

whose roots in the facts of social life
sustain a trust of theories

No one can deny that the idea is fascinating—the idea of subduing the phenomena of politics to the laws of causation, of penetrating to the mystery of its transformations, of symbolizing the trajectory of its future; in a word, of grasping destiny by the forelock and bringing it prostrate to earth. The very idea is itself worthy of the immortal gods. . . . If nothing ever comes of it, its very existence will fertilize thought and enrich imagination.

—CHARLES A. BEARD

PREFACE TO SECOND EDITION

IT IS almost two decades since *The Political System* was conceived. Before its publication in 1953, the concept system was only accidentally applied to those aspects of society on which political science focused its attention. Since that time this concept has grown in popularity. By 1955 I had formulated the major outlines of my ideas on an empirically oriented theoretical approach to the analysis of political life, subsequently published in my article "An Approach to the Analysis of Political Systems," 9 *World Politics* (1957), 383–400. The opportunities that this conceptualization seemed to provide for the generation of theory helped to encourage the reception of a systems orientation in the discipline.

By the 1970s, positive theory has carved a firm niche for itself in political science, and in the area of this kind of theory, we have moved from rags to modest riches in no less than a single generation. The continued elaboration of positive theory has now gained it a life and legitimacy of its own. It hardly needs to be said that when I first began to grope toward an interpretation of what was wanting in the discipline in 1950, only on the wildest flights of imagination could I have fantasied that so rapid and varied a growth could have occurred in less than twenty years.

In retrospect we can see that *The Political System* was a response after World War II to fundamental changes that were taking place in political science, but that at the time were only faintly recognizable for what they were. The first sounds of the behavioral battle had been heard, but neither the nature of the conflict, nor its outcome, were as yet clear. At this very early and ambiguous stage in the behavioral revolution, *The Political System* strove for an interpretation of what was happening and offered suggestions that hopefully made some small contribution to hastening the transformation.

The Political System contributed to the changes that were even then obscurely under way by arguing for the need to improve the reliability of political knowledge and understanding. Reliability, as I proposed in *The Political System,* must rest not on the development of a new technology of research alone, but on the self-conscious effort to elevate one component of traditional political theory, the empirical part, to a position of prime importance. Hence, as stated in the Preface to First Edition, the ostensible purpose of the book was to help "in some small way to win back for theory its proper and necessary place" in political science. As it turned out in the succeeding years, this plea did more than encourage the development of empirically oriented (causal) theory. It joined with a new research technology in facilitating the reception of a new phase in American political science, one that is now familiarly known as behavioralism.

The end of World War II is a convenient dating point for identifying when the behavioral revolution got under way in earnest. In the quarter of a century since then political science has undergone profound changes. Behavioralism has been accompanied by an increasingly complex technology; it has also flowered into an unexpected variety of empirically oriented theories. If articles in the *American Political Science Review* indicate anything about transformations in the perspectives and aspirations of the discipline, they reveal that political science of the 1940s is scarcely recognizable in the publications of the 1970s.

The discipline has not been united in its acceptance of behavioral innovations, whether technical or theoretical. Dissatisfaction has always been present, particularly among those who would reject the possibility of ever developing a science of society and politics. In the 1960s, however, new and louder rumblings of discontent began to be heard. The voices this time did not come only from those who would turn the clock back to traditional intuition and non-methodology. They were now joined by others who saw deficiencies in behavioralism, but who sought, by building upon the existing behavioral foundations, to provide a more secure and useful footing for political research.

At the beginning of the 1970s the nature of the changes that these new challenges to behavioralism will encourage are, as yet, only dimly discernible. The outcome of this new movement for reform of our discipline is at this time certainly not predictable. Even so, its potential seems to me to be undeniable for the continuing evolution of political science as a discipline that must, like all sciences, prove its ultimate utility for society. These new criticisms of the aims, ambitions, and assumptions of the discipline have indeed appeared to be so central for the continued growth of the discipline that I took advantage of my presidential address to the Annual Meeting of the American Political Science Association in New York, September 1969, to seek to identify and assess their major import. My address, entitled "The New Revolution in Political Science," has been included in this new edition, after the last chapter.

Like *The Political System* itself, this address is clearly a response to events and incipient changes in the discipline and in society, this time in the late 1960s. The theme of this added piece is that times have indeed changed and with them our image of the tasks of political science and political scientists, that is, of the discipline and the profession. It has not seemed to me premature, therefore, to focus attention on the transformation now occurring, in order to try to understand its assumptions and perspectives. Nor has it seemed inappropriate to give it a distinctive name, the *post-behavioral revo-*

lution, so that we may identify it the more easily and encourage greater self-consciousness in its own continuing evolution.

Some may object to characterizing this new movement as a revolution and argue that if anything, it is only a shift in emphasis. Whether it in fact penetrates far more deeply than a change in emphasis must be left to history to decide. It does seem to be encouraging profound changes in the character of the discipline, and this is all that I would imply in labeling it a revolution. But to avoid arguments about degree, it would be equally acceptable to speak of the *post-behavioral reformation.* The only important point for us to recognize is that as we move into the 1970s new and powerful winds of change are sweeping through our discipline.

If behavioralism once denoted intense dissatisfaction with traditional research, post-behavioralism is itself a sign of mounting discontent with important aspects of the behavioral revolution. Behavioralism sought to improve the reliability of political explanation and understanding. To do so it turned to new methods for the collection, collation, and analysis of data and to the elaboration of concepts and theoretical frameworks for the identification of significant areas of research. Without denying the crucial importance of these concerns, many post-behavioralists are turning from the problematics of method to unsettling questions about the subject matter of research and from the quest for explanation to doubts about the uses of political knowledge. Priorities for research are being reassessed without behavioral objectives necessarily being abandoned.

If my presidential address correctly perceives the existence and nature of a shift under way in our discipline during the 1970s, it is clear that *The Political System* and this address identify two turning points or watersheds in political science within the last quarter of a century. But just as *The Political System* went beyond the mere effort to describe what was beginning to change within the discipline and sought to prescribe for the tasks of the day, so in my address I seek to do more than merely identify the beginning of new changes. In it I propose courses of action that seem mandatory if we are to begin to measure up to the demands now being thrust upon all the social sciences by a world in a state of continuing crisis the outcome of which is in grave doubt.

It would appear to be useful to have in a single book one person's efforts to mark out an early course for two succeeding major phases of political science in the twentieth century. The juxtaposition of these two efforts should serve to highlight the similarities and differences between the two transformations that political science appears to be experiencing within the short span of a generation. At the same time, the fact that the original book and the new essay each marks a different stage offers dramatic proof that, like all science, our discipline has a built in capacity for change even in the face of those vested interests that institutions inevitably spawn over the years. Although those of us who have struggled to consummate the behavioral revolution have hailed it as perhaps the most significant transformation in the whole history of political science, it did not herald the millennium. It has now become evident that behavioralism has been but one stage, although a profound and vital one, in the continuing evolution of our discipline.

Finally, the inclusion of my presidential address offers me an opportunity to undertake what I would like to have included in the address itself. Lack of space and time made it impossible for me to attempt to delineate the continuities and differences between my thinking in the 1950s and my point of view today. To some, a casual reading of my address might leave the impression that I have drifted away from one or another of the basic assumptions and convictions which informed *The Political System*. This new edition has permitted me to write an entirely new essay, as item B in the Epilogue, in which I face up to these possibilities. I have satisfied myself, and hopefully will be able to do the same for the reader, that although for the most part my assessments and prescriptions for the 1970s are certainly different from what they were for the 1950s, they are also an extension of basic points of view already expressed and elaborated in *The Political System* itself.

PREFACE TO FIRST EDITION

THIS study deals with the condition of the science of politics as it is known in the United States today and with the relation to it of general political theory, both moral and causal. In earlier centuries a student of political systems would have been hard put to distinguish his theoretical inquiries from his general political research. Today in the United States, however, it has become increasingly difficult to appreciate why political theory should continue to be included as a central part of political science. Theory has become increasingly remote from the mainstream of political research. This study will have served a useful purpose if it helps in some small way to win back for theory its proper and necessary place.

In the preparation of this work I owe a particular debt to two colleagues: to Professor Herman Finer for his insistence that my preliminary re-examination of theory might be of interest to a broader audience and for his kindness in subjecting large sections of the study to his sensitive political insights; and to Professor Leonard D. White, from whose tolerant wisdom and unfailing encouragement my manuscript gained measurably both in form and content. Others, too, were generous of their time, effort, and advice: Professors C. Herman Pritchett and Edward C. Banfield read large portions of the manuscript; Chapters 9 and 10 profited from the friendly criticism and challenging scholarship of Professor Leo Strauss; Chapter 11 underwent the rigorous scrutiny of Professor Julius Margolis, and reflects in some slight measure, I hope, my numerous discussions on its general theme with Professors Theodore Morgan and Kenneth J. Arrow; and the manuscript had the good fortune of coming under the discerning and judicious editorship of Professor V. O. Key, Jr. This study has also been shaped in many subtle ways through the efforts of my wife who contributed to its substance, helped to clarify its structure and meaning, and edited successive versions. Needless to say, aside from my wife, I dare not incriminate any others in the views set forth.

Parts of this book are borrowed and adapted without benefit of quotation from my previously published articles entitled: "Harold Lasswell: Policy Scientist for a Democratic Society" and "The Decline of Modern Political Theory." These essays appeared in the *Journal of Politics* for the years 1950 and 1951 respectively. Chapters 6, 7, and 8 have been published in abbreviated form in 4 *International Social Science Bulletin* (1952), 107–23. I am grateful to the Social Science Research Committee of the Division of the Social Sciences at the University of Chicago for the funds it contributed to help defray clerical expenses incurred in preparation of the manuscript. And for helping with many of the chores involved in preparing a manuscript for publication I wish to thank also Mrs. John Greene, Dr. T. Tsou, and Messrs. R. Scigliano and E. Rizzo.

D.E.

Contents

The Political System

AN INQUIRY INTO THE STATE OF POLITICAL SCIENCE

Chapter 1

Mood and Method

My theory has always been, that if we are to
dream, the flatteries of hope are as cheap,
and pleasanter than the gloom of despair.

Thomas Jefferson

FROM the days of Aristotle, political science has been
known as the master science. Although political scientists today
might be accused of being overambitious or imperialistic if they
were thus to cast their net so broadly, their subject matter is
nevertheless central to the solution of our present social crisis. For
the moment, therefore, they might well set modesty aside and confess to a belief in the transcendent value of their research, in
that of all the social sciences, for the destinies of man. Yet, in the
light of what society demands from them and of what is in fact
possible for political science, they would be compelled in equal
honesty to set all pride aside and confess that in its achievement
in research American political science has grave difficulty in
measuring up to the tasks imposed upon it.

Many cogent reasons could be offered for the disappointing results of a discipline already twenty-five hundred years old. It
is the burden of this study that among these reasons and at the

3

forefront we must place the constant reluctance in American political science to adopt and teach seriously the standards of valid thinking, observation, and description which today we are prone to associate with something vaguely called scientific method. Acceptance and introduction into ongoing research of the fundamental postulates and assumptions of this method would reveal the following: A major source of the shortcomings in political science lies in the failure to clarify the true relationship between facts and political theory and the vital role of theory in this partnership.

All mature scientific knowledge is theoretical. Obviously this does not mean that facts are immaterial. At the present highly empirical stage in the development of the social sciences, there is little need to insist that scientific knowledge must be well-grounded in facts. What does need emphasis, however, is that in and of themselves facts do not enable us to explain or understand an event. Facts must be ordered in some way so that we can see their connections. The higher the level of generality in ordering such facts and clarifying their relations, the broader will be the range of explanation and understanding. A set of generalizations that orders all the kinds of facts we call political would obviously be more useful for purposes of understanding political activity than a single generalization that related only two such facts. It is for this reason, among others to be discussed later, that the search for reliable knowledge about empirical political phenomena requires ultimately the construction of systematic theory, the name for the highest order of generalization.

Clearly, if political science could arrive at such a general theory, the understanding of political life that it would give would be both profound and extensive. There is no need consequently to point out that such a theory would be desirable because of its utility. The only thing that is not apparent, however, is that the formulation of such a theory is a possible and necessary step along the road to reliable and perceptive knowledge about politics.

No such theory is visible on the horizons of political research in the United States today; nor would I be presumptuous enough to say that I intend to offer such a theory in this work. The merest hint of a theory that does emerge is incidental here to the main purpose. My objective, rather, is to suggest that political science is too little sensitized to the need for inquiring into the problems that stand in the way of the development of such a comprehensive or general theory of political activity. I shall urge that the neglect on the part of American political science to identify the role that theory plays in the attainment of reliable knowledge has helped to imperil its attempt to understand the major problems of political life. Without a conscious understanding of the role of theory and its possibility, I shall argue, political research must remain fragmentary and heterogeneous, unable to fulfill the promise in its designation as a political *science*. In the light of this interpretation I shall be led to inquire into a few of the major problems that would emerge if American political science were to devote some of its intellectual resources to the study of general or systematic theory.

If it were not for the fact that today we are confronted with a growing disillusionment about the whole of scientific reasoning as a way of helping us to understand social problems, we could step immediately into a discussion of our central topics. We could examine at once some major consequences for American political science that flow from the neglect of systematic theory and a few of the problems involved in the construction of such theory. But since at this very historical moment dissent against scientific method is growing strong, it would be superficial, if not naïve, to expect hospitable acceptance for the conclusion that political science requires more rather than less of this kind of reasoning. At the outset I am therefore compelled by present suspicions about scientific method to try to probe to the roots of this mood.

It is a curious fact that even though as a group, American political scientists reflect this mood quite strongly, in large part they have been committed to a vague image of themselves as scientific students of political life. Although there are important exceptions to whom I shall refer in a later chapter, the majority in political science has expressed at least the faint hope that it pursues a social science in the best meaning of the term. And yet, in spite of this assumption, historically we find among American political scientists a decided reluctance to introduce into their research the strict techniques and prerequisites of scientific method, much less to identify the crucial task of scientific inquiry as one of formulating general theory. We have, in consequence, the peculiar condition among the members of this discipline of nominal acceptance of their role as scientists, with the rejection in practice of the recognized logic and techniques of scientific method. Today this historical reluctance to commit themselves to a scientific approach to social knowledge shows few signs of decreasing; indeed, because of the present intellectual mood in Western society as a whole, it is actually growing.

The continued and increasing doubt among political scientists about the merit of scientific method for helping men to understand how they act in political situations mirrors the mood of our age. It is the argument of this chapter that in the face of the manifest strides through scientific research in other social disciplines, the continued reluctance today of large numbers of political scientists to insist upon a search for universal generalizations through the introduction of scientific method in their respective fields does not flow from an objective appraisal of the validity of this approach. It derives rather from their subjection to a mood in Western civilization directed against the use of scientific reason. I shall suggest that even those social scientists, and not political scientists alone, who have in the past favored the application of this kind of reason to their problems, now, under the pressure of this mood, see more restricting limitations on the possibility of attaining generalized knowledge than are justified by the facts.

This flight from scientific reason, especially in the area of political knowledge, is displayed in two distinct ways: as a movement away from the rational attitude towards life, implicit in the use of scientific method, and towards a greater dependence upon emotion or faith and upon tradition; and as an increasing willingness to entertain as criticisms of scientific method arguments that rest less on logic than upon the mood of the day. But before looking at these two consequences of the growing doubt about the adequacy of scientific reason in social matters, we must glance briefly at the well-known history of the role that scientific reasoning has played in the modern Western world. This historical retrospect will put us in a better position to understand the character and objectivity of some specific criticisms now being lodged against scientific method.

1. *Enchantment with Reason*

The present epoch may well be the beginning of a long period of the decline of men's faith in reason, as Pareto and Spengler among others have predicted, or it may simply be a passing phase from which society will emerge unscathed and improved. Whatever the outcome may be, it is clear from the present historical vantage point that from the seventeenth to nearly the end of the nineteenth century, the Western world became increasingly imbued with a faith in the ability of the kind of reasoning implied by scientific method to solve social problems, empirical and even moral.

For two thousand years after Aristotle, the first significant scholar in the West to treat facts seriously, few great social thinkers turned to empirical research. When they finally did feel the need to examine the behavior of men more closely, the method of the physical sciences stood as a model. In its origin, contemporary social science was a response to the work of men like Copernicus, Kepler, Galileo, and especially Newton. In his three laws of motion, Newton summarized and synthesized the work of earlier scientists. From the fragmentary state of knowledge about the motion of heavenly bodies, he abstracted a few principles, thereby explaining in synoptic form a comparatively large body of apparently unrelated data. From his few basic principles of motion it now became possible to explain and predict a multitude of facts.

The very symmetry, economy, and architectonic quality of the Newtonian system at once impressed itself upon students of society, and it became the ideal towards which the social investigator strove. For the first time, it became apparent in Europe that perhaps the successes of the physical sciences could be duplicated in the social world, if—and this was the vital premise—the basic procedures of the physical sciences were adopted into social research. The assumption was that the physical and social worlds were at least sufficiently similar so that the basic method of reasoning applicable to one could be transferred with appropriate modifications to the other. Today, of course, this has been and is being challenged, but at the time it was a widely accepted assumption and conclusion.

In application, however, little research into social questions did reflect the method of physics because a strange misconception of the nature of that method took place. Students of society saw the finished product rather than the painful, meticulous work that had gone into the search for the miscellaneous physical theories out of which Newton created his synthesis. Newton's laws of motion had summarized the efforts of his predecessors who had devoted untold hours to the laborious task of observing the activity of physical bodies. But in customary lay distortion of scientific research, students of society mistakenly believed that Newton had really begun with his assumptions and from these had spun out, like the spider of Bacon's analogy, an intricate web of conclusions.

With this ill-understood conception of the procedure used in the physical sciences, there is little wonder that people like Hobbes and Spinoza thought they too stood in line with the best of the scientific tradition. Thus they felt a part of this tradition when they built up elaborate doctrines resting largely on casual empirical observation from which axioms were then speculatively derived. Out of these axioms, by a process of largely rational speculation, tempered with some attention to facts but not geared to a real attempt to stay with them by a process of controlled observation, they elaborated theories about political life. It is a tribute to the genius of these thinkers that, in spite of the shortcomings of their method, their insights into the nature of politics, among other matters, was such that they did not stray too far from the reality with which they were familiar. But the method they used, which they thought was scientific in the pattern of the physical sciences, turned out to be at the level of pre-scientific thinking. In its structure it resembled not empirical science out of which the laws of motion had been induced, but mathematics, in which, from *a priori* axioms, a vast body of theory is elaborated.

This dependence on mathematics was not accidental. Mathematics was a vital prop in the foundation of physics and appeared to be the basis of its method. Mathematical axioms are not of course always entirely imaginative. In various mathematical systems there is an undeniable empirical relevance in the axioms; otherwise they might be so remote from reality that they could never be used in the daily operations of living. But the distinctive quality about the mathematical approach is that its starting point need not reflect the real world; it can be purely imaginative without disturbing the validity of the system.

The mathematical or rationalistic quality of early modern social science can be clearly seen in the work of Hobbes. He begins with the axiom "know thyself." Knowledge of self is the beginning of political research. But Hobbes assumed too much: namely, that one could really understand human behavior from casual introspective observation, that what was true of himself was true of others, and finally that the truth about human nature could be summed up in one principle. This introspectively derived and universally applied principle, he thought, was that men fear violent death. In the true spirit of a science conceived in terms of mathematics, from this simple beginning Hobbes spun out his whole political order. In it the fear of violent death leads Hobbes to argue the necessity of granting almost unlimited authority to a sovereign.

The conclusions of Hobbes's generation can scarcely be said to offer the degree of verification that we have come to expect of social generalizations today. It was not the results, however, but the spirit in which the research was conducted that counted. Hobbes and many of his contemporaries thought at least that they were adopting for social phenomena the standards of valid reasoning of the natural sciences. Rebelling against the scholastic heritage from the Middle Ages, they consciously favored the use of scientific method, as then conceived, for the solution of social problems. Scholasticism had discerned truth in revelation and commentary upon Aristotle, not in original research spurred by a quest for experiential knowledge after the pattern of the physical sciences.

The eighteenth century is a projection of and a commentary on the method of its predecessor. As in the earlier period the intention means more than the result. A broad intellectual movement of the period, utilitarianism, epitomizes the hold scientific reason had over the thought of the age. On the theory that it could be proved empirically that men valued happiness and would pursue it, the utilitarians, especially Bentham and his disciples, laid the political foundations of modern democracy. If men desired happiness, they concluded from their observations, then the political and economic orders must be adjusted to gratify a basic irrepressible impulse. Quite consciously and deliberately Bentham sought to drive out of his thinking any hint of *a priori* knowledge. Every premise must be based on facts.

In France during the Age of Reason Rousseau, it is true, rebelled in his own way against the growth of technology and the ubiquity of reason; but in spite of this, his basic concept of the natural man demonstrates that the premise from which he thinks he starts is not *a priori* but the result of observing what he felt human nature to be like in its primitive, unsophisticated origin.

Helvetius, Condorcet, Diderot, Montesquieu, and the other luminaries of this great movement for the application of the mind to social issues, were, of course, by our standards more speculative than empirical. But by the criteria of the day and in the light of the slow movement towards the use of controlled, first-hand observation as a basis for understanding, they made their own contributions to the emergence of a belief in the necessity of scientific reason. Most acted as if the mere self-conscious use of reason, casually focused on the way men behave, was the essence of science.

If the seventeenth century, overshadowed by Newton, was the age of physics, and the eighteenth the age of the enlightenment, then the following century was indeed the age of scientific method. The tremendous hold that the mere desire to be scientific maintained over men's minds finally became the source of an outpouring of social research. The nineteenth century showed an ever-increasing tendency to lean on observation, in large part historical in the beginning, but later in increasing measure related to contemporary social behavior. Comte, Marx, and Spencer are the triumvirate who dominate the century. Each in his own way tries to analyze society from the starting point of experience, consciously seeking to exclude *a priori* intuitive premises.

Comte set the tone for the age and in fact went further in his conception of the possibilities of scientific reason than most social scientists would go today. He created what one might call a closed scientific system. He felt that there was no question confronting society, factual or moral, that science could not solve. To arrive at this conclusion he was compelled to make a number of assumptions. First, the world is rationally ordered, a cosmos, not a chaos; there are laws of social development and social interaction which can be discovered. Second, this discovery is possible since men have sufficient reason to perform this task. Third, not only are men rational enough to perform this task, but they are even reasonable enough creatures to use their knowledge in their own interests, a point of view that Comte borrowed from the utilitarians. And finally, not only does reason permit us to discover the laws of social behavior, but it even enables us to discover the concrete goals towards which men do in fact strive and therefore towards which they ought to strive. Trust of scientific reason could carry an advocate no further than this. So convinced was Comte of the rational nature of man and society in the sense just described that he had no doubt that the ultimate millennium of a scientific utopia would be achieved in his own day or shortly thereafter. Reason became almost an autonomous force carrying society along to its inescapable although happily beneficent goal, the positive (scientific) polity, as Comte named it.

Comte both mirrored the spirit of his age and contributed to its intensification, but he was not the only student of society to be swept along in this torrent of rationality. Marx, a true son of the enlightenment, likewise accepted the basic assumptions of the period. He too thought that appropriately mastered tools of inquiry, historical and dialectical materialism, which he developed from Hegel, would reveal the nature of inexorable social laws and the goals towards the realization of which these laws tended. Whereas Comte in his law of evolution concluded that society passed through three stages, the religious, the metaphysical, and the positive, in that order, Marx sought to prove that it evolved basically from primitive communism to feudalism to capitalism and must eventuate in socialism. And Spencer joined Comte and Marx in this search for the laws of development and interaction.

Whatever the relative merits of their conclusions, and especially of their preoccupation with premature system-building, the complete immersion of these thinkers in something called the scientific approach distinguishes and links them. No one of them would have agreed with the other on the nature of this special kind of reasoning called scientific to distinguish it from common sense. But, in spite of their own fondness for speculative systems, they would each have agreed that without some special, painstaking application to the facts of experience—the positive data of the senses as against the negative or airy data of pure imagination—no progress could be made in understanding society.

They would each have agreed, too, about the immodest claims they would make for social science. There was no generalization too vast that could not be subjected to the test of scientific historical research. Thus they advanced massive theories of social transformation which consumed the energies of innumerable students for decades, especially in the case of Marx, whose generalizations have, of the three, longest held the interest of men. The very gargantuan nature of these laws of social change demonstrates the infinite confidence these theorists of the nineteenth century had in the ability of scientific reason not only to give understanding but also to direct human efforts.

Perhaps the most telling index of the state of mind during the last century consists of the theories of progress. These theories were essentially novel for western Europe. During the eighteenth century men did believe in human perfectibility but they did not view this as a genuinely developmental process. Instead, education and reform were thought sufficient to improve mankind. This view of human change lacked the notion of transformation through time; it was static rather than historical, as though each man was solely the product of his experiences and owed nothing to the past, and as though each institution could be torn up by its roots and a new one planted in the old soil to grow entirely according to present plans. There was little sense of the role of history and of the force of the past in molding human institutions. There was the feeling, also a product of the scientific revolution, that men had only to decide on their wants, specify their objectives, and social ingenuity could do the rest with little regard for custom. There was no lack of protestants to this view, for in spite of its utility as a weapon against an old social order, feudalism, there were men of wisdom like Burke who saw that no age could entirely remake the world in its own image. But until the beginning of the nineteenth century, with exceptions like Burke, scientific reason interpreted society as though it could.

By the turn of the century, however, Burke's insistence on the need for a look into the past was quickly absorbed by the very type of reasoning against which he himself declaimed. Social science turned to history as a new way of understanding society. And the optimism of scientific reason infected the historical method. The great optimism of science in the eighteenth century poured over into the next century and led men to substitute for the notion of human perfectibility the theory of human progress. The steady advance of the physical sciences and the technology with which they were interrelated, together with the continuing utilitarian conviction that man was sufficiently reasonable to use his knowledge for his own advantage, that there was no *a priori* reason why men could not improve themselves without foreseeable limit, led to the assumption that society must automatically evolve to a millennium in the not too distant future. Until nearly the end of the century progress served as a fundamental and pervasive hypothesis in social research.

The age was so ecstatic with its own presumed success in the use of science that it seemed that progress occurred not simply as a matter of chance or as a reward for continued labor judiciously applied, but as the automatic outcome of a rationally ordered world. In a sense scientific reason was used to demonstrate its own helplessness. In Comte's theories, for example, the laws of social change work inexorably; each country in western Europe must pass through the three stages. And in Marx's scientific socialism, until modern Marxist modifications corrected an obvious intrusion in his thinking of the mood of the nineteenth century,[1] we find the same conviction. Given human nature as Marx saw it, socialism could not be avoided as the culmination of social evolution from primitive to industrial communism.

[1] See L. D. Trotsky's law of combined development in his *History of the Russian Revolution* (New York: Simon & Schuster, 1932), 3 vols., esp. Vol. I, pp. 6-15, 50-1. Here Trotsky amends Marx's law of social development, to indicate that historical change can jump stages. However, Trotsky in this period still assumed the inevitability of socialism. Later, after the rise of Hitler, he became willing to acknowledge a reversion to barbarism as an alternative. Retrogression then became possible.

Although it had discovered the natural tendency towards progress, social science did not deny itself a further, useful role. The task of scientific reason quickly became one of discovering the exact course of this development and the means with which best to smooth the path. The direction and movement was predetermined by the nature of man in society, but the rate of development still depended on the extent of conscious human effort. In a sense, the very rationality of the world was sweeping man along to a fate whose approach he not only welcomed but, by his own rational efforts, encouraged. Optimism in the fruits of human reason could have achieved no greater heights.

2. The Blighted Hope

Contrast now the optimism of the nineteenth century with the often-observed pessimism of our own age; this will offer a clue to understanding the present concerted attack against the use of scientific method in the social sciences. Today we have lost faith in the ability of men to use scientific reason for the common welfare. Scientific method is no longer associated with social good. This pessimism is easily illustrated by a simple, even though it be an extremely hypothetical, example. Suppose Hiroshima had been gutted by an atomic bomb in the middle of the nineteenth century. Suppose too at that time, that the only set of blueprints for the manufacture of fissionable atomic material had accidentally fallen into the hands of the average informed layman. To the extent that he expressed the spirit of his age, there can be no doubt that he would have returned them to the officials originally responsible for them. He could have experienced little doubt that in spite of the disastrous military potentials of atomic energy the kind of human beings he imagined his fellow men to be would never permit the energy to be used for anything but beneficent purposes.

Today we are no longer certain what the layman might

have done with the blueprints after the first reports of Hiroshima and especially at the conclusion of the Pacific war. It is not inconceivable that if he, too, were representative of the mood of our age he would ponder into the small hours of the night the desirability of destroying the blueprints, in spite of their potential value as an irreplaceable aid to human welfare. He would doubt whether men were sufficiently rational in their outlook to conciliate their conflicts so as to bring about that harmony necessary if the knowledge was not to be used for self-destructive purposes. In fact, six months after Hiroshima, when the magnitude of the damage and suffering had been movingly reported by John Hersey,[2] I put the hypothetical problem to a number of people; a sizable percentage would have destroyed the blueprints on the grounds that it is better to live and deny ourselves the productive fruits of atomic energy than to seek our immediate improvement but risk our ultimate annihilation.

At this level of common popular experience we no longer trust ourselves and our friends, let alone our foes. In the last century, whatever misgivings one might have had about the competence of political leaders and whatever suspicions one might have entertained about the enemies of his country, there was nevertheless a strong feeling that all nations in western Europe, at least, belonged to one family, the family of nations, as it was actually called. One at least knew what to expect in dealings with others. In contacts with western Europeans a person could normally trust others to live by a customary code of conduct underwritten by good reason. Today it is commonplace to recognize the loss of this consensus and harmony.

This pessimistic mood reveals itself in innumerable ways, especially in the thoughtways of our time. Large parts of the intellectual world, at least, are no longer in agreement with the nineteenth century that the world is rationally ordered. In fact, with the development of the schools of logical positivism, some philosophers have retreated entirely from the question, arguing

[2] *Hiroshima* (New York: Knopf, 1946).

that it is impossible to tell not only what the real world is like, but even whether there is such a thing as a real world. All we can say, these philosophers argue, is that we order something we call experience in terms of certain categories and this seems to help us understand our present experiences and explain our future ones.

Others, highly sensitive to the latest developments in physics, suggest that since the behavior of each neutron is now conceived to be indeterminate, there is no real order even in the physical world. Hence it is we who impose order on the external world. In this way the crisis of indeterminacy in physics has transferred itself to the social world. It has undermined the nineteenth-century belief in a rationally ordered, palpable world whose existence had come to be accepted. Such new philosophies as these have proved sufficiently unsettling to suggest that a transition is in process to some new kind of synthesis. In the meanwhile they reflect and in turn contribute to the loss of faith in a rationally ordered world whose order men need simply discern with their own scientific reason.

Political philosophy similarly gives evidence of this less optimistic mood. Our century has given up the illusion that progress is inevitable. There is, first, the humanistic feeling that scientific development, either social or physical, does not always lead to desirable moral effects. This strand of feeling was not missing in the nineteenth century, but it has become ubiquitous in our thought today. What was a matter of protest in the last century is today generally accepted. Today, too, not only is the conception of progress challenged but for the past fifty years social scientists have devoted considerable efforts to proving that no one can legitimately state, in terms of any one set of moral standards, that progress is either inevitable or even highly probable. Students such as Pareto or Sorokin have undertaken to demonstrate, as a sounder hypothesis, that social change fluctuates aimlessly. Each historian today has his own view as well, but whatever the variegated theories may be, it would only be the egregious exception who would any longer believe in the inevitability of progress. The future looks too dark and forbidding.

The disproportionate emphasis on violence in the twentieth century also stands witness to our polar distance from the previous age. Behind new attitudes towards violence lies the disenchantment with the old utilitarian theories of man as an essentially reasonable creature who would naturally use accumulated knowledge for his own improvement. There is a feeling that perhaps men will not necessarily do the right thing at the right time and accordingly it may be necessary to resort to violence. What the rational theorists of the last three centuries had usually considered to be the vice of violence, justifiably used only as a last resort, recent social doctrines have converted to a virtue. Violence, to use Marx's phrase, becomes the necessary midwife of social change.

It is true that Marx had already preached such a theory of violence in the nineteenth century and others had accompanied him in this. But Marx did regret the necessity of its use. He did not glory in it for its own sake, nor did he see in it any other virtue than its instrumentality towards a new and higher form of social organization. But as contemporary problems begin to emerge, the mood changes. Violence changes from a weapon of last resort to a desirable therapy for an ailing civilization. Sorel expresses more than his own attitude in his *Reflections on Violence;* he crystallized a growing sense of frustration that sought expression in violence, not only as a necessary outlet, but as a desirable one. Psychoanalysts have discovered this phenomenon in neurotic patients who find violent action a release for their sense of insecurity. In a similar way, while all of us deplored both world wars, a search of our innermost attitudes would confirm the suspicions of the psychoanalyst that war did not lack its fascination and gratifications.

This changed conception of the nature of progress and the emerging role that violence has begun to play in social action demonstrates, in contrast to the last three hundred years, the pessimism about the usefulness of reason that has permeated our age. It is of slow growth but it unmistakably denotes a marked change in social outlook.

3. Flight from Reason

Today this pessimism is mirrored in the increasing dependence that social thinkers place upon arousing emotions and upon the authority of tradition. Let us look in turn at each of these two attitudes towards life that are gradually displacing the earlier rational approach.

In arguing, not without justification, that scientific reasoning is unable to show the way to the solution of all our social problems, especially moral ones, the critics of scientific method have insisted upon the need for a revival of an emotional attachment to high spiritual ideals. It has frequently been observed that the contemporary loss or confusion of faiths by which men live has been hastened by the growth of scientific reasoning in the natural and social sciences. The fact that natural science taught men to look to experience for the moral basis of life left them with little but a faith in the hard, impersonal facts of observation. To the contemporary sceptics of science this is no faith at all. It lacks the warm touch of emotion and the constantly elusive but alluring spirituality out of which, it is often felt, an appealing faith must be constructed.

In part, this desire for greater spirituality finds its outlet in the existing movement back to theology; institutional religion has profited in membership and popularity from the disillusionment with scientific reason in the last few decades. But not all critics of science turn to revelation. Others see the need to arouse in men once again broad, secular emotions which fire them with a sense of purpose and collective unity, a "culture religion" [3]

[3] R. H. Gabriel, *The Course of American Democratic Thought* (New York: Ronald Press, 1940), p. 385.

rather than a theology. For them scientific reason has failed and by its nature must fail to instill a passion for purpose in human behavior. They seek to revive religion in the sense in which Rousseau wrote when he appealed for the need of civil faith or a secular myth to weld the political unity.

The novelty of this appeal to unreason cannot be minimized. At one time, in the nineteenth century in particular, it was thought that men could be moved to action by an appeal to the reasonableness and rationality of a new purpose. John Stuart Mill could argue for the support of democratic government on the grounds that it had fewer defects than other political forms and, therefore, any rational person could see at once that it offered a more promising social order. His epoch sought to subject to logic and clear analysis all possible questions and in this way placed its hope in rationality.

The sweet reason and rational standards of his epoch, however, are vanishing from contemporary political appeals. In their place the ardent democrat now feels within the temper of the times if he strives to stir up the less rational currents of action. For him, "the essence of the [democratic] formula is faith." [4] If dictatorial regimes, like fascism, could establish themselves on the foundations of secular unreason, then, by deed if not by conscious decision, the democrat seems to say that democracy too ought to avail itself of the blind faith of which the people seem capable. The flight is from a political order, sought for its rational conformity to social and individual purposes, to an order founded upon a myth and maintained through the periodic revitalization of this myth. Democracy is to outbid its competitors in appealing to passion. Patient instruction in the virtues of a democratic social order for serving accepted purposes, until truth becomes firmly rooted conviction, is displaced by quick persuasion, through the arts of propaganda, in the virtues of a myth.

[4] Ibid., p. 382; see also W. A. Orton, *The Liberal Tradition* (New Haven: Yale University Press, 1945), and R. M. MacIver, *The Web of Government* (New York: Macmillan, 1947).

The movement away from a rational attitude and towards emotion-laden myth has crept upon democratic theory in unobtrusive silence. Traditionalism, on the other hand, voices its despair with social science in firm, confident tones. It deliberately defends a kind of social blindness, a belief in the virtues of the intuitive art of the statesman as against the conscious deliberations of the social scientist. A foremost representative today appears in the *Cambridge Journal,* which is published, ironically, under the editorship of a man recently a member of the faculty at Cambridge University and now at the London School of Economics and Political Science—schools that owe their reputation in considerable measure to their association with the development of science and scientific method.

The main theme of traditionalism is simple and direct. The critical ailment of Western civilization since the Renaissance is its rationalism, which has led to the conviction that controlled reason alone can bring about an understanding of all significant political relations. It implies, so the argument runs, that each person or leader or class is equally competent as long as he has learned all the techniques that the science of society can teach him. Michael Oakeshott, the editor and a leading representative of this point of view on the *Journal,* sees this attitude as the source of our social failures today.[5] Reason, he holds, must yield to the greater wisdom of prejudice, tradition, and accumulated experience knowable largely through history. Knowledge of political life is obtained through the act of politics, not by learning from books, and at most from the history of acts, not from the other social sciences.

There are few social theories that do not show some insight into the problems they seek to solve, and neither emotionalism nor traditionalism is entirely without merit. But aside from the truth or shortcomings of these positions, the point here is that these schools of thought are not isolated in a hostile intellectual

[5] M. Oakeshott, "Rationalism in Politics," 1 *Cambridge Journal* (1947), 81-98, 145-57.

22 / *The Political System*

environment. Rather, they express and enlarge the sentiment that has been growing up over the last few generations. They convey the endemic disappointment of our period at the failure of the rational attitude, associated with social science, to keep us from the edge of the abyss upon which the world at the moment seems to be poised. Whether or not the social sciences are genuinely to blame for this outcome is not the question. What is important is that in a mood of despair people do place blame on scientific reason and the outlook associated with it; they seek to escape from its authority and use. Scientific reason as it is used to understand social life is made responsible for the unresolved dilemmas of our own day.

The crisis in method to which this disillusionment has led is especially apparent in the field of political science. Although at various periods in the nineteenth and twentieth centuries students of political life sought to identify themselves with the youthful scientific movement in the social disciplines,[6] it has not been until quite recently, with a few notable exceptions, that a limited number of political scientists have undertaken to re-examine the conception of science[7] in political research. In terms of a sophisticated understanding of the prerequisites for scientific research, political science is probably the last of the social sciences to feel the effects of scientific reason in its most developed form. Even though the movement towards more exacting standards of inquiry has as yet gained little momentum in political research, because it is a recent development it has had a curious reception from the main body of political scientists. Efforts are being made to introduce the study of politics to rigorous scientific reasoning and investigation at the very time that the honeymoon enchantment with sci-

[6] See, for example, W. W. Willoughby, "The Value of Political Philosophy," 15 *Political Science Quarterly* (1900), 75-95, esp. p. 81.
[7] See the early work of G. E. G. Catlin, *A Study of the Principles of Politics* (New York: Macmillan, 1930); the recent attempt of H. D. Lasswell and A. Kaplan to systematize empirical political hypotheses in their *Power and Society* (New Haven: Yale University Press, 1950); and H. Simon, *Administrative Behavior* (New York: Macmillan, 1947) which develops a theory for the field of administration.

entific method has passed away in the other social sciences. At the very time that an attempt is being made to introduce a more exact conception of science into the study of politics, many social scientists and philosophers have begun to grow extremely cold and sceptical about its effectiveness in social research as a whole. In all social research a forceful challenge has gone out about the use of this method and its goals. As a result, the question of the adequacy of rigorous method for political research has become bound up with the problem of its fruitfulness for social science as a whole.

It is, therefore, only through an analysis of this social mood that the origin of the problem of method can be understood. In the heyday of men's enchantment with reason there could be little occasion for a serious general questioning of the fundamental basis upon which social research was being carried out. But once the underlying props had disappeared, it was inevitable that the method of social science, dependent as it was on a firm conviction about the use of reason, should be subject to relentless attack. Despair about the use and the fruits of reason, the hallmark of our epoch, has bred disillusionment with scientific method. Where complete disillusionment has not set in, it has at least led to a hostile examination and appraisal of this method as it appears in the social sciences.

The kind of criticism now being lodged against the use of scientific reasoning in social research demonstrates clearly the intimate connection between such criticism and this mood of our age. Social science in the nineteenth century laid itself open to the charge that it sought to warrant human goals by reference to empirical evidence. Indeed, even today implicit in much social research we find the suggestion that the facts, once discovered, will themselves suggest the kind of political or social life men ought to lead. In a subsequent chapter I shall explore more fully the need to assume that scientific reasoning cannot determine what values we ought to hold. But contemporary criticism passes beyond this justified correction. It seeks to show the impossibility

of discovering generalizations about human activity that correspond in universality and durability to the laws of the natural sciences.

Our own epoch has, therefore, increasingly turned away
from confidence in the usefulness of a rational outlook to help
solve the problems of the world. In the more limited area of the
social sciences this mood is reflected in a declining conviction
about the ability of reason to help us understand social life in the
way it has aided us with the physical world. Although in the past
the claims of social science had never been wholly accepted without challenge, today the doubts are increasing in scope and intensity. Even social scientists themselves have begun to respond
so faithfully to the new temper of the times that they too show an
increasing willingness to admit the presence of hitherto unad-
mitted kinds of limitations within scientific method.

4. The Self-Fulfilling and Self-Denying Prophecy

Attention to a crucial limitation which some social scientists[8] now claim to see in the use of scientific method will point up
the extreme degree to which the general loss of confidence in reason has been carried today. It has led to deep misgivings about
the ability of social science to perform its fundamental task,
namely, to discover reliable, universal knowledge about social
phenomena. Not that lesser problems are entirely ignored. There
is a derivative distrust in such matters as the techniques that social scientists use for making their obervations or the terminology
they employ in describing their data. The most sophisticated crit-

[8] See, for example, F. Knight, *Ethics of Competition* (New York:
Harper, 1935); R. Anshen, *Science and Man* (New York: Harcourt, Brace,
1942); H. Morgenthau, *Scientific Man vs. Power Politics* (Chicago: Univer-
sity of Chicago Press, 1946). In defense of science against scientism, see
R. Bendix, *Social Science and the Distrust of Reason* (Berkeley and Los
Angeles: University of California Press, 1951).

ics, however, are not particularly concerned with such problems. The latter are considered peripheral and incidental to the main issue: Can the kind of knowledge which the social sciences seek through the rigorous logic and rules of science ever be obtained?

The argument is that reliable theoretical knowledge, the kind that all science, social and natural, must ultimately seek, is simply not attainable. There are no laws describing social interaction to be discovered. The goals of scientific reasoning in relation to society are thus a chimera; such reasoning must in the end expose its own hollowness.

Clearly, if true, this criticism would succeed in reducing the usefulness of scientific method to the most limited proportions. The purpose of scientific rules of procedure is to make possible the discovery of highly generalized theory about any given kind of empirical phenomena. If such generalizations are by the nature of things unattainable, then a general theory of politics, much less a science of society, could of course never be achieved. It is therefore worth while pausing for a moment over this presumed limitation to indicate the extent to which the answers to the issues it raises flow, not from the evidence, but from the social mood within which the criticism is raised.

One of the forms that this criticism often takes has been quite appropriately called the law of the self-fulfilling or self-denying prophecy. According to this criticism social laws must inevitably be less permanent than physical laws. Enduring generalizations about social action can never be made. All theories must be of temporary and usually short duration. The reason for this is simply that once the social law becomes known, the individual can and may change his behavior in such a way as to destroy the validity of the generalization. Every time we offer a prediction based upon a theory of human behavior or state a law of social action, knowledge of this so-called law and the prophecies or predictions flowing from it, when known by the actors in the situation, become new factors in the situation and must change the outcome.[9] As W. B. Munro put it in his presidential address to the American Political Science Association: "Every increase in the knowledge of human nature results at once in a modification of human nature; hence it is rather optimistic to hope that social psychology will ever point us the way of explaining, much less controlling, the actions of men in the body politic." [10]

This criticism is a generalized version of a very common phenomenon which R. K. Merton has called the "self-fulfilling prophecy." [11] As he describes it, our actions are influenced by the way in which we define a situation. We predict a certain outcome and the very fact of the prediction then becomes another element in the definition of the situation and thus may guarantee the emergence of the anticipated results. But without the prediction, the results might never have occurred.

Assume that on the basis of a social generalization that "wartime Presidents are always ousted at the cessation of hostilities," we predict the defeat of a certain President in a forthcoming election. If this prediction is believed widely enough it may well so convince people of the inevitability of this event, that they will vote the incumbent candidate out of office. Knowledge of the law is itself a factor in the situation and helps to lead to confirmation of the law. This is a case of the self-fulfilling prediction.

The contrary may similarly be true, so the adherents to this position maintain. Knowledge of a social generalization may lead people to act contrary to the behavior described and related in the generalization itself. We may conclude, for example, as Gosnell[12] did in an early study, that an impartial non-partisan ap-

9 This criticism of social science has become associated with some kinds of American pragmatism. See J. Dewey, *The Public and Its Problems* (Chicago: Gateway Books, 1946; first published, 1927), pp. 196-9; and also C. M. Perry, "Knowledge as a Basis for Reform," 45 *International Journal of Ethics* (1935), 253-81.

10 W. B. Munro, "Physics and Politics—An Old Analogy Revised," 22 *American Political Science Review* (1928), 1-11, on p. 8.

11 R. K. Merton, "The Self-Fulfilling Prophecy," 8 *Antioch Review* (1948), 193-210.

12 H. F. Gosnell, *Getting Out the Vote* (Chicago: University of Chicago Press, 1927).

peal to an electorate will serve to increase the number of voters. Once this generalization becomes known, consciousness on the part of the voters that they are being appealed to in this way may well negate the effect of the appeal and the generalization will lose its validity. This can be called a case of the self-denying prophecy. The fact of predicting that non-partisan stimulation of voting will lead to increased voting serves to destroy the efficacy of such a measure.

This version of the limitation on discovering valid and universal social generalizations or theories seems to throw social science into a state of confusion. A generalization can be expected to maintain its validity only so long as it does not become part of the common culture. It can describe the way people behave only while they are ignorant of it, while it is not part of their definition of their situation.

But there is even worse to come. Suppose that we phrase our generalization in such a way that it takes into account the effect of knowledge of the situation. The statement could then be made that wartime Presidents are voted out of office when people are convinced that this law is true. But this rephrasing of the generalization does not materially help us out of the difficulty. It simply throws us one stage further back. We are now confronted with the need to determine the effect on voting behavior of the new generalization. That is, how will people respond under the new conditions in which they are convinced of the validity of the proposition that "wartime Presidents are voted out of office when people are convinced of the truth of the law." It is obvious that this kind of reasoning could be pushed back at each stage in an infinite regress of effects. Like the limitless vista of images on two opposed mirrors, knowledge of each revised generalization produces a new condition which must be taken into account and results in a new set of circumstances to be considered—and so forth to infinity.

This theory of the effect of our definition of the situation on subsequent behavior fundamentally challenges the social sciences. It is clear that Merton does not carry his argument this far. He uses it for other purposes, to strengthen rather than to undermine the use of scientific method in the social sciences. But as elaborated by others, this theory appears to deny the possibility of stating universally valid propositions. This is not true, of course, in the natural sciences. There the mere fact of prediction has no influence on the occurrence of an event. In astronomy, for example, a prediction of the time, character, and course of a solar eclipse does not influence the behavior of the sun, earth, or other heavenly bodies. In society, since men have consciousness they will presumably alter their behavior in the light of their knowledge of the way they are said to behave.

The assumption underlying this mode of reasoning is not difficult to locate. When the theory of the self-fulfilling prophecy is used to prove the impossibility of discovering anything but temporary principles of behavior, there lurks behind this theory what is really a curious conception of free will. In effect it suggests that men can change their behavior, if not at will, at least whenever there is introduced whatever knowledge social science has to offer about a situation. Once men know what social science has to say about their behavior then presumably this factor will be of sufficient importance to change their subsequent behavior materially. As suggested, this would lead to such a degree of indeterminacy in behavior as to nullify any attempts at discovering enduring social generalizations. Social science would be reduced to uttering opinions or principles which in time, as they spread throughout the community, would gradually lose their truthfulness.

This conception of the character of scientific generalizations about social life stems from a misunderstanding of the nature of social theory. When we say that a social law is universal we are merely stating elliptically that one class of events is related to another class under specified conditions. Behind Gosnell's generalization, for example, there lies the unstated premise that non-partisan appeal stimulates voting, given two conditions, namely, the kind of people or "human nature" we have in the United States at this particular time and ignorance of the generalization itself. This generalization is definitely restricted to time and place; it is culture-bound. This raises a more general problem of social science which we shall discuss fully in a moment. The universality of Gosnell's generalization is not limited, however, as long as we recognize that the hypothesis, to be complete, should include the two specified conditions under which it is valid. All Gosnell has really been saying is that, under the given conditions, it is impossible for people to escape the influence of a certain kind of voting stimulus.

There are other kinds of hypotheses, however, the validity of which does not depend on the knowledge or ignorance of those to whom they apply. Certain consequences of the division of labor, for example, cannot be avoided, however widely they may be advertised. The fact of ensuing industrialism is a result that no amount of human knowledge can alter, as long as a division of labor prevails. And the consequence of accompanying technological change has been equally inescapable, given the condition that society early decided to intervene only peripherally in the whole process of industrialization. Once knowledge of the effects of urban concentration and industrialism has been dispersed throughout the population, it does little to change the relationship between industrialism and urban concentration. Indeed, we have known of this relationship for a long time, we have deplored the results, and yet we have not been able to change them by any mental *tour de force*. The generalization still prevails that undirected industrialization leads to vast congregation of human beings in small areas. It is so elementary a proposition that, like the medical axiom that survival requires nutriments, we seldom bother to identify it as an important premise in our thought.

We must, of course, be careful to distinguish between the existence of an invariant relation between events and the avoidance of the results of a certain event. For example, in the natural sciences, it is known that because of gravity and the various laws of tension, a bridge made of specified materials will bear only a certain weight. This is a result of inescapable laws of matter. But if we wish the bridge to carry a greater weight, we can avoid a collapse of the bridge by using the same laws to build a stronger structure. Similarly, meteorology provides us with certain generalizations about the behavior of the atmosphere. If we dislike the results of the operation of the atmospheric laws, we have found that we need not accept them fatalistically; seeding of clouds, however doubtful its success, does hold out some promise of avoiding a few of the effects of the weather. Here we use our knowledge of atmospheric laws, not to change them, but to alter their effects. We change our behavior without thereby destroying the validity of our generalizations.

Similarly, in the social sciences we can expect to find generalizations that will continue to be true in spite of our awareness of them and yet will stimulate us into changing our behavior. Knowledge of such generalizations can help us modify the conditions of external existence. To use the previous illustration, industrialism need not force us into what we consider to be the evils of urban life. Knowing what the effects of undirected industrial development are, we can use relevant generalizations to help construct a new pattern of life. The relation between undirected industrialization and urbanism is still valid; we simply need to change the conditions by introducing guided industrialization to avoid some of the undesirable results. Zoning laws, housing programs, and industrial decentralization are in a very small way attempts to do just this. Here we seek to improve conditions of life without however thereby destroying the truth of the initial generalization.

I am not suggesting that awareness of a presumed social generalization will, in all circumstances, have no effect on its own subsequent validity. Certainly, some propositions about human actions will be stated which, when known, will materially alter the behavior of the actors. The task of social science here is twofold. First, it must be able to identify and distinguish such principles from the more enduring social theories, knowledge of which makes little difference to their continued truth. And second, it must discover the way in which the definition of the situation, especially when some presumed social law is involved, actually does change behavior. This second line of research, which Merton supports and which was the occasion for his discussion of the self-fulfilling prophecy, obviously should lead to a kind of theory which, even when known, would have little effect on its own validity.

The extent to which such universal and enduring theories, patterned after but not slavishly aping the laws of the natural sciences, can be discovered is less a matter of certainty than of expectation growing out of the whole philosophy of the social sciences. If we continue in the long tradition of the social sciences there is no doubt that we shall be more likely to find reason for believing that such generalizations can be discovered than if we fall victim to the social pessimism characteristic of our period. There is grave danger that the wish will father the conclusion and the search for such enduring theories will be aborted.

5. Culture-Bound Science

The argument that it is impossible to discover valid theoretical social knowledge of the kind found in the natural sciences frequently appears in a second major form. Some social scientists would argue that, at most, political science, like its sister disciplines, can hope only to discover principles of politics true for a particular time and place. These principles must lack the universality we associate with theories of science.[13] At first sight what seems like a potent argument is advanced. The kind of human beings we are depends on the culture in which we live. As the culture changes so do our natures. Therefore any generalizations

[13] See, for example, the work of Karl Mannheim, especially *Ideology and Utopia* (New York: Harcourt, Brace, 1949) and *Man and Society in an Age of Reconstruction* (London: Kegan Paul, 1940).

are true only under the particular conditions of the culture.[14] At time T under conditions P, X is related to Y. This would be the abstract way of expressing a social generalization. But since T is always changing and P, the culture, is never the same from decade to decade, what is true of the way people behave today will not be true tomorrow.

Essentially this is what John Stuart Mill was hinting at in the first half of the nineteenth century when he suggested that in order to lay down laws of social change and interaction it would be necessary first to develop the science of ethology, a science calculated to reveal the influence of national character, or national sub-culture as we might call it today, on the behavior of people within each nation.[15] If Mill and contemporary critics are correct, then it would be impossible to find anything but very limited social uniformities restricted to a particular kind of human nature at a particular time. Social generalizations would be in constant flux, not because with the development of social science they were gradually being improved and strengthened in their validity, but because as the culture changes, the old principles would of necessity yield to new ones. The changing social environment, operating on the plastic nature of man, is constantly creating people who respond differently to similar situations. Accordingly, what was true of human reactions in the past need no longer be true today. This means that it is hopeless to seek enduring generalizations about society. At most, such generalizations would be rules of thumb to guide policy-makers in each epoch, and the rules of one generation would be of limited value for the policy-makers of the next.

This criticism does possess considerable strength. In a sense it is a sophisticated elaboration of the self-fulfilling prophecy kind of argument. Each prediction contributes to change in the

[14] Early in the nineteenth century G. C. Lewis distinguished truly universal from culture-bound generalizations. See his *A Treatise on the Methods of Observation and Reasoning in Politics* (London: J. W. Parker and Son, 1852), Vol. II, pp. 25, 87-115.

[15] J. S. Mill, *A System of Logic*, Book VI, chapter 5.

culture and, accordingly, under changed conditions people behave somewhat differently. Furthermore, an honest appraisal of the generalizations in most of the social sciences today must show that in large measure they are of just this historically conditioned nature.

Economists and political scientists, to choose only two disciplines, have consistently felt that their conclusions applied to all peoples everywhere. But increasingly economists are realizing that their laws of supply and demand are valid only in our contemporary culture[16] and that it is possible to find cultures in which, under conditions of otherwise perfect competition, constant prices will be maintained even when supply falls off sharply. A people more bound to customary modes of living than we are in the West, will look askance at a society that permits its prices to fluctuate with the supply and demand. In economics the assumptions with regard to the motivations of human activity reflect not a general psychological theory of the way human beings behave but largely the way in which Western people were thought to behave. Economic theory is culturally conditioned at least to this extent.

Similarly, in political science the small body of rigorous generalizations that we may have applies to the way in which human beings act in our own culture. Numerous authors discern in the search for power a universal trait of mankind; but even if this theory were true, it would at most be true of Western culture and the Western character structure. It is possible, however, to discover even among subgroups within our own culture and certainly in exotic societies patterns of behavior which deny power as a primary drive in political life.

Not only statements concerning motivations but also most generalizations in political science are limited to a particular culture. Without seeking to make invidious comparisons among

[16] R. Firth, *Primitive Polynesian Economy* (London: Routledge, 1939); E. Heimann, *Communism, Fascism or Democracy* (New York: Norton, 1938), pp. 53 ff.

fields of political research, it is clear that most of the propositions in public administration are derived from a study of Western civilization, especially within recent times. Virtually ignored are the administrative experiences of exotic and other non-Western cultures; even the experiences in historically earlier variations of Western culture, such as medieval administration, have received too little attention.

To this extent, then, the critics are right. Much of social science is culture-bound. Although theories are thus limited today, it does not follow that they must so remain. Once we become aware of the fact that most generalizations are valid, if at all, within the limits of a particular cultural situation, it becomes necessary to define this culture more carefully and to separate the truly universal propositions from the more limited ones. A beginning has been made[17] but social science at present requires that a conscious and concerted effort be exerted to extract from available data those generalizations that apply to other cultures as well. If none do apply, then special study must be made of other cultures to find theories that are truly universal. It is still far too early to draw any definite conclusions from the research executed or under way. But the studies show so much promise that it would indeed take the prejudiced eye of the pessimist to deny the possibility of drawing together such cross-cultural theories.

An optimistic view of the development of social science would hold that a large number of generalizations, true for all cultures, will be discovered and will be useful in practical problems in each particular culture. The argument that most generalizations today are true only within our own culture is not necessarily an argument against the development of a science of society. It is rather an exhortation for the need to develop a cross-

[17] See for example recent studies on character structure by E. Fromm, A. Kardiner, R. Linton, and D. Riesman; and a revealing volume on political systems in nonliterate societies by M. Fortes and E. E. Evans-Pritchard (eds.), *African Political Systems* (New York: Oxford University Press, 1940).

cultural science or for the need to test theories which we feel are true for our own culture against the behavior of people in other cultures. The fact that most generalizations are limited by time and place is simply an indication that until the last twenty-five years at most, the vast majority of social scientists were not aware of the need to check their theories with other cultures. Undoubtedly the growing impact of social anthropology on the other social sciences will lead the political scientist to recognize the need to take into consideration the experiences of other cultures.

The disillusionment with scientific reasoning, especially in the search for theoretical knowledge, as suggested in these criticisms of social science, does not stem only from the intellectual movement against the use of reason. Broader cultural and political tendencies are at work; the decline of confidence in reason is a manifestation as well as a contributing factor. Undoubtedly this decline also reflects a sense of frustration, after the sanguine expectations of the nineteenth century, at the genuine limitations upon all social knowledge. It is clear now, as it was to the most thoughtful students in the last century, that certain kinds of social data, necessary for the discovery of generalizations, are unfortunately inaccessible. Because of the practice of secrecy in political affairs, for example, vast areas of social information are denied the social scientist. Furthermore, social variables are so numerous that not even all the social sciences could hope to be exhaustive in identifying and relating them. And finally, scientific reason excludes from its scope and skill the discovery of the kind of ultimate values a society ought to pursue. It thereby removes from its competence a crucial area in human affairs.

But whatever the underlying sources of the growing misgivings about the possibility of discovering universal generalizations about society, there is manifest a tendency to turn away from reason to emotion and tradition. In the social sciences this has become associated with the tendency to deny the fruitfulness of searching for universally valid general knowledge. Without bearing constantly in mind the fact that the mood of the day runs against trust in scientific reason, that in political science criticism rather than approval of scientific method and its cognitive objectives is almost imperceptibly becoming the criterion in many circles for judging the worth of a study of method, the chapters that follow would lose much of their meaning and cogency.

Chapter 2

The Condition of American Political Science

> *As a result of this backwardness in what may*
> *be called the pure science of politics, there*
> *has been almost no applied science of*
> *government worthy of the name.*
>
> William B. Munro

THE analysis in the preceding chapter has suggested that universal generalizations about social relations are possible and that the growing movement today to doubt their possibility is less an outgrowth of persuasive evidence than of a social mood. In this and the succeeding chapter I shall explore what appear to be reasons for the failure of political science to address itself directly to the search for such valid and useful generalizations about political life. The conclusion will be that while there are individual exceptions in political science, as a discipline it has misconstrued the nature of the tools required for the attainment of reliable, generalized knowledge. For the necessary task of developing verifiable theory, it has substituted the accumulation of facts and the premature application of this information to practical situations.

37

1. The Malaise of Political Science

Since the Civil War, American political science has come a long way in company with other social sciences. In the last quarter of the nineteenth century it was scarcely discernible as a separate teaching or research discipline.[1] While there are no exact data on the number of college and university instructors devoting most of their time to the study and teaching of politics, one author suggests that in 1900 they did not exceed a hundred.[2] As late as 1914 a typical large university offered at most twenty courses devoted to political science; and in a sample of three hundred universities and colleges, only thirty-eight maintained separate departments for the study of politics.[3]

Today the figures alone testify to the tremendous strides taken in political research. Full-time teachers of the subject exceed a thousand and the number of teachers engaged in one way or another in teaching it reaches almost five thousand.[4] It is not unusual to find the larger universities each offering thirty to forty courses in the subject. Certainly no university or college of repute could afford to be without an administratively independent department of political science. This numerical strength of political science and its crystallization as a discipline are simply an index of the vast corps of workers now available for inquiry into the various aspects of domestic and international relations. Research has in fact ranged from the minute problems of personnel selection for municipal government to the unbounded horizons of international conflict, and from the activity of the individual in local politics to the interaction of national collectivities in a world society.

[1] A. Haddow, *Political Science in American Colleges and Universities* (New York: Appleton-Century, 1939).

[2] W. Anderson, "Political Science Enters the Twentieth Century," in A. Haddow, op. cit., chapter 14.

[3] Ibid.

[4] Report of the Committee for the Advancement of Teaching, American Political Science Association, *Goals for Political Science* (New York: Sloane, 1951), p. xiv.

This wealth of accessible knowledge has helped to carry the political scientist into the turbulent stream of policy formation. At the turn of the century, training in political science alone was seldom sufficient to bring an invitation from official public agencies for consultation. Statesmen, complained Lowell early in the century, do not turn to professors of political science for advice.[5] Today the ties between national or state capitols and university circles are strong and numerous. The historic report of the President's Committee on Administrative Management was almost exclusively the work of specialists with formal training in political science; and the recent Hoover Commission on the Organization of the Executive Branch of Government drew heavily upon their knowledge. The frustrating fact, for many political scientists, that their advice about means has often fallen on deaf ears is as much a commentary on the vagaries of policy conflicts within the political process as on the validity of the suggestions. It is true that with the exception of public administration, formal education in political science has not achieved the recognition in government circles accorded, say, economics or psychology.[6] Nevertheless, the demands made on political scientists during the recent war were heavy enough to raise the question in not a few universities as to where the immediate obligation of the teacher in political science lay, to his students or to his government.

Yet, in spite of undeniable accomplishments, and in spite of the fact that every year there are millions of valuable and talented man-hours devoted to political research and its communication to others, the condition of American political science is disturbing and disappointing, if not in absolute results at least in terms of what is possible. That it falls short of what is needed is not subject to dispute; that it has failed to maximize its inherent and available potentialities is a more controversial matter.

[5] "Physiology and Politics," Presidential Address to sixth annual meeting of American Political Science Association in 4 *American Political Science Review* (1910), 1-16.

[6] L. B. Sims, "Social Scientists in the Federal Services," *Public Policy* (1940), 280-96.

To each generation its crucial political problems seem never to have been matched before; nevertheless, by any measure, a civilization has seldom been faced with a crisis weighted with graver consequences than that confronting us today. In the face of an urgent need for some reliable knowledge as an aid in solving our perplexities, whatever the enthusiasm and admiration for the present accomplishments of political research, honesty would compel an unimpassioned observer to confess that the fund of political knowledge falls far short of what is required. Other social sciences can still offer little enough; the whole corpus of social research is at so early a stage in its growth. Over twenty years ago Frederic Ogg complained in a biting evaluation of the trends in social research that "the meagerness of first-rate American contributions to philosophy, philology, political science . . . reveals the immaturity of our culture. Plenty of research work, of a kind, is all the time in progress. Quantitatively, there is little ground for complaint. But a considerable proportion of the studies undertaken are ill-planned, crudely executed, and barren of significant result." [7] Since that date great strides have been taken in the study of politics, but it lags far behind the other social sciences.

If the condition of political science represented the exhaustion of its present potentialities, then there would be little justification in voicing any concern about it. But comparison with the level of achievement of other social sciences demonstrates what political science could be doing. However much students of political life may seek to escape the taint, if they were to eavesdrop on the whisperings of their fellow social scientists, they would find that they are almost generally stigmatized as the least advanced. They could present society, they would hear, with at least a slice of bread but they offer it only a crumb. However hard this may fall on their ears, and however incendiary it may be to their professional pride, it must be the starting point for a

[7] F. A. Ogg, *Research in the Humanistic and Social Sciences* (New York: Century, 1928), p. 17.

forthright, even though at times distressing, discussion of the present condition of political science.

Political research has still to penetrate to the hard core of political power in society. Each revision or reaffirmation of social policy, if it is to be effective, must depend on reliable knowledge about the distribution of social power. Without this knowledge, there can be little assurance about the way in which political decisions will be formulated and about the degree to which, once adopted, they will be realized in practice. In spite of the intensive research activity of the last seventy-five years only limited knowledge can as yet be offered on the fundamental distribution of power among the basic social aggregates. Instead, in examining the way in which social groups interact in the creation and execution of policy, there has been a pronounced inclination in political research to assume the stability of the basic power pattern within which this interaction takes place. As a whole, political science has viewed the fundamental patterns of influence as given and has sought largely to trace the way in which the political process functions within this pattern. Not that it has disregarded the broader problem entirely, for there are numerous insights, supported with evidence in varying degrees, to suggest that the bulk of power lies with a political class, with the bureaucracy, or in some vague way with the people. But the energies of the discipline as a whole have not been given to developing consistent and integrated research in order that it might identify the major variables affecting power relations and the significant kinds of data to be observed. Solutions to these problems are inescapable prerequisites for the description of the basic power distribution in society.

However fashionable it may be today to talk about power and the power struggle, only occasionally have these lacunae in political research been observed. V. O. Key has complained that "the pattern of the allocation of values through politics has not been explored enough to permit ready collation" for a "study of politics as status [that] would furnish for a given moment a picture of the pattern of power and of the distribution of those ends or objectives that are gained through political power."[8] But research still concentrates on the trees.

Without reliable knowledge about the configurations of power, the determinants and knowable consequences of policy will continue to be vague and scientifically unforeseeable. Indeed, such is the state of political research that it is not uncommon to hear that many a Washington columnist has an intimate insight into and reliable knowledge of political life envied by most political scientists. The same cannot be said about the businessman's knowledge of economics or the visitor's insights into a foreign culture as compared with the respective generalizations of the economist or the cultural anthropologist. Unless political research is able to throw some light on the sources and knowable consequences of policy to give a more reliable picture than the insight of the well-informed layman—in this case the politician, the administrator, and those, like top-level columnists or lobbyists, whose job it is to know—the existence of a special political discipline will indeed take a good deal of explaining.

Not only is there a lack of knowledge about the locus of political power, but students of political life have also been prone to forget that the really crucial problems of social research are concerned with the patterns of change. No social institution is stationary; it is in continuous, if at times imperceptible, change. The idea of stationary conditions is an artificial abstraction necessary only as a means for simplifying changing reality. Its value lies in the fact that ultimately we shall be able to explain how we get from one moment to another in history. Yet, in spite of the acceptance as axiomatic, of Heraclitus's well-known propositions about change, over the last seventy-five years political research has confined itself largely to the study of given conditions to the neglect of political change.

Aside from a brief period in the twenties and thirties,

---

[8] V. O. Key, *Politics Parties and Pressure Groups* (New York: Crowell, 1945), pp. 4-5.

when it was fashionable to study revolutions as climactic moments in a process of change, and with the further exception of a sporadic and minor interest in the genesis and course of political movements, political science has viewed its task as one of discovering how political institutions function today and what may happen in the immediate tomorrow. Although political scientists are taught to criticize fifth-century Greek thought for its dangerous and indeed fatal search for the conditions of stability, it is a tragedy of contemporary research that it too stands committed to the investigation of similar conditions. In fact, the preoccupation of contemporary political research with stationary conditions has even graver consequences than the similar preoccupation of the Greeks. The critical inclinations of the latter stand in marked contrast to the strong predisposition in American political research to view the going political system as though, with all its avowed imperfections, it were the best of all possible practical worlds. For this reason it is in Candide's tutor, Pangloss, not in the hypercritical Greeks, that we see the image in caricature of the modern political scientist.

Political research was not always thus chained to the present. In the great age of liberal speculation and inquiry, especially in the early nineteenth century, the going political systems were always under the questioning scrutiny of skeptical social philosophers. As the work of any of the prominent nineteenth-century social philosophers, such as Comte or Marx, illustrates, they were interested in projecting present trends into the future. They stood on top of their world to see what a new world might be like; this was the occasion for an abortive attempt to define the laws of social change. Today political research seldom transcends the frame of reference of its own age. However painful it may be to admit, political research leaves the impression that the study of the sources and the direction of basic change is not of great consequence or urgency.

Furthermore, if we look at this research for its exactness of meaning and concreteness of reference, we find that here too *it* is wanting. At the earliest stage in the growth of social science, the stage out of which we may hope it is now passing, propositions are inevitably formulated as insights rather than as research statements. The initial identification of relevant variables and their relationships is always the work of a talented, uncurbed imagination.[9] At this exploratory stage the important thing is to grope one's way to a vague and not necessarily precise discovery of the vital elements and their connections, to obtain the insights. The activity of the imagination here is largely a matter of art about which we know little[10] and it is of course the difference between keen imagination and pedestrian perception that separates the great from the mediocre political scientist. But whatever talent the insights may mirror, the first stage in any social science is clearly that of discovery, without too much concern for the rigor of the formulation of the propositions or the precision of meaning of the concepts.

When we look at the greater part of political research over the past several decades we cannot help but conclude that it shows evidence of still being in this earliest stage and what is disturbing, it seems to be perpetuating this condition today. It exerts little effort to raise itself to the next stage. The major concepts, for example, are still frustratingly unclear. A science, it is often said, is as strong as its concepts; and if this is true, the vague, ill-defined concepts unfortunately so typical of research in political science reduce the discipline to a low position on a scale of maturity in the social sciences.[11] It is the rule rather than the exception to find difficulty in referring political concepts back to the things to which presumably they refer.

[9] Cf. R. Redfield, "The Art of Social Science," 54 *American Journal of Sociology* (1948), p. 181-90.

[10] That we do know something, however, is the conclusion of R. W. Gerard, "The Biological Basis of Imagination," 62 *Scientific Monthly* (1946), 477-500.

[11] This has been a recurring complaint, reflected in a comment by W. W. Willoughby at the beginning of the century. "In these days . . . ," he wrote, "it is a reproach to any science that its essential terms should not have precise meanings; yet this is precisely the condition in which political science finds itself. . . ." "The Value of Political Philosophy," p. 86.

Part of this difficulty results from the very scope of the terms. Concepts such as "dictatorship," "class," "sovereignty," "responsibility," [12] and the like convey such broad meanings that it is possible for a number of students to use them apparently with reference to the same social phenomena but in fact with reference to considerably different things. In other cases the concepts such as "freedom," "liberty," "equality," "rights," "democracy," and so forth provide the additional difficulty of conveying both factual and distinctly evaluative meanings in research which presumably seeks to be primarily empirical. If, for empirical research, we define a good concept as one that refers to an identifiable set of facts and that can be explained in terms of the operations needed to discover these facts, then a good part of the terminology used in political science falls far short of this standard.

The imprecision of the concepts explains in large part the reasons why there are such differences about political generalizations. With ambiguous terms the generalizations themselves become very broad and vaguely worded; the consequence is that definitive confirmation or invalidation for any given time is impossible. One set of political scientists can argue that planning and dictatorship are unalterably associated; another can demonstrate the contrary. One can maintain that the separation of powers acts as a restraint on political power; another can prove that it really makes possible the capricious and irresponsible exercise of power. It is possible to do for the whole of political science what one student has done for public administration; namely, to show that, like folk proverbs, for each principle supported by considerable evidence there is a contradictory one supportable by evidence of equal weight.[13] The result is that all too often we have propositions, the subjects and predicates of which are so poorly defined that the meticulous student of politics finds it impossible to judge between conflicting statements.

[12] See a recent preliminary attempt at clarifying this concept in H. Simon, D. Smithburg, and V. Thompson, *Public Administration* (New York: Knopf, 1950), p. 513.

[13] H. Simon, *Administrative Behavior,* chapter 2.

I do not intend these remarks to depreciate the value of existing political knowledge. On the contrary, traditional political science has attracted and continues to attract to its approach some of the brilliant minds of each generation. In consequence it could not help but offer penetrating insights into the nature of the political process and the operation of political institutions; nor could it fail to identify crucial variables that must be examined more systematically. Twenty-five years ago such knowledge was at the forefront of the social sciences. Today it is still vital. But political research has now reached a point where it is possible to take what are essentially insights, to refine them, and to began to examine them more rigorously. It is not a matter of discarding or spurning the results of what has come to be called traditional political research. It is a matter, wherever possible, of using the available knowledge as the point of departure for the next stage of development, namely, to increase its reliability. Knowledge of method for the study of human activity has now made it mandatory and feasible, in preparation for this next period, to attack the problem of reformulating political knowledge with all the resources that can be spared or commanded, so that it becomes more easily verifiable. In this way it will become possible to determine which insights to reject or to accept as valid.

The value of social science ultimately rests in its attempt to transcend ordinary insight by testing it, and where it proves erroneous, by correcting it; and where, even when correct, it does not explain fully the phenomenon under scrutiny, by penetrating to deeper levels of understanding. If the experience of some of the social sciences, such as economics or psychology, or of the natural sciences is a guide, research such as this ultimately demands the gradual creation of a new meaningful vocabulary, to be distinguished from artificial and unnecessary jargon, the refinement of current concepts, and the development of special techniques for observing and reporting data, collating and testing them.

The search for these indicia of scientific sophistication in the study of political life is in vain. Most works on politics do not pass beyond the comprehension of the ordinary well-educated person, untutored in political science. This has a merit, of course, in that communication between the political scientist and his clients, usually governmental administrators or legislators, is not difficult because it requires no translation from technical to lay language. On the other hand, the sophistication and progress of a discipline varies in direct ratio to its technicality, and the virtue here of communicability appears as the obverse of a greater fault.

2. The Source

It is not difficult to see that political research is wanting in its substantive knowledge and in the formulation of the insights it does have. To what is this lack of progress due? One is inclined to reply, with perhaps some exaggeration: The American political scientist is born free but is everywhere in chains, tied to a hyperfactual past.[14] The lack of more reliable knowledge flows directly from an immoderate neglect of general theory.

We cannot, to be sure, place on this neglect the sole blame for the slow advance of political science towards reliable knowledge and understanding of political life. We could explain its slow pace in a number of different ways, each of which would throw some quantum of light on the matter. It can be argued that we live in an age of action rather than of contemplation and as a result all the social sciences must suffer. They are doomed to draw

[14] For suggestions along other lines see UNESCO, *Contemporary Political Science*, (Paris: Unesco, 1950), articles on American political science; American Political Science Association, Committee on Instruction, *The Teaching of Government* (New York: Macmillan, 1916); C. E. Merriam *et al.*, "Report of Committee on Political Research," 17 *American Political Science Review* (1923), 274-312; T. H. Reed, "Report of Committee on Policy of the American Political Science Association," 24 *American Political Science Review* (1930), supplement; C. E. Merriam, *New Aspects of Politics* (Chicago: University of Chicago Press, 1925); P. Appleby, "Political Science: The Next Twenty-five Years," 44 *American Political Science Review* (1950), 924-32; P. Herring, "Political Science in the Next Decade," 39 *American Political Science Review* (1945), 757-66.

on the store of ideas and methods inherited from the recent past rather than to make contributions of their own. This explanation has a core of truth. In a world of turmoil, men are compelled to seek a solution for their immediate problems on the basis of the available inventory of ideas. The atmosphere for leisurely and exacting research into fundamentals is missing.

A small but insistent part of recent thinking in political science places the blame for the latter's slow development on the absence of serious attention to methods of research. The term "method" has always been a slippery concept laden with a varied store of meanings. In each of its numerous senses, shortcomings in method do contribute to some glaring deficiencies in research, although I shall urge that today these weaknesses are secondary when compared with the absence of a theoretical orientation.

We might attribute part of the cause for the inching pace of political research to the relative lack of concern for questions of methodology, the logic behind the scientific procedures which political scientists often say they are using. Such questions of logic are as relevant to political science as they are to all the social sciences and, for that matter, as they are to all the biological and physical sciences as well. Indeed, methodology is of particular importance for political science. The latter is the last of all the social sciences in the United States to feel the influence of rigorous scientific procedures. Since it is the last, it has been subjected to scientific treatment at the very time, as we saw in the preceding chapter, that the use of scientific method for an understanding of social problems is coming under renewed severe attack. The result is that there is a tendency for political science to become the battleground where the advocates and opponents of the use of scientific procedures fight out their issues. The preceding chapter explored part of these issues.

Although methodology has a special importance in the catalogue of problems of method in political science, it is only one of the many causes to which the present underdeveloped state of political research has been attributed. We might correctly deal at some length with matters of technique. American political research is still quite unsophisticated in this respect.[15] It still tends to collect and relate data in a casual, uninstructed way. The repertoire of techniques for controlled observation, such as the varieties of highly developed forms of interview and objective participation, the correlation of data, experimentation, and the testing of theories, so familiar to other social sciences, still finds only an irregular, almost accidental, place in the curriculum of students of politics.[16]

The absence of special concern for techniques has had the secondary result of keeping the research student from intimate contact with his material. Relatively few political scientists have the opportunity to participate extensively in high-level politics at the national and state capitols; a slightly broader group eddy about these scholars.[17] For the vast bulk of the profession this is manifestly impossible. But for this group it is often forgotten that a broad scope for direct field research of equal, if not overriding, importance exists in local politics. In their early training political scientists are rarely impressed with the need to make personal observations in the field according to acceptable standards for the collection of data. One could readily trace the damaging effects of this lack of intimate knowledge about political activity on the products of research.

It is possible to explain shortcomings in subject matter, and even in method, as the extravagant results of professional insensitivity to change. Fundamentally such deficiencies have their origin in the late nineteenth century. In the light of the stage of development of political science and of social science in general in that

[15] Cf. H. D. Lasswell, "Psychology and Political Science in the U.S.A.," in UNESCO, *Contemporary Political Science*, pp. 526-37.
[16] See Report of the Committee for the Advancement of Teaching, A.P.S.A., op. cit., pp. 266 ff. where the Committee recommends that "One of the ways to improve the effectiveness of budding political scientists is to provide a good course on the scope and methods of political science as an introduction to all graduate work."
[17] J. P. Harris *et al.,* "The Relations of Political Scientists with Public Officials," 35 *American Political Science Review,* (1941), 333-43.

century, the problems selected for investigation and the procedures of research had their historic explanation and justification. Their continuation today, however, reflects the prestige that an ancestral way of life has for contemporary political science. Essentially political science today is traditionalist. Where a discipline develops a professional character, its attitudes and premises of research frequently strike deep roots. Its professionalism shelters its members from the vitalizing influence of the community as a whole. Even new recruits to the field who have by their own efforts sought training in the advanced techniques of the other social sciences are normally discouraged by the thick crust of tradition from transferring their knowledge to the study of political life. As a discipline political science has tolerated innovation; it has not encouraged it. The result is that inadequate procedures or formulations of substantive questions, once founded in the profession, have continued in spite of their manifest shortcomings, simply because the lore that has been bequeathed by teacher to student receives the protection of professional sanctity.

The traditions of a discipline as congealed in a professional outlook, however, can explain only the closest institutional source of current dominant conceptions of research in political science. Other social sciences are exposed to the same force and yet have not been victimized to the same extent. There is a deeper social reason for the failure of political science to transcend its limitations. It lies in the proximity of political research to the social forces that determine social policy. The findings of psychology, sociology, or economics, for instance, are less intimately connected with revealing the actual locus of power in the community or the channels whereby existing power formations struggle to influence social policy. However inadequate its success in this respect, political science is reaching towards an understanding of the very things that men consider most vital: their differences over what in Chapter 5 I shall describe as the authoritative allocation of values. Entrenched power groups in society, those who have a firm hold on a particular pattern of distribution of social goods, material and spiritual, have a special reason to look askance at this probing into the nature and source of their social positions and activities. They are prone to stimulate research of a kind that does not inquire into the fundamentals of the existing arrangement of things.[18] In varying degrees this is necessarily true of any society. History has yet to show us empowered groups who welcomed investigation into the roots and distribution of their strength. Such knowledge is at least discomforting, if not inherently dangerous; the underlying unifying myth concerning the location of power is seldom borne out by the facts.

It would be a mistake, of course, to insist that there is a direct and invariant causal relation here between the pace and depth of political research and its potential danger to those who actually possess social power. Political research has obviously remained neither static nor stagnant. The only point here is that the institutional matrix within which this research must be conducted has shaped and directed the growth of political science as a field more than it has the other social sciences. By the very nature of its research interests, political science is in a particularly exposed position, hence its virtual extinction in dictatorial countries. I am suggesting that elsewhere its proximity to sensitive areas of political power has helped to keep it close to the level of achievement attained at the beginning of the twentieth century, when it began to feel its first strength as an independent field for empirical research.

Many more reasons could be offered to explain the present state of political research. As I suggested at the outset, however, one stands out for its primary importance: the absence of a theoretical orientation to provide the basis for the kind of understanding of their data that students of political life seek. A keen sense

---

[18] Compare a related criticism by Ratzenhofer, over half a century ago, quoted in A. W. Small, *General Sociology* (Chicago: University of Chicago Press, 1905), p. 319. Here Ratzenhofer accuses politics of being a pseudo-science, a conclusion with which the penetrating American sociologist A. W. Small undoubtedly agreed, because it "displayed decided reluctance to use the probe relentlessly in research within political conditions."

of where and how to look for the locus of power and its influence, a clear perspective on the fundamental problems of the logic behind scientific method, unambiguous terminology, the introduction of new techniques and a deep awareness of the need to seek out intimacy with observed phenomena, even the growth of a professional spirit that in research seeks to rise above the value premises of the political system that research students may approve as citizens—these must all add up to little in the absence of a conceptual framework or systematic theory to give meaning, coherence, and direction to ongoing research. To the lack of no other single factor can we trace such grave consequences for the present condition in political science.

3. The Role of Theory[19]

"Theory" can be used to mean many things. In political science it is customarily used to refer to discussion of political values or the philosophy of politics. To distinguish this meaning of theory from its other meanings, I shall call it value theory. In later chapters I shall have something to say about the place in political science of this kind of theory. Here however I shall speak primarily about another kind, causal theory, which seeks to show the relation among political facts. As we shall see in a later chapter, it is deceptive to counterpose value to causal theory; in practice each is involved in the other. The distinction between these two classes of propositions is logical only. But a statement may be heavily weighted on the side either of causal analysis or of moral (value) judgment; hence for purposes of discussion nothing is lost if we speak as though causal and value propositions each did appear apart from the other. This looseness of expression is only for purposes of convenience in discourse, however, and ought not to be interpreted to mean that causal or value statements do exist in

[19] See the four essays on the relation of political theory to research in 13 *Journal of Politics* (1951), 36-100.

a pure form. Although this caveat is not of immediate relevance to this chapter, its importance will appear at a much later stage in the discussion.

The importance of causal theory lies in the fact that it is an index of the stage of development of any science, social or physical, towards the attainment of reliable knowledge.[20] Very briefly, causal theory is a device for improving the dependability of our knowledge. If we should begin with the assumption that reliability depends primarily on the techniques for collecting and collating data and on the clarification of concepts, we would soon run into the difficulty of explaining the nature of the facts so accumulated. No matter how indifferent a research worker may be to causal theory, the logic behind the selection and accumulation of facts inevitably implies the existence of a theory, even if it is below the level of consciousness.

In methodology this is so axiomatic that we need not labor the point here. In strict use of the term "fact" there is no such thing as a pure fact. What we have in the concrete social world is a series of events in which human beings are involved. It is obviously impossible literally to describe an event however long we might take or however limited the event in time and space. There is an infinite level of detail possible about any event. The aspect of the event selected for description as the facts about it, is determined by the prior interest of the observer; the selection is made in the light of a frame of reference that fixes the order and relevance of the facts. When raised to the level of consciousness this frame of reference is what we call a theory. In this way even those who may feel they are interested exclusively in facts must nevertheless be making some theoretical assumptions, otherwise it would be impossible for them to select meaningful facts. A fact is a particular ordering of reality in terms of a theoretical interest.

[20] For suggestive insights into the role of theory, see the writings of T. Parsons, *The Structure of Social Action* (New York: McGraw-Hill, 1937), Part I, and his *Essays in Sociological Theory Pure and Applied* (Glencoe, Ill.: Free Press, 1949), Part I; also, R. K. Merton, *Social Theory and Social Structure* (Glencoe, Ill.: Free Press, 1949), Part I.

The event of a policeman giving a ticket to a person driving through a red light, for example, could never be fully described in its totality. Even my description of the event here does not take into account the whole event. I have ignored the participants' style of clothing, which would be of unique interest in some cases to a cultural historian or an anthropologist, the attitudes of the individual violator towards the policeman, the health of the participants, and so on; each aspect of the event is of concern to some specialist in human knowledge. My own description indicates my bias towards political research rather than an accurate report of the event. And this so-called bias in turn indicates that I operate with a broad theory about the nature of what the political is; it is for this reason that I choose to study the power and authority aspects of this event. And if I had gone on to describe this aspect of the event in greater detail, behind my selection of this aspect—that is, these facts—would lie some narrow theory which would make sense out of my selection of these particular facts as being relevant. Facts therefore imply theory. And to parody Poincaré, since we make such theories without knowing it, we are powerless to abandon them.[21]

Although there are many secondary characteristics that distinguish scientific reasoning from common sense, the primary one is this deliberate attempt to bring to the surface what common sense leaves permanently concealed. "It is the aim of all natural science," Morris Cohen has written in this regard, "to attain the form of a theory or system in which all propositions are logically or mathematically connected by laws or principles. Loose words about science being practical, experimental, and inductive cannot permanently obscure this truth, made evident in the history of every branch of physics and biology. No science, for instance, can seem so hopelessly empirical and so immediately practical as chemistry, yet its whole growth through the Periodic and Mozley's Laws has been in the direction of a deductive [theo-

---

[21] H. Poincaré, *The Foundations of Science* (Lancaster, Pa.: Science Press, 1946), p. 134.

retical] system." [22] The accumulation of data through acceptable techniques does not alone give us adequate knowledge. Knowledge becomes critical and reliable as it increases in generality and internally consistent organization, when, in short, it is cast in the form of systematic generalized statements applicable to large numbers of particular cases.

In this broad sense the concept of causal theory has a special meaning. Causal theory has been used to describe so many different relations that its use here must be carefully delimited. It often carries the simple meaning of hypothesis, as when a person claims that he has a theory about the cause of a certain phenomenon. Since this is its most generic and undifferentiated meaning, in this sense it applies to all generalizations. Every description of a uniformity is an attempt to state in propositional form the assumed relation between two or more variables. Such a proposition is hypothetical in the ordinary sense of science, namely, that however numerous, varied and intensive the confirming data may be, the truth of the proposition never transcends some degree of probability less than one. Since the revolution in physics at the turn of the present century, it has become axiomatic that however much it may be retained as an ultimate ideal, the absolute truth sought by earlier physical and social scientists cannot be achieved through the method of the sciences. Every generalization is in this sense a theory; it is a statement of a relationship which is only probably, not certainly and finally, true.

If any kind of proposition about the relation between variables is a theory, there are three kinds of statements that can be distinguished in terms of their scope. Traditionally the concept of theory has come to be reserved for only certain of these. There are first, singular generalizations, which in the strict sense ought not to be called theories. These are statements of observed uniformities between two isolated and easily identified variables.

[22] M. R. Cohen, "The Social Sciences and the Natural Sciences" in W. F. Ogburn and A. Goldenweiser (eds.), *The Social Sciences and Their Interrelations* (New York: Houghton Mifflin, 1927), pp. 451-2.

Since from such a statement, few deductions can be made that go beyond the actual observed uniformity, this places singular generalizations on the first rung of theoretical thought. A carefully verified proposition by Gosnell, mentioned earlier, is an illustration of this kind of generalization.[23] Derived from what is now a classic experiment in voting behavior, it states that non-partisan stimulation of voting will increase the number of people who vote, given certain specified conditions. Such generalizations are without doubt the least difficult to obtain, in spite of the manifest labor and time involved, and yet there are relatively few such rigorously formulated propositions available in the whole literature of political science.

At a higher, intermediary level stands synthetic or narrow-gauge theory. Theory, in this sense, consists of a set of interrelated propositions that are designed to synthesize the data contained in an unorganized body of singular generalizations. But in the process of synthesis, the theory that is developed goes beyond the actual data included in the original cluster of generalizations. It becomes possible to understand not only the phenomena to which these generalizations originally related, but also other phenomena which had hitherto been shrouded in doubt.

Consider the iron law of oligarchy as an illustration of this kind of theory.[24] It arose initially as the result of the desire of Michels to indicate in a brief form the fact that all organizations with specific ends, containing human beings of the kind we know in western Europe, tend to concentrate power into the hands of a few. The so-called "law," therefore, emerges out of an attempt to synthesize a considerable number of empirical observations relating to party organizations. By transcending the limits of his observations, Michels was able to generalize and apply this law to all social groups organized to fulfill specific ends, including the political system itself. It is a theory, therefore, since it has broader

[23] H. F. Gosnell, *Getting Out the Vote.*
[24] R. Michels (trans. E. and C. Paul), *Political Parties* (New York: Hearst's International Library Co., 1915).

implications than the actual facts which it was designed to draw together. If it is true, we should be able to deduce that even in a direct democracy, after Rousseau, the bulk of power would still not reside in the hands of the people. If true, it might also help to explain the source of political apathy and other related problems.

At the highest level, there stands broad-gauge or systematic theory, the conceptual framework within which a whole discipline is cast. Since no social scientist can be interested in all the facts, the most general order of facts that enlists his interest will depend upon the conceptual framework used. Now conceptual framework is a badly abused and overworked term. It has become part of the easy jargon of methodology in social science and often serves to conceal rather than illuminate meaning. In spite of this excessive burden already imposed on the term, its use is nevertheless inescapable if we are to describe the ultimate objective in the search for reliable general knowledge.

But first, what exactly is a conceptual framework? In a sense it is a sieve which helps to sort out, select, and reject observed facts; or a compass which indicates the direction in which research is moving; or a gauge which reports the state of development of a science at a particular time. Although it has all the virtues of these mechanical contrivances to which, in the mental sphere, it is analogous, it has none of their defects. In place of the rigidity of a mechanical apparatus, it is flexible, in a state of constant flux. It is a body of theory which changes in the light of the facts that it collects or that suggest it.

Less metaphorically, a conceptual framework consists of those theories and assumptions which an investigator uses in undertaking an analysis within a given field. It serves as a theoretical model to test the relevance of succeeding research. It is a system of working hypotheses, adopted and used only as long as it helps to orient empirical research in such a way that socially significant problems are better understood. There is nothing sacrosanct about a theoretical scheme such as this, and the same one need not be adopted to help understand different problems. The supreme test is its utility in understanding phenomena. The systems of hypotheses which can direct research to the greatest variety of significant problems and which, accordingly, can help to unify and give meaning to apparently diverse kinds of research thereby form the best framework. All too frequently the broadest theories which underlie a particular piece of research, not being stated clearly and openly by the investigator, must be inferred by the reader. But this lacuna cannot be taken to mean that the investigator lacks such a structure. The mere fact that he was not aware of it, that he did not delineate it carefully, or that he denied its existence would be an index of possible methodological innocence or confusion rather than an indication of total absence of guiding criteria for selection.

Since theory of this order is designed to help select the specific variables that are vital to an understanding of the problems confronting a discipline, the more developed the framework, the more precisely will these variables be identified and related. It differs from synthetic theory only in that it is broader in scope and, in its sophisticated state as found in physics or economics, it is deductive. It begins with a few postulates of empirical reference and from these deduces a series of narrower generalizations. From these in turn stem singular generalizations capable of empirical proof. This is a theoretical system which serves as an analytical model of the concrete political system. It is conceivable that some day in the social sciences such a framework might reach the stage of maturity associated with theory in physics, for example. In the latter science, from a few basic premises, empirically derived, it has proved possible to formulate deductively a whole body of intermediate theory and from this in turn, to predict the occurrence of empirical events. From such predictions the ultimate validity of the parent conceptual framework is then either affirmed or denied in whole or in part.

At the present stage of development, with the exception of economics, the attainment of such advanced theory in social science is still in the distant realm of aspiration. Nevertheless, one cannot deny that behind all empirical research there are those basic assumptions with regard to the major variables in the field and their relations and that one way of promoting the maturation of a discipline is to raise these assumptions to the point of consciousness for purposes of careful examination.[25] The main core of political research is imbedded in just such a theoretical matrix, the equilibrium theory, and in a later chapter I shall examine this theory in considerable detail.

I am not suggesting, of course, that it is either probable or possible that we can immediately chance upon a body of theory that even approaches in architectural form or intrinsic explanatory value the theories of such natural sciences as physics, chemistry, or biology. To pose as an immediate goal the attainment of the methodological rigor and precise formulations of the physical sciences, which are centuries ahead of the social sciences in their theoretical and factual maturity, would be to fall victim to scientism, the premature and slavish imitation of the physical sciences.[26] All social research cannot yet be conducted with the methodological rigor familiar to the natural sciences or in terms of the systematic frameworks resembling the model of physics. There is yet to appear an advocate of scientism who in his published research has measured up to his own *a priori* scientific standards, simply because in most areas of social science this is either impossible or, where possible, the financial and other resources to do the massive research necessary are just not available. If political science were

[25] "The importance of the development and comprehension of a more or less systematic general view or theory of politics needs perhaps to be emphasized. The universal belief of undergraduates that there is no value in knowing 'facts' points to the significance of a general, over-all theory of politics. Knowledge of an isolated 'fact' may be quite useless erudition; the isolated 'fact' must be related to a larger theory of political behavior before the significance of the 'fact' may be perceived. Throughout the volume a consistent effort is made to relate the 'facts' to a theory or general conception of political behavior. 'Facts' and 'events' are described usually not for their own importance but for their value in illustrating some general idea or proposition. The degree to which any particular 'fact' or 'event' may be understood depends in large measure on the comprehension of its position in a general scheme of politics." V. O. Key, op. cit., p. 12.

[26] F. A. von Hayek, "Scientism and the Study of Society," *Economica*, New Series, 9 (1942), 267-91; 10 (1943), 34-63; and 11 (1944), 27-39.

to insist upon universal adherence to technical rigor, at the present time, as the only kind of adequate research, there is little doubt that, in attending so mechanically to form, all life and wisdom would be squeezed from even the existing insights into political life.

What is possible, however, is a constant orientation in all fields of political science to problems of theory together with the allocation of part of the research and financial resources in political science to the special problem of theoretical analysis. The absence of theory is, of course, no indication *a fortiori* that a piece of research lacks the merits of good scientific procedure; it is quite possible to discover vital empirical generalizations and to construct classifications and morphologies from data. But the research worker can maximize the returns from this empirical work only if he bears in mind that where science has achieved a high level of development, where, in short, it has transcended to a high degree the reliability of knowledge derived from common sense alone, there the critical enabling instrument has been theory.

A word of explanation must be interjected at this point. To single out systematic theory as a vital source of present shortcomings in political research is to assume that we can speak of such a thing as a political *system*. It is sometimes argued, on the contrary—even by political scientists, at least verbally, if not in print—that the study of political life can never reach the level of the other social sciences because it does not constitute a distinctive theoretical field such as economics or psychology. Talcott Parsons is only one of a number who question "whether 'political theory' in a scientific rather than an ethical and normative sense should be regarded as a fundamental element of the theory of social systems. It seems more logical to regard it as a field of application of the general theory of social institutions but one which is sufficiently differentiated to be treated as an independent discipline for many purposes." [27]

If this statement were true, then the development of politi-

[27] T. Parsons, *Essays in Sociological Theory Pure and Applied*, p. 40.

cal science would be so dependent upon the other social sciences that little blame could attach to it for the level of its insights, the nature of its methods, or its neglect of theory. The question of the existence of a political system—an analytical tool designed to identify those integrally related aspects of concrete social activity that can be called political—is so vital to the development of political research that I shall set it aside for further discussion in the next chapter. For the moment I shall assume that political science does constitute a distinct field of research, not for problems of application alone, but, what is more signficant, for analytical and conceptual purposes as well.

For a variety of reasons a theoretical framework is essential to an adequate analysis of the political system. In the first place, as I have indicated, through such a theory it would be possible to identify the significant political variables and describe their mutual relations. Once the research worker became aware of these relations through an analytical scheme, he would have a master plan, as it were, for empirical research. It would give research a meaning and a coherence unattainable when each set of generalizations must stand or fall by itself. Research today does of course have a coherence, but it is a connection that arises, at the broadest level, from the fact that in one way or another all research deals with something vaguely called political or governmental problems.

As a result, there is little theoretical relationship in the research conducted by the various scholars in the field. It is seldom indeed that two important works can be compared in the same terms even though they deal with closely related topics. Commensurability depends to a large degree on the presence of explicit theoretical assumptions. Where research explicitly indicates its theoretical framework it becomes possible through analysis to establish whether dissimilarities in conclusions or interpretation flow from the use of different major variables or from a differing conception of the relations of the same variables. Work apparently far apart could in this way be brought to the same level for comparison.

In the second place, not only does theory facilitate comparison of research, but it maps out the areas in which additional or new research is badly needed. Without systematic theory such matters are necessarily decided in a hit-or-miss way.[28]

In the third place, theory adds to the reliability of the results of both new and old research in a way impossible without the existence of a relatively consistent body of concepts. Prediction is not the only function of scientific generalizations, and the mere fact that a social science is unable to offer successful predictions about the course of events need not in itself be proof of its low level of development. However, where research has been quantitatively and qualitatively adequate to permit of prediction, its success is geared neatly to the existence of a comprehensive body of consistent theory. Where this exists, prediction takes its validity from the consistency of anticipated consequences with an integrated body of theory. The result is that if the prediction should fail, a complicated network of ancillary theory, each part of which presumably had been substantiated on other grounds, must fall as well. Knowledge becomes more reliable because it becomes part of a web of theory, each strand of which helps to support the other and has, as well, independent bases of proof. This is of course the ideal; however imperfect the actual achievement of a theoretical structure should prove to be at a particular historical moment, it would nevertheless add to our knowledge a degree of reliability not yet attainable. And even if the actual formulation of an acceptable systematic theory does still lie in the far distant future —a contingency about which we can only guess since, as a group, political scientists have united their efforts so little in search of such a theory—it would still serve as a goal for particularistic research activities now and nurture the soil out of which a theoretical structure might arise.

．　　．

[28] For some consequences of the lack of theory in the study of voting behavior, see S. J. Eldersveld, "Theory and Method in Voting Behavior Research," 13 *Journal of Politics* (1951), 70-87.

There is today in American political science pervasive discontent with the condition of research, and considerable soul-searching is under way. There is a danger, however, that the self-questioning may be answered in purely technical terms; suggested remedial measures may be confined to ways of collecting data, of using statistics, of describing political facts, and the like. It is the burden of this chapter that while such proposals are valuable in themselves, their incorporation into political research would not in itself go far towards solving the major problem of obtaining reliable, socially useful knowledge. Such measures will have meaning only if they are welded to a concurrent attempt to identify and relate the most significant variables found in the political aspect of social life. Political science today is confronted with the need to recognize that scientific understanding of political life is ultimately possible only by clarifying the broad theoretical premises of research.

Chapter 3

Conceptions of Science and Theory in Empirical Research

> The Fact is the first thing. Make sure of it.
> Get it perfectly clear. Polish it till it shines and
> sparkles like a gem. Then connect it with
> other facts. Examine it in its relation to them,
> for in that lies its worth and its significance.
> . . . To counsel you to stick to facts is not
> to dissuade you from philosophical
> generalizations, but only to remind you—
> though indeed you as trained students
> do not need to be reminded—that the
> generalizations must spring out of the facts,
> and without the facts are worthless.
>
> James Bryce

BY and large, students in political science have not considered it worth while to allocate even a small part of their collective energies to systematic theory. Not that they have neglected all
kinds of theoretical thought. There are ample illustrations of an interest in theory in the work of Merriam with regard to power, of

64

Friedrich in relation to the basis of constitutional democracy, of Simon in connection with administrative behavior, of Lasswell and the power of the oligarchy, of Key and Truman in their syntheses of the role of interest groups in a democratic political system, and in the work of others. But the research of these theorists centers in synthetic theory whereas our discussion here relates to a generalized mode of analysis.

In political science there has been little deliberate effort to formulate a conceptual framework for the whole field. It is possible, of course, to identify considerable concealed general theory. In a completely inarticulate way the forces that drive us towards logical consistency have led students of political life to assume what in a later chapter I shall call an equilibrium theory as the fundamental mode of analysis in political research. But since as a group political scientists have not recognized this theory for what it is, it is still true to say that they have closed their eyes to general theory.

While it is not easy to explain why political science has been reluctant to inquire into such theory, there stands out at least one reason of consequence: the conception of science prevalent in political research over the last fifty years has deflected attention from theory. For the most part, as we saw earlier, political science has sought to identify itself with the general tendency to apply scientific method to social matters. It has conceived of science, however, in very narrow terms. It has construed it as an imperative first, to accumulate facts with great zeal, and second, in the name of theory to discuss problems concerning the application of knowledge. Theory has been interpreted to mean the discussion of alternative mechanisms for improving the political structure and processes rather than the identification of the major variables in political life and their relations. This chapter will examine this conception of science that has been dominant in the last half-century or more. It will help us to understand why general theory has played so small a part in political research.

1. Hyperfactualism

Examination of the important political literature over the last half century or more reveals that students of political life have been captive of a view of science as the objective collection and classification of facts and the relating of them into singular generalizations. Only recently has a movement got under way to synthesize these generalizations into narrow-gauge theories, but even now such efforts are not yet considered essential to scientific procedure. With the exception of the work of a few, like those already mentioned, whose efforts are consciously directed to codifying and synthesizing, the significant characteristic of most political research is that each piece is likely to stand alone with little conscious relation to the work of others in the field. This results from the prevailing view of science.

Where research has sought to be scientific, the underlying conception of science, in part, has been that the task of the political scientist is to describe the way in which people act politically together with the determinants of this activity: how and why people vote as they do, what role political leaders play, how propaganda functions, the way the president performs his legislative, executive, and other duties, the steps followed in the passage of a bill through Congress and the various forces acting at each stage, and so on in an indefinite list of subject matters about which the objective facts have been and continue to be collected. Of course, research workers do not collect and catalogue facts as though they were building a political directory. They do seek to show a relation between the occurrence of given events with that of others. They gather data to show that variable A is related to variable B and so forth. They are constantly searching for new variables to explain more fully why political activity takes any given form. But most factual research is concerned with singular generalizations, not with a broader type of theory. Such research is what we can call the pursuit of the facts about political life.

Whether and why the data so collected really belong together, other than for the fact that they are vaguely related to government or an undefined idea of the political, is seldom asked. In the last few years the appearance at regional and national conventions of the American Political Science Association of panels on conceptualization in various fields, such as public law or political parties, does show an emerging discontent with inventory building. Nevertheless, when a group of scholars comes together to talk about research, the typical discussion is more likely to move in the direction of improving techniques for gathering facts and identifying new variables or matters suitable for investigation, than of inquiring into the theoretical matrix for research. As a result there is now a vast and still growing inventory of research monographs, each of which may have meaning in its own right and each of which reports the facts about a particular political situation; but the general relationships of these studies have yet to be vigorously pursued. The task here is to explain more fully the nature and source of this conception of science as the pursuit of facts and their immediate relations.

In the last half-century political science has undergone a radical transformation. No one single factor has had as much to do with this change as the empirical revolution[1] in Europe which took root in the nineteenth century. By the turn of the century it had so firmly seized the minds of American political scientists that they too sought to emulate the natural sciences in building what was conceived to be a field of knowledge anchored in facts.

Not all political scientists lent their support to this empirical movement. From the very beginning there were protests against what were conceived to be the strictures of scientific method on the free play of insight into human relations. Woodrow Wilson, who was more a part and product of the scientific revolution than he realized, nevertheless inveighed against this infatuation with rigid procedures. "I do not like the term political science," he protested. "Human relationships, whether in the family or in the

[1] The apt phrase of H. D. Lasswell and A. Kaplan in their *Power and Society*.

state, in the counting house or in the factory, are not in any proper sense the subject-matter of science. They are stuff of insight and sympathy and spiritual comprehension." [2] Later, as the enthusiasm behind the scientific movement approached its crest, Beard too sought to mark the importance of the uncurbed creative spirit in political research. It is the "imaginative process," he wrote, "which often makes the poet or artist a better fore-teller and statesman than the logical master of detail and common-sense." [3]

But these were voices in the wilderness unable to drown out the chorus in favor of fact-finding scientific techniques. And there were others, fewer in number and influence, such as George Catlin and W. B. Munro,[4] who approved of scientific techniques but who complained of the indifference to the role of theory as a guide to the relevance of political problems and to further research. But neither those who rejected the scientific approach entirely nor those at the opposite pole who were committed to science but saw theory as its foundation and capstone were able to stem the factual tide.

For American political research the factual conception of

[2] W. Wilson, "The Law and the Facts," 5 *American Political Science Review* (1911), 1-11, on pp. 10-11.

[3] C. A. Beard, "Time, Technology, and Creative Spirit in Political Science," 21 *American Political Science Review* (1927), 1-11, on p. 9. Elsewhere he wrote: "Where do we stand now? The conclusions thus far advanced may be quickly summarized in the following formulas. No science of politics is possible; or if possible, desirable. There is no valid distinction between descriptive politics, political science, political theory, or political philosophy. They all represent more or less serious efforts to think about a phase of life called political. The method of natural science is applicable only to a very limited degree and, in its pure form, not at all to any fateful issues of politics. What we have, therefore, and can only have is intelligence applied to the political facets of our unbroken social organism." C. A. Beard, "Political Science," in W. Gee (ed.), *Research in the Social Sciences* (New York: Macmillan, 1929), pp. 269-91, on p. 286. See also E. S. Corwin, "The Democratic Dogma and the Future of Political Science," 23 *American Political Science Review* (1929), 569-92.

[4] G. E. G. Catlin, *The Science and Method of Politics* (New York: Knopf, 1927); W. B. Munro, "Physics and Politics, An Old Analogy Revised." As the earlier reference to Munro in chapter 1 indicates he was more optimistic about a science of politics than about one of social psychology.

science had its birth in the period following the Civil War. Prior to that time the building of factual inventories was practically unknown; after that time there sprang up a view of science that became the basis for modern political research. In this view the essence of science lay in the collection of objective data, the hard facts, about political life. Fundamentally it arose in revulsion against the speculative kind of system-building prevalent in the nineteenth century, especially in Europe and specifically in Germany, where most prominent American social scientists either were trained or drew their inspiration. Part of this speculation took the form of rationalistic jurisprudence which ended in the blind alley of legal positivism. Its limitations for helping to understand society were becoming apparent by the eighteen eighties. But a considerable part of this speculation, typical not only of political science but of all the social sciences, was engrossed in the construction of vast systematic theories of social and political life. These systematic theories were, however, substantive theories or philosophies of history, not theoretical modes of analysis depicting the major variables and their possible relations. Where they did touch on modes of analysis it was in most cases accidental, not intentional. They were designed to provide a body of substantive data to explain political and social change. Comte, Spencer, and in political research, especially Hegel, were the early prototypes for students. Traditionally, empirical research into the minutiae of problems attracted little attention or interest, even though at the same time historical positivism was beginning to make inroads into broad speculation.

The rise of industrialism and its complex problems of mass civilization, which became most marked after the Civil War, made American social scientists keenly aware that the solution of urgent social problems required more than broad historical syntheses or logical analysis of legal obligations and rights. Practical action demanded increasing attention to the factual elements in social situations. Quite rapidly it became evident that even minimum reliability in social knowledge depended on closer proximity to facts.

On the intellectual plane, this new need slowly drove philosophies of history into disfavor, until recently, in the whole Western world; and in the United States the aggravation of the stresses of industrialism by the Civil War and its associated causes accentuated this trend.

Specifically, the Civil War and its attendant problems turned American political research towards facts in two ways. First, it taught that concern primarily for the goals of social behavior, a major object of philosophies of history, would not help us to understand how to reach those ends; and second, that what had to that time been considered the facts of political life were only the legal forms that cloaked political activity.

After the Civil War, American students of political life began to feel that in the past they had been inordinately immersed in speculation on the good life. At the beginning those who sought to concretize political investigation did not deny the utility of such thought, but they did argue for the need to increase attention to political realities. Beginning with the eighties, therefore, the literature is filled with exhortations that research should be devoted to what is, rather than to what ought to be. Understanding came to mean knowledge of what happened in social life rather than what ought to happen. The facts came to take priority over the goals. It has left us with the contemporary problem of how once again to bring speculation about ends into harmony with research into the facts of political life.

But American political scientists found even more urgent reasons for opening their minds to facts. It took the Civil War to awaken them to the realization that the law surrounding the Constitution did not provide an adequate explanation of political life. Until the latter part of the nineteenth century, where political research was not preoccupied with history or the good life, it dealt largely with the legal aspects of political relations. The reason for this is clear. The actual power structure was so intertwined with the formal division of powers in the Constitution and so indeterminate because of the process of judicial review, that since the days of *The*

Federalist the student of politics had considered legal forms to be at the heart of research. Constitutional law had become the raw data of political study. It was not until the social upheavals of the Civil War brought to light the fact that legal analysis did not necessarily reach the real seat of power that a general interest was sparked in penetrating beneath legal forms. After the trauma of the Civil War, American political science, which was just making the first efforts to stand on its feet as an independent discipline, became sharply conscious of the need to loosen the hold of jurisprudence on research and it therefore welcomed, as a means, the new intellectual trend towards the factual reality.

The major work of John Burgess, *Political Science and Comparative Constitutional Law* (1890), brilliantly illustrates the legal character of research typical of the nineteenth century. Its appearance after the stimulus of the Civil War, however, doomed it to a rapid decline in favor because of its indifference to the new role of hard facts. In this work Burgess had dealt with the very two kinds of subject matter against which feeling was rising, values and constitutional law. Of course, Burgess continued to be used and admired for some time because the teaching of political science is always more catholic than its advance guard will approve and also because courses of instruction usually take a substantial period to catch up with the data and outlook of latest research. Burgess was never publicly excommunicated; his work just quietly slipped into neglect because of its irrelevance to newer research. A sympathetic reading of Burgess would have revealed that he was aware of the limitations of his efforts; he was always careful to distinguish between constitutional law and what he called political science, the study of the social forces underlying the law. But in the nineteenth century few, with the exception of the political historians, made this meticulous distinction. Most tended to act as though the study of the distribution of power as delineated in the Constitution constituted the core of political research.

It was James Bryce who opened the way to the new view

of science in the study of politics in the United States. Although a Scot, he so influenced the course of American political research that there need be no apology for intensively examining his approach. Although he was not the first student to break through the legal barriers to the hitherto neglected underlying activities, his work in *The American Commonwealth* nevertheless carried this approach so systematically into the most significant aspects of American political life that the impact was incalculable. An understanding of the relation between fact and theory in this work will shed considerable light on the source of the contemporary view of political research. Not that Bryce has become the conscious model for political science; most political scientists would deplore any suggestion that they had not left Bryce far behind in the sixty years since the first edition of *The American Commonwealth*. But it is an astounding fact that political science has moved so slowly in redefining its conception of science that Bryce could fit comfortably into any modern university. He would only have to be brought up to date on the additions made to the inventory of political facts and singular generalizations since his death and on the newer technical devices available for collecting and relating the facts.

The strange part about Bryce's influence is that he does not neglect theory to the extent apparent in later political science. It is an index to the way in which a culture will select aspects of a scholar's work for its own purposes that American political science was actually inspired by Bryce. He endeared himself to the changing American environment because of his own aversion to system building, especially German philosophies of history, and legal analysis, "idle logomachies" as he called them. Political science, he frequently points out, "is not a deductive science any more than it is a branch of speculative philosophy. Some writers have treated it as a set of abstractions. They have tried to create by efforts of thought, and to define, such general conceptions as sovereignty, the State, the origin of political right, the ground of political obligation, and so forth, following the methods of metaphysics and keeping as far from the concrete as possible. . . . How vague and cloudy are many of the German treatises of the last sixty years on the theory of the State? . . . What can be more windy and empty, more dry and frigid and barren than such lucubrations upon sovereignty as we find in John Austin and some still more recent writers?" [5]

But Bryce did not intend to disparage all theory. He scorned rather the kind of theory associated with legal analysis and value construction and would have substituted for it theories weighted by facts. He was British, and in spite of the common assumption about British empiricism—a myth difficult to verify by reading the literature in political science—larded throughout his work are acknowledgments of the need to collate facts through hypotheses and theories. He is clearly unhappy about leaving himself open to the accusation that he intends "any disparagement of historical generalizations or political theory. The study of facts is meant to lead up to the establishment of conclusions and the mastery of principles, and unless it does this it has no scientific value." [6] He speaks of the need to identify the substance under the diversity of facts.[7]

In spite of his occasional plea on behalf of theory, however, it is apparent from his writings that Bryce had an image of himself in political science as a concretizer. He sought to reformulate theory to give it an empirical orientation and, in the process, theory became far subordinate to the accumulation of facts; in the end it was almost lost from sight. In *The American Commonwealth* (1893), for instance, he goes so far in the direction of the facts that one searches in vain for an explicit theory to cover the whole enterprise. As he himself writes, his purpose was "to paint the institutions and people of America as they are . . . to avoid the

[5] "The Relations of Political Science to History and to Practice," 3 *American Political Science Review* (1909), 1-19, on p. 9.
[6] Ibid., p. 10.
[7] J. Bryce, *Studies in History and Jurisprudence* (New York: Oxford University Press, 1901), pp. 619-20.

temptations of the deductive method, and to present simply the facts of the case, arranging and connecting them as best I can, but letting them speak for themselves rather than pressing upon the reader my own conclusions." [8] And elsewhere, as in *Modern Democracies* (1921), in spite of his own hypothesis about the role of human nature, his enthusiasm for the facts runs to such heights that he speaks in the words of an unrestrained factualist. There he rhetorically exclaims that "it is Facts that are needed: Facts, Facts, Facts. When facts have been supplied, each of us can try to reason from them." [9] This book, he says in the introduction, is not meant "to propound theories," but "to supply [the readers] with facts." [10] Seldom has a writer relished the idea of a fact with such delight; he turns the word over and over on his tongue to savor its tempting flavor.

His passion for the facts of political life is not strange, as he himself was a product of historical positivism of the late nineteenth century, a methodological movement which is still very much alive and which stresses the accumulation of positive data as the means of recreating the past. To parody Ranke's famous formula, Bryce sought to depict political life "as it really was." His intention was to make political science descriptive rather than theoretical or explanatory in the way history had become in the hands of Hegel and others. He approved of the historical method because, as he interpreted it, it could always "be relied upon to give us facts." [11] In thus reacting against the theorizing of philosophers, historical positivism passed to the other extreme of crude empiricism. It was remarkable that Bryce, as a historian, could escape the influence of this movement to the limited extent that he did in his refusal to rule out theory entirely or to consider it a purely accidental element. He escaped historical positivism only in part, however, for although he was quite clear about the rela-

---

[8] *The American Commonwealth* (New York: Macmillan, 1926, ed.), 2 vols., Vol I, p. 4.
[9] (New York: Macmillan, 1924 ed.), 2 vols., Vol. I, p. 12.
[10] Ibid., p. viii.
[11] *Studies in History and Jurisprudence*, p. 624.

tion between fact and theory,[12] the age in which he lived led him to give facts a prominence far beyond their due.

In retrospect we can see that the reverence for the fact, to which Bryce contributed so heavily, reached its peak during the twenties of this century. As one critic wrote: "Political science has been slow to admit the importance of political facts—too slow, indeed, to prevent other sciences from establishing themselves in its proper domain. It has not undertaken anything like the patient accumulation of data on which the natural sciences have been erected." [13] While there is evidence that facts are being displaced by an increasing interest or at least a growing awareness of the need to be interested in theories,[14] the factualist movement has not yet lost its momentum.

Early in the twenties, under the inspiration of a Committee on Political Research of the American Political Science Association, although not under its auspices, a series of meetings was held in 1922, 1923, and 1924 called the National Conference on the Science of Politics.[15] The basic conceptions running through the reports of these meetings reveal that those most keenly interested in developing a science of politics assumed that the task of political science at that stage was to gather new information. The brief reports of the Conference indicate that the participants devoted themselves to identifying what they considered to be "important" problems upon which research could be undertaken and to devising techniques, statistical and otherwise, for obtaining accurate knowledge about these problems. The Conference devoted no special attention to the role of theory as a device to help to establish

[12] See the quotation at the head of this chapter, taken from "Relations of Political Science to History and to Practice," in *Studies in History and Jurisprudence,* pp. 10-11.

[13] R. T. Crane, "Research Agencies and Equipment," 17 *American Political Science Review* (1923), 297-8.

[14] See most recently the attempt by H. D. Lasswell and A. Kaplan in *Power and Society* to codify into a body of related propositions the main discernible theories in political science.

[15] See the reports of these meetings in the *American Political Science Review* for the years 1923-5.

the relevance or importance of a question. Importance only meant relevance from the point of view of social policy. The test of the significance of a problem stopped at the point of determining whether research in such an area would help in the solution of social problems: what light would it throw on the "best," the most "effective" or "efficient" way to organize political institutions?

We cannot cavil with this as an initial criterion of selection; unless research is directed to human needs, it has little justification. But the mere identification of a problem as socially meaningful does not of itself transform it into a theoretically meaningful subject. I shall have more to say about this matter in the next section of this chapter, but at the moment we can see that it is quite conceivable that a particular politically crucial problem can be best understood, not by plunging into a description of the variables at work, but by an analysis of variables found here as types in all political situations. By relating a number of apparently diverse situations in this way, a particular problem can often be initially understood, prior to factual investigation, largely on the grounds of earlier theoretical analysis. The task of subsequent factual research would then be to improve the theory by testing and modifying it. It is not a matter either of facts or of theories but of a judicious combination of both.

The Conference on the Science of Politics, however, committed itself largely to facts. The topics of the panels held at the various annual meetings indicate a preoccupation with the areas of factual research. "Obviously," the chairman of the Conference wrote in his first report, "there can be no real science of politics until we have developed a fact-finding technique that will produce an adequate basis for sound generalization." [16] They were devoted, among other things, to the study of psychology and political science at the empirical level, problems and methods in the civil service with special reference to efficiency ratings, the legisla-

[16] A. B. Hall, Chairman, National Conference on The Science of Politics, Madison, Wisconsin, Sept. 3-8, 1923, Introduction to Report, 18 *American Political Science Review* (1924), 119-22, on p. 120.

ture as an area of research, nominating methods, and so forth. In most cases the reporters for the panels left little doubt that the recommended pattern for future research included continued additions to an already bulky inventory of information, an intensification in the accumulation of new facts.

With this as the major assumption about research, it was logical for the Conference also to agree on the need to adopt and develop new techniques for the collection of data. The emphasis on technique flows from this fascination with the fact. It almost appears that the essence of science lies not in the logic of its procedure, which would show the true place of theory, but in the techniques devised for the objective observation and collection of new quantities of facts. For example, running throughout the three conferences were panels that explored, as part of the general problem of measurement, statistics as a technique for measuring public opinion; other panels sought to understand the appropriate techniques for studying legislative leadership. It was felt that the development of techniques of impartial observation and collation would uncover the facts and the facts would speak for themselves.

After the hiatus of the First World War, this view of science, that for very good reasons had its start in the latter part of the nineteenth century, reached a new peak in the Conference just examined. Today political research continues to function under the impetus given this view of science in the twenties. A survey of typical subjects in the conventions of the American Political Science Association over the last quarter of a century would bear this out. Although, as I have said, within the last few years these conventions have evinced a slight interest in the matter of conceptualization in some fields, by and large where panels on empirical research are not involved in policy questions—to which we shall turn in a moment—they continue to devote their time to gathering evidence about old problems or to discovering problems that have hitherto been neglected.

In the training of political scientists, this theoretical malnutrition and surfeit of facts has serious consequences for the mat-

uration of political science as a discipline. It has concealed from
students of political life the need to view the political system as a
whole and it has deprived them of the analytical tools necessary for
such a task. With their gaze fixed steadily on the particular problems requiring solution, they are less prone to see the relation of
each significant problem in the political system to related questions
and to the system as a whole. Reliability of knowledge and understanding requires us to anchor thought firmly in empirical data;
theory without facts may be a well-piloted ship with an unsound
keel. But when preoccupation with fact-gathering siphons away
energy from seeing the facts in their theoretical significance, then
the ultimate value of factual research itself may well be lost.

2. A Premature Policy Science

If the prevailing factual view of scientific research has contributed to the suppression of a theoretical perspective, it has not
been alone to blame. This suppression can be attributed equally
to the reluctance in political inquiry to separate, both in logic and
in practical research, pure science from what is variously called
practical, prescriptive, or applied science.[17] The scientific revolution
has never penetrated thinking among research workers to the degree necessary to persuade them to divide their research into these
two categories. On the contrary, they have felt free to spend a
good part of their research energies, not on the discovery of uniformities in political life, the objective of pure science, but on the
apparently less remote task of establishing principles to guide society in revising its political structure. Even when research workers are most alert to the exactions of objective investigation, it is
the rule rather than the exception that they gather their material

[17] See the recent symposium entitled "Applied Social Research in
Policy-Formation," 16 *Philosophy of Science* (1949), 161-349; R. Dahl,
"The Science of Public Administration," 7 *Public Administration Review*
(1947), 1-11; H. Simon, "A Comment on 'The Science of Public Administration,' " ibid., 200-3, and also his *Administrative Behavior*, pp. 248-55.

with the immediate objective of putting it to use in suggesting some projected reform of the political structure or process. At the same time as new factual relations are uncovered, the investigator feels free, even compelled by the orientation of his discipline as a whole, to pass judgment on how this new knowledge ought to be used. In political research scientific method has therefore been conceived as involving, on the one hand, the accumulation of new information about the political system, and on the other, the acceptance of these facts for the purpose of showing at once how they can be used to revamp some part of the political structure. If some judgment must be passed, it would seem that those interested in the immediate application of their knowledge are predominant today in political research.

It is customary in political science to describe these suggestions for reform as theories. In this sense, therefore, it would be true to say that facts are indeed collected within a "theoretical" framework. Clarity about the nature of political research, however requires us to distinguish just what we mean when we call the application of political knowledge, theoretical thinking, and to show its relation to causal theory.

When students of political life speak of theoretical discussion in relation to political structure and activity, they usually mean that someone has an idea or a "theory" about how to overcome what he considers a defect in political life. This use of the word appears very early in literature, in Bryce, for example who hoped that his *Modern Democracies* would "be serviceable to those who are interested in the practical [meaning factual] rather than the theoretical [meaning reformative] aspects of politics." [18] Theory in this sense is entirely different from causal or conceptual theory, the theory of pure science. Here differences oc-

---

[18] *Modern Democracies,* Vol. I, p. 8. Of course, in spite of his best intentions, Bryce is just as much interested in remedies as he is in the description of what he finds. Cf., for example: "To find the type of institutions best calculated to help the better and repress the pernicious tendencies is the task of the philosophic enquirer, who lays the foundations upon which the legislator builds." Ibid., p. 10.

cur over "theories" or proposals for reform, not over generalized modes of analysis for empirical research.

When we speak of theories in this reformative sense we are performing two kinds of mental operations. In the first place, when we suggest that a particular reform, such as the centralization of authority over most governmental agencies in the hands of the President, is desirable, we imply that we have a standard of preference in terms of which this reform can be approved. The theory involved here, therefore, is in part value theory. We are proposing that our preferences be accepted as desirable and that they set the objectives for reform. Our proximate goal may be centralization of administrative authority; but our ultimate goal is related to something we call good government, and presumably we could elaborate, in terms of a broad value theory, just what we mean by this phrase. To take a further example, when a theoretical discussion arises as to the role of pressure groups, it often takes the form of dispute over whether or not they are desirable and necessary in a democracy. This is essentially a problem in value theory and, as we shall see in a later chapter, has its own rules of procedure. The issue is whether the existence of pressure groups is compatible with various constellations of values of the disputants.

But proposals for reform involve, in the second place, another kind of mental operation. We take whatever knowledge we have of the way in which institutions function and use it to specify the kind of changes necessary in our structure and activity if our goals are to be achieved. We theorize or speculate on the relation of various alternative procedures to the given goals. We often describe as theory this speculation on the application of knowledge to a specific situation. Theoretical differences in this respect mean, therefore, disagreements about the results of proposed changes in political structure. Presumably the differences are termed theoretical because they refer to a future situation the results of which can be contemplated only in the abstract. Reformative theory consequently involves both an implication about one's ultimate moral position and a statement of the proposed means for realizing it.

This is usually called applied theory or, properly, applied science.

A review of the literature reveals the amazing extent to which preoccupation with applied or reformative theory has tended to act as an intellectual substitute for the utterly different task of conceptual theory, even though ultimately the merit of the latter lies in its usefulness for social reconstruction. There are of course numerous important exceptions in which pure causal analysis has played the predominant role, as for example in the early work of Merriam and in a good deal of the work of Lasswell, Key, and Gosnell, to mention a few. But the vast bulk of research has dealt with problems of reformative or applied as against pure science.

It sounds perhaps inconsistent to speak here of the reformative orientation of political research when I mentioned earlier that contemporary research shows a strong commitment to the *status quo*. The fact is, however, that proposals for reform have for the most part been confined to minor adjustments in the existing mechanisms, rather than to the contemplation of the value of more drastic revisions or to research into the fundamental generalizations explaining political change. Furthermore, it may seem anomalous and even perverse to speak of the policy interest of political science as a handicap in any sense when the latest tendency of contemporary social science is to try to reach out to practical life, in these critical times, and to emerge from the ivory tower into which it has sometimes been accused of retiring. Students of society are now seeking to link all social science to social policy. However, my point will be, not that political science must now refrain from using its knowledge, imperfect as it may be, to help solve social difficulties, but that in using it in this way political scientists ought to reconsider carefully what they are doing—the relation of their activity to pure research and the extent to which their limited collective resources ought to be devoted to each legitimate phase of research.[19]

[19] For the continuing value of applied science even for purposes of social theory see S. A. Stouffer, "Some Afterthoughts of a Contributor to 'The American Soldier,'" in R. K. Merton and P. F. Lazarsfeld (eds.), *Continuities in Social Research* (Glencoe, Ill.: Free Press, 1950), pp. 197-211.

We can dip again into the background of contemporary re-search to see how, at an early time, a pattern was set that has since prevailed, even with respect to the mingling of the discovery and application of knowledge. Woodrow Wilson's *Congressional Government* is an admirable example of this tendency; the early date of its publication is secondary because a description of its orientation applies equally well to a large portion of contemporary research. Indeed, it is especially significant since it stands near the beginning of the scientific movement in political research and yet deliberately outside it. But in spite of the fact that art appealed to Wilson as the most fruitful approach to human relations, his at-titude toward the use of his common-sense knowledge fell into the same pattern as a large part of subsequent scientific work.

Contrary to his own image of his work as one in which he was "pointing out facts—diagnosing, not prescribing remedies," [20] Wilson is reformative rather than purely descriptive in his study. He is interested in demonstrating that only a particular kind of political organization will meet the standards of the political system he pre-fers. His goal is responsible use of power, and by this he seems to mean strict accountability to the electorate for the use of political power. Accordingly, his approach to the Congressional system is, What kind of institutional arrangements will help to produce the kind of results in which I am interested? He is not concerned to ask questions like the following: How can I analyze the various factors determining the way in which the American political system func-tions? What kind of theory or set of related hypotheses can I state to guide me in my selection of relevant data?

These two kinds of questions are of course not contradic-tory but rather supplementary. The latter is posed in order to be able to answer the former. Wilson, however, asks the first kind of question and expects to answer it without first explicitly having tried to discover the solution to the others. He sets the cart before the horse. He wants to discover how to achieve a given goal without

[20] *Congressional Government* (Boston: Houghton Mifflin, 1885), p. 315.

first having discovered the way in which the institutions he wishes to manipulate do in fact operate. This failure to put first things first has a confusing effect upon his whole analysis. It means that the reader is never quite certain whether the result is desirable and whether the means advocated will achieve this result if desired.

The technology of his argument can be summarized very briefly, especially as it offers a substantive formula common among one category of political scientists today. By using a new, realistic approach to politics as a means of penetrating behind the formal constitutional arrangements, Wilson seeks to show that no longer was power divided among the three branches of government, as the founding fathers had intended, but that it was now concentrated in the House of Representatives and within that body it was scattered in bits and pieces among the various committees. To this point he is simply describing certain facts. He then interprets the facts by drawing the conclusion that this divisiveness of power prevented the electorate from being able to locate just who was responsible for the legislation enacted. Clearly, without being aware of the fact, he is here stating a singular generalization, namely, that there is a relationship between the power of committees in the House of Representatives and the attitudes and opinions of the population. More precisely, his hypothesis is that confusion about the locus of blame is correlated with the fragmentation of power in the House. "The more power is divided the more irresponsible it becomes." [21] This is his major hypothesis upon which the whole analysis turns. But instead of confronting himself with it for purposes of direct examination, he adopts it as his *assumption*.[22]

From this point forward, his argument must be convincing. Accepting this assumption as true, then to achieve his goal, steps must be taken to collect the bits of power together and put them into the hands of someone or some group that can be easily identified. For this purpose he suggests the institution of what

[21] Ibid., p. 93.
[22] See also A. L. Lowell's criticism of Wilson in *Essays on Govern ment* (New York: Houghton Mifflin, 1892), pp. 46-8.

amounts to the British system of responsible ministries. One could analyze this proposal to demonstrate that it too rests on certain assumed hypotheses which Wilson fails to examine consciously. In effect, what Wilson has done is to base his argument—for it is an argument rather than an analysis—on two unexamined premises: that fragmentation of real power confuses an electorate and that a responsible ministry concentrates power and clarifies responsibility under all circumstances. Assuming the validity of these premises, the conclusion is obvious, and it is for this reason that his *Congressional Government* appears to be so cogent and convincing. He has assumed the premises of what he sets out to prove.

Analysis of many contemporary political works would reveal the same unhappy circular kind of reasoning. The major theoretical assumptions are not elevated for careful statement and subsequent proof before the value-oriented task of suggesting changes in institutional arrangements is undertaken. We can see here that causal theory is crucial if only because it makes the research worker conscious of his assumptions or theoretical premises, and it thereby indicates the order of priority in research. Before attempting the applied task it was incumbent on Wilson to prove the hypothesis upon which his reformative suggestions were to rest. This is simply a matter of good logic, not of any abstract compulsive called scientific method.

A random selection of any contemporary work on politics would show the prevalence today of the same prescriptive or reformative approach to the subject matter. The primary question has been, not "how do the various institutions function?" but "how ought they to be improved?" Political research has sought to answer such questions as how we are to avoid the defects of the separation of power, to strengthen the two party system or obtain more responsible parties, to activate an apathetic citizenry, to create a strong public opinion, to improve the administrative services, or to centralize responsibility and blame when the national government acts. To discover answers to these questions it has been necessary to uncover facts about the various kinds of political relations involved. But a paramount interest has been not in conveying information and theories about these relations but in suggesting how the political structure ought to be transformed.

There is, to repeat, nothing inherently wrong with this procedure as long as the research worker is aware of what is taking place. Indeed, questions oriented to reform are the essential stimulus to pure research. Without this prompting to achieve a particular goal there would be little point in conducting research into the variables assumed to be related to that goal.[23] As we shall see in a later chapter, the moral framework of the investigator sets his problems and thereby the major social incentive for any research. Furthermore, however inadequate causal knowledge may be, there is the constant pressure of the immediate need for political action to induce, and indeed, within almost any conception of social duty, to oblige political scientists to offer whatever information they have for the solution of these problems. Political life does not wait upon the social scientist but insists upon eliciting whatever solutions are available at the time. Attempts, therefore, to propose new means for achieving given objectives ought not to be deplored simply because they are oriented towards reform.

Here, however, the desideratum involves the extent to which the resources of political science ought to be devoted to matters of reform. At the least, the application of knowledge ought not to overshadow the discovery of general causal relations; at the most, it ought to play only a secondary role in the first stages of a social science. Essentially the prescription of the means towards the achievement of a specified end is the most difficult part of science. It assumes that political knowledge is sufficiently exact to permit of prediction, whereas even in the more advanced biological and natural sciences, such as in the medical sciences, with all their theory and capacity for experimentation lacking in political science, prediction is very treacherous and un-

[23] H. S. Dennison, "The Need for the Development of Political Science Engineering," 26 *American Political Science Review* (1932), 241-55.

certain. The degree of success attainable in these fields, however, is a function of the reliability of the descriptive knowledge and the level of theory. This makes it possible to indicate the probable means for the attainment of a given goal, such as good health.

To the extent that excessive attention to questions of political reform siphons off resources that might otherwise be devoted to the search for uniformities in political relations, the development of research towards theory is thereby retarded. I would stress again that nothing can be said against even the premature application of political knowledge; it is obviously vital to the ultimate utility of all research. My point is that the discussion of how political knowledge can be used to attain given objectives—what is often meant by theoretical inquiry—ought not to be substituted for general theory. The premature application even of causal knowledge ought not to be allowed to divert interest from the prior task of formulating theory in terms of which political science can heighten the reliability of its conclusions. It is dangerous to the maturation of a discipline if discussion of problems in application, although necessary and desirable by any standard, is allowed to crowd out research into conceptual theory based on causal knowledge. For purposes of research we must recognize each as a distinct, even though in the end related, matter.

We can appreciate fully the separate roles of pure as compared with applied research if we speculate on how we would draw up a curriculum for political science, assuming that we had complete freedom and insisted upon institutionalizing the various logical aspects of the discipline. We could set aside part of our resources for the study and teaching of the pure science of politics. A hypothetical School of Pure Political Research would be devoted to the search for the various levels of generalizations discussed earlier and would ultimately attempt to cast all research into a general conceptual scheme. At the same time, however, it would be shortsighted and unrealistic to refuse to recognize that however inadequate the knowledge retailed by the school of pure science, the pressure of necessity would demand its continuing utilization. Therefore, if we were to be ruthlessly logical in institutionalizing the two realms of research we would be compelled also to establish a School of Applied Political Research.

The primary tasks of this school would be, first, to achieve some consensus on the goals for which political knowledge was to be used, since without this agreement the school would be divided into interminably disputing factions. In medicine and engineering, for example, the objectives are clear enough to permit action on the part of doctors and engineers, although from time to time a process of clarification and redefinition takes place. The second task of the applied school, however, would be to use whatever generalizations were available for the purpose of instructing its students on the application of the scientific knowledge to specific situations.[24] Whether this task could be met by a school of applied politics alone or whether the problem of practical political reform is so complex that only a school of applied *social* science as a whole would prove effective is a separate question. Whatever the case, we can conceive of a separate resource devoted to problems of application. As in the medical and engineering schools, their concentration on the special problems of application does not prevent the inclusion within their

[24] We ought to note carefully that the goal of an applied school would not be to train statesmen. Statesmanship is an art, not an applied science. It calls for the use of prudential in addition to scientific judgment in applying knowledge to specific cases. Where a social scientist seeks to act within the limits of his knowledge he can offer advice only to the extent that science can help to show the consequences of various alternatives. Since decisions must be made in practical affairs, where, even at its best, science is usually ignorant of some of the consequences, then the choice must include foresight based on prudence; it becomes the application not only of scientific but also of prudential knowledge. Morris Cohen put this well when he wrote: "The foregoing considerations suggest the element of truth in the Aristotelian view that while physical science depends on theoretical reason (nouns), practical social science involves more sound judgment (phroneisis). Sound judgment means ability to guess (or intuit) what is relevant and decisive, and to make a rapid estimate of the sum of a large number of factors that have not been accurately determined. In practice the statesman, the businessman, and even the physician may often find the suggestive remark of a novelist like Balzac of greater help than long chapters from the most scientific psychology, since the latter deals with elements, whereas in conduct we deal with whole situations." M. R. Cohen, op. cit., p. 465.

walls of scientists devoted to pure research, but the emphasis and tone of the schools are towards application.

The mere fact that we do not have such a division into pure and applied institutions in political research, that it is unlikely that such a division will be introduced within the foreseeable future, and that there may be no real need to set up separate organizations devoted to each kind of activity does not destroy the lesson behind this speculation. Whatever the organizations we might adopt for the training of political scientists, we ought to recognize the different natures of these two kinds of research.

Today in political science there is little clear distinction between pure and applied research; in the same classroom and in the same research worker attention must be divided between the two areas. As a result research workers have overlooked the intrinsic difference between the two. Efforts at application are always initially the more appealing and in a short-run sense, because of the tremendous difficulties confronting pure research, the more easily undertaken. The study of causal relations as a distinct enterprise has therefore been jeopardized and the whole problem of systematic theory has been driven deep into the recesses of political research, where it is scarcely visible.

In conclusion, we can say that the knowledge today available in political science for an understanding of political life falls far short, not so much of what is desirable, which is obvious, but of what is possible with the tools of analysis and research at hand. There is, of course, no single source of these shortcomings. But certainly one vital cause is the deep-seated indifference in political science as a whole to its conception of the nature of political research. In the large, students of political life have shown a continued reluctance to question the methodological premises of their research. For this reason it has been possible for them to adopt quite unwittingly a conception of research that has necessarily narrowed the scope of their conclusions and the returns for their efforts.

As we have just seen, over the years political science has emerged as a fact-gathering and reforming discipline. While verification of theory obviously requires the accumulation of facts and social utility demands the application of knowledge, nevertheless excessive emphasis on these aspects of research has both reflected and contributed to the concealment of the necessary theoretical foundation for any mature understanding of the political system. In concentrating on the accumulation of facts, political science has neglected the general framework within which these facts could acquire meaning to transcend any particular time and place. And in becoming preoccupied almost exclusively with problems of applying this factual information, political science has impeded its own movement towards a fundamental understanding of political life, a kind of knowledge that would place the relation of means to ends on a secure foundation.

Chapter **4**

The Orientation of Political Research

Although the nuclei of sciences can be profitably pointed out, the boundaries are an experimental matter to be determined by the limits of fruitful and coherent investigation.
George E. G. Catlin

IN the discussion up to this point I have sought to show that useful knowledge about actual political relations, an understanding of the way people act in political life, requires sustained attention to systematic theory. Although some social scientists today are prone to challenge the possibility of obtaining the kind of generalizations required for the construction of mature theory, I have suggested that such knowledge is in principle well within the realm of achievement. At the same time, however, as the preceding two chapters have brought out, by the very nature of the way American political science has conceived of its research in the past half-century, it has aborted the development of any major interest in theoretical inquiry. Since it has seldom paused to examine the methodological premises of its own research, political science has been able to offer little guidance about the kind of understanding of political life it either sought or considered desirable.

Now that we have discussed the kind of knowledge necessary for a reliable understanding of the way the political system functions and some general characteristics of the knowledge actually available in political science, we are prepared to move forward to another class of questions. These deal with problems that would arise if political science were to address itself deliberately and seriously to the task of formulating a conceptual framework.

There is an almost unlimited range of problems confronting such theoretical research. From these, for reasons that will become apparent as we proceed, I have selected only three: the basic concepts needed to orient research to political as distinct from other kinds of subject matter (Chapters 4 and 5); the categories of data that must be taken into consideration in any piece of research (Chapters 6, 7, and 8); and finally, the role that value judgments play in the formulation of theory (Chapters 9 and 10).

As I have indicated, these problems are by no means exhaustive or exclusive of those that require discussion; they are just three among a number of urgent ones. They will, however, be sufficient for present purposes. The reason is that the limits of this work relieve me of the obligation to inquire into more than a sampling of the issues raised in the formulation of theory. My purpose has not been to sketch even in broad outline a possible theory of the political system but simply to urge consideration for the need to undertake an examination of such a theory. The discussion here of a few of the barriers to a general theory is offered, therefore, only as an illustration of the areas into which the quest for theoretical knowledge must move research. And even with regard to these matters, although a substantive answer to them will in fact appear, my primary interest will really lie in the kind of issues they raise.

From this starting point it is apparent that disagreement with what follows could conceivably take one of two forms: It might challge the importance of the problems that I identify as relevant to the construction of theory; or it might accept their importance but reject or take exception to some parts of the substantive answers. From the viewpoint of this work, objections of the latter sort would in the long run be less consequential. Let us assume that the reader should conclude that political science is not what I suggest it is, that my classification of data for analyzing a political situation is totally inadequate, and that I have misinterpreted the moral foundations of research. My long-run purposes would nevertheless be fulfilled if the reader should agree first, about the place, need, and general properties of systematic theory in political research, and second, that on any scale of relevance the points raised here are central to the development of such theory.

1. The Need for Orienting Concepts

If we direct our attention to systematic theory, clearly the preliminary question facing us would be "just what are we to talk about?" The question is so obvious and elementary that it seems almost ridiculous to ask it. Presumably we might answer, "political science," but of course this reply does not carry us very far. What we would need to know is how we are to orient ourselves to the things that we have learned to call political. Where does the political begin and end, and how is it distinguishable if at all, from other kinds of data that we call economic, sociological, psychological, and so on through the whole catalogue of the established social sciences. The very idea of systematic theory, in other words, raises the question of the gross outlines of the concrete empirical system to which a system of theory is to refer.

Initially the outline must be gross for the simple reason that if we sought a refined version of all the significant variables included within a concrete political system, then at the very start we would need to have what we were setting out to find, a conceptual framework. We seek the latter because through it we would be able to identify the significant variables necessary to explain political activities and to show their interrelations. This is a task of the highest order of intellectual abstraction, and failing the instantaneous illuminating flash of insight of a political Newton, we must begin with the very simplest frame of reference. This frame of reference consists of those broad concepts which help to orient us to political data so that at the outset we have a rough sketch of the ground we must traverse. In political science this has traditionally been called the study of the nature and scope of the discipline.

Discussion of the limits of political science has today fallen into disrepute. At one time, at the turn of this century, when political science was still in process of discarding its swaddling clothes, it was a popular enterprise to inquire into the general characteristics of this new offspring. Political scientists sought to convince themselves and others that it was a legitimate progeny of social science. But within a short time, having established itself as a full-fledged and undoubted member of the family of social sciences, there was no further point in pursuing this line of self-conviction and self-justification. With morale high in the discipline, discussions of scope as a live topic could pass out of the journals into the introductory or concluding chapters of texts, where they now usually appear as a more or less sterile issue about which custom demands a few words. Once political science became a separate teaching field in the United States, the important part of research was to get down to the business of investigating the facts of political activity, not to dispute interminably about its boundaries. In the long run political science has become what the political scientist does, and political science today reflects this expedient apathy concerning its limits.

For sound reason dispute over the province of political science all but vanished. When the discipline was younger as an empirical science in our modern sense, the reservoir of factual knowledge was slight, the need for plunging into the collection of more data was great, and talk about the metes and bounds of political research was artificial, even presumptuous, when so little empirical investigation had actually been undertaken. Premature definition at this stage might easily have led to the narrowing of the horizon in research. And further, since factual data were so scarce, much of the discussion of what the limits of political science ought to be were pure guesses, expressions of prejudice or speculation in a vacuum.

The deep and almost bitter sarcasm with which Arthur Bentley—whose contribution to the evolution of American political science we are only now just beginning to acknowledge—refers to the writings about scope, suggests that those who wanted to get on with the task of actual research had been driven to the limits of their patience. "Ought we not," he queries, "to draw a distinction in advance between [the study of politics] and other varieties of social activity, so that we can have our field of study defined and delimited at the outset? The answer is No. Many a child, making paper toys, has used his scissors too confidently and cut himself off from the materials he needs. That is an error to avoid. Instead, we shall plunge into any phenomena or set of phenomena belonging to the roughly recognized field of government. . . . If any of these things lead us to interesting paths we shall be prepared to follow them, heedless of definitions. Who likes may snip verbal definitions in his old age, when his world has gone crackly and dry." [1]

Bentley's evident frustration at the importance attached in his day to the scope of politics clouded a usually clear intelligence. However much he himself sought to avoid mentioning the scope of political research, at the appropriate stage in his own volume on *The Process of Government* he was compelled, in spite of his

---

[1] A. F. Bentley, *The Process of Government* (Bloomington, Ind.: Principia Press, 1949, 1st publ. 1908), p. 199. A. W. Small in his "Fifty Years of Sociology in the United States (1865-1915)," 21 *American Journal of Sociology* (1916), 721-864 on pp. 820-3, shows how equally surfeited another social science was becoming with agitation about the boundaries of the various disciplines.

verbal brickbats, to question himself about the limits of his own data. He felt the need to explore the meaning of "political phenomena," [2] a concealed way of talking about scope. By coming at the matter indirectly and implicitly he managed to deceive himself about the utility of such an inquiry. The real problem that he faced, therefore, was not whether he should postpone the question of limits to an old and senile age, but whether he was to sneak it in through the back door or introduce it as a legitimate topic. Since he was anxious to get on with the examination of political phenomena, a task obviously prior for his period, no serious objection could be raised to his inconsistent and devious procedure.

Today, however, the condition and quantity of political knowledge has changed radically. Political science has accumulated bulging inventories of facts and their insistent pressure drives it towards an effort to draw these facts together into some meaningful whole. Political research is now, however, suffering the consequences for the failure to clarify, at the time when discussions of scope were prominent, the true relation of its facts to an understanding of political life. Political scientists are led to misconstrue the earlier historically conditioned need to set aside questions about the limits of political science as a sign of the permanent sterility of such inquiry.

Furthermore, it has become much more difficult to revive this question for permanent incorporation into analytical inquiry because the trend today is to search for the unity among the social sciences, not their elements of differentiation. The result is that if political science were to raise again the question of boundaries, it would appear to leave itself open to the accusation of displaying an invidious narrowness in relation to social research, seeking, like the medieval monopolistic guilds, to stake out a claim to a private jurisdiction. It would appear to be excluding others for purely arbitrary, self-centered, and professional reasons from grounds that ought to be common to all. To revive questions of scope, therefore, is to bring down upon oneself the threat of ex-

[2] Ibid., p. 259.

communication by the avant-garde in social research which seeks for elements of unity rather than differentiation.[3] And yet, in spite of the historical decline of interest in the question of limits and in spite of the jeopardy in which political scientists might place their reputation among fellow social scientists, the concern for systematic theory irresistibly leads back to an inquiry into the province of the political discipline.

It would, however, be too ambitious at this juncture in political research, when theory has been relegated to the background, to attempt to define the core of the field to the satisfaction of most students. This task must wait until a much later date when systematic theory has been brought to some level of maturity. We can nevertheless undertake to stake out some of the broadest concepts to orient us to political data and to serve as an initial guide in developing systematic theory. We require a few fundamental or key concepts to help us locate political science on the general map of social science; otherwise we would have no point of departure from which to begin any attempt to formulate theory.

2. The Idea of a Political System

Essentially, in defining political science, what we are seeking are concepts to describe the most obvious and encompassing properties of the political system. As I indicated earlier, the idea of a political *system* proves to be an appropriate and indeed unavoidable starting point in this search. Although there is often uncertainty about the unity of political science as a discipline, most students of political life do feel quite instinctively that research into the political aspects of life does differ from inquiry into any other, sufficiently so to constitute a separate intellectual enterprise. These students have been acting on the unexpressed premise that

[3] L. Wirth (ed.), "The Social Sciences, One or Many," *Eleven Twenty-Six* (Chicago: University of Chicago Press, 1940), pp. 113-52.

the phenomena of politics tend to cohere and to be mutually related. Such phenomena form, in other words, a system which is part of the total social system and yet which, for purposes of analysis and research, is temporarily set apart.

In the concrete world of reality not everything is significantly or closely related to what we call political life; certain kinds of activity are more prominently associated with it than others. These elements of political activity, such as governmental organizations, pressure groups, voting, parties, and other social elements related to them, such as classes, regional groupings, and so forth, all show close enough interaction to be considered part of the political process. They are, of course, part of the whole social process and therefore are part of analytical systems other than the political. But they do show a marked political relevance that is more than purely accidental or random. If they were accidental there would be little point in searching for regularities in political activity. The search for recurrent relationships suggests that the elements of political life have some form of determinate relation. The task of research is to discover what these are. In short, political life constitutes a concrete political system which is an aspect of the whole social system.

We must recognize, as I have intimated, that ultimately all social life is interdependent and, as a result, that it is artificial to isolate any set of social relations from the whole for special attention. But this artificiality is imposed upon political scientists by the need for simplification of their data. Since everything is related to everything else, the task of pursuing the determinants of any given relation would be so vast and ramifying that it would defy any tools of investigation available either to the social or physical sciences. Instead, political science is compelled to abstract from the whole social system some variables which seem to cohere more closely than others, much as price, supply, demand, and choice among wants do in economics, and to look upon them as a subsystem which can be profitably examined, temporarily, apart from the whole social system. The analytic or mental tool for this purpose is the theoretical system (systematic theory). It consists, first, of a set of concepts corresponding to the important political variables and, second, of statements about the relations among these concepts. Systematic theory corresponds at the level of thought to the concrete empirical political system of daily life.

It is now clear why an initial step in developing systematic theory must be an inquiry into the orienting concepts of the system under investigation. If the object of such theory is to identify all the important variables, some criteria are required to determine relevance or importance. We require some knowledge at the outset about the kind of activity in general that we describe as political before we can examine political life more closely to identify its components. Without some guide to the investigator to indicate when a variable is politically relevant, social life would simply be an incoherent wilderness of activities.

At first sight, to be sure, and, for that matter, even upon closer examination, political science does not seem to possess this systemic coherence. There seem to be no broad variables common to the whole discipline; instead there seems to be a large number of heterogeneous fields. For the sake of illustration we might notice that the list of doctoral dissertations in progress at any one time seems to be made up of a fantastic agglomeration of subjects. In one year dissertations dealt with such diverse subjects as the following:[4] the effect of humanism on American thinking, content-response analysis in magazines, impact of war on government publicity, philosophy of Niebuhr, majority rule and minority representation as provided by the electoral system of the limited vote, case study of the *Nation,* development of prize law, study of methodology in the social sciences, informational activities of the State Department, political aspects of birth control, foreign policy of the American Legion, Senate Judiciary Committee, violence in labor disputes, removal of public officers, problems of non-voting, the Chinese Foreign Office, welfare

[4] 42 *American Political Science Review* (1948), 759-80.

clause of the Constitution, patents and copyrights, third-degree practices in the administration of justice, municipal licensing, county functions, woman's rights movements, fear of Bonapartism in France, international federation, and the interposition of states on behalf of nationals having interests in foreign corporations.

A search for unity out of this variegated manifold does indeed tax one's ingenuity. Throwing up their hands in defeat when confronted with such heterogeneity, some political scientists have ventured the opinion that this is the great weakness of their discipline: it lacks the intrinsic unity necessary to make a science. Without this essential unity there can be no cohesion of subject matter. It cannot constitute a system. If it is true that political science is fragmentized into a large number of fields, related only in that they deal with men in society or with something loosely called governmental problems, then certainly from the very beginning the search for a few central, common concepts would turn out to be futile.

One thing, however, is certain. Political scientists are not interested in all kinds of facts in the world. Some process of selection does take place. Quite instinctively, if only as a result of slavish adherence to their training, they turn their attention to a kind of fact that differs radically from the kind other social scientists usually study. For example, a political scientist, if he is wise, does not attempt to voice a professional or authoritative opinion on the relation of the breakdown of family life to personal insecurity common in modern society, or on the relation of fluctuating price levels to depressions. His interest leads him to focus on other matters related to these and yet distinctively apart. However diffuse political science may appear to be, there can be no doubt that "political" refers to a separable dimension of human activity.

The origins of this separable interest lie buried in the differences that distinguish all the social sciences, each from the other. This means that in order to appreciate fully the individuality of political science, and its systemic character, we must turn for a moment to the broader question of the historical and logical reasons for the the separation of the various social sciences into independent fields of study. This will provide the clue essential for the discovery of the major orienting concepts implicit within political research.

3. The Divisions Among the Social Sciences

The historical need for a division of labor in social research accounts in some measure for the separate and independent[5] existence of any social discipline. If this were the only reason, however, there would be little ground for disputing the contention of some historians that the growth of specialization in the social sciences is largely, if not purely, a matter of historical accident. The work entailed in the study of society required some kind of division, and from the historical point of view one kind might seem just as logical or expedient as the other. Yet, ordinary acquaintance with the social sciences does suggest, and close examination confirms, that the original, common, and undifferentiated body of social knowledge underwent a logical development of its own and that, under the impact of the rapid expansion of knowledge, this evolution ultimately led each of the social disciplines to branch off from the parent stem. There is, to be sure, a purely historical basis for the division of knowledge as we know it today, for without the progressive accretions to the fund of social data in each generation, there would be no need or purpose behind specialization. But the intrinsic logic of the development is the vehicle which gave direction to the historical process of fragmentation and specialization.

In elaboration of these conclusions the following discussion ought not to be interpreted as a plea for the continuation of con-

[5] "Independent" does not mean that the problems of any social science are unrelated to the other social sciences; it means only that there are systemic differences appropriate and necessary for the purposes of simplifying complex social data.

temporary specialization in the social sciences. Rather, I adopt as a premise and a continuing conviction that specialization has in fact been carried to such an extreme today that the whole body of social knowledge threatens to disintegrate into a multitude of intellectual feudalities. Each specialist is sovereign in his own field. Each specialty appropriates its own concepts, jargon, and its unique techniques, with the obvious result that each area of specialization is virtually a foreign domain to its neighbor. Today this condition has stimulated a movement towards a re-integration of our compartmentalized knowledge which should go a long way towards remedying these defects.[6] But even if the social sciences, for teaching and applied purposes, do achieve a measure of integration and unification, there can be no doubt that to continue creative additions to social knowledge at the higher levels of inquiry, the distinctions among various areas of research will have to be maintained. Even though the future must witness an increase in the rate of cross-fertilization and in the degree of co-operation among the social sciences, there are few realists who envision the ultimate fusion and disappearance of all specialties into one body of knowledge.

To telescope into a few brief phrases the evolution of the social sciences towards their present excessively specialized state cannot do justice to its complicated, tortuous nature. Over the past twenty-five hundred years the central body of knowledge about social matters has undergone a complete transformation. At one time this knowledge was unified and largely undifferentiated, and it was the proper topic for discussion by any articulate person who wished to contribute his share to an understanding of society. Today, in contrast, the original body of unspecialized knowledge has gradually been reduced in quantity and scope by the divorce from it of the separately organized contemporary social sciences. From an era, several centuries ago, of integrated, unified knowledge, we have today arrived at a period of extreme specialization. The weight of all empirical knowledge has become too

[6] See L. Wirth, op. cit.

heavy for any one person to carry and too intensive for any one scholar to digest and develop in creative research.

In no small degree this trend towards specialization has been imposed by the historical accumulation of knowledge to which we are heirs. Until the eighteenth century, the moral sciences, as the social sciences were then known, possessed greater unity than diversity. So broad was the range of subject matter with which the moral philosopher dealt that he was truly a universal student of society. But with the increase in the rate of research by the beginning of the nineteenth century, economics, through the efforts of Adam Smith, and sociology, in the work of Auguste Comte, began to pry themselves loose from the main body of social thinking. Psychology, too, had by that time made some progress in separating itself from philosophy. And by the end of the century, anthropology, inspired by the work of the Scottish school at an earlier period, emerged from its swaddling clothes.

Of all the areas of social life, politics was the first to win the concentrated attention of men. The overwhelming interest of the ancient Greeks centered in the nature of the political system; Plato's interest in human nature, for example, and in problems of education and other matters stemmed from his concern for the *polis* as a whole. Since an understanding of political life was thus the source of inspiration for the study of society, it might have been expected that political science would be one of the first to break away from the main body of moral philosophy. But the truth is that it was the last. Only after the other well-recognized social sciences had drifted away from the general body of knowledge, leaving a residue composed essentially of politics and general philosophy, did the growing weight of political data finally force political science as well to branch out on its own.

Thus the purely physical need for a division of labor helps to account for the distinctions among the social sciences. This fact, however, cannot be used as a means for explaining the genuine deep-going differences in the data of these sciences. It could be argued, and often is, that the social sciences have grown up as

separate disciplines because—and only because—of this historical necessity. The actual allocation of subject matter to the various
disciplines is simply a matter of accident. It follows from this view
that if the social problems with which the various disciplines now
deal had been farmed out in a different way, what is today economics might conceivably deal, not only with typical economic
problems, but also with what has usually been identified as typical anthropological or political issues. Just as soon as the implications of the historical view are spelled out in this way, it becomes apparent that the division among the social sciences owes
its existence to more than historical accident and the accumulation of knowledge. The separation and withdrawal of the various
bodies of knowledge each from the other have a rationale of their
own.

Distinctions in social knowledge have existed from the beginning of human inquiry into society. They are implicit in the
works of the earliest social philosophers even though, as already
mentioned, the paucity of actual information about human activity left it possible for any one individual to assimilate and comment upon the whole body of knowledge. These distinctions arise
from the elemental fact that we are human beings who live in an
organized society. To survive and continue any given mode of
life we are confronted with the need to solve a variety of problems at a given time and in a given place. As a result of the nature of this social life, men have been compelled to direct their
attention to certain recurrent typical problems. The fact that we
can turn to Plato or Aristotle or Machiavelli for insights into
contemporary social problems vouches for the latter's recur-
rence. To answer these questions about the functioning of society
itself and about the biological and psychological basis of human
conduct, social investigators had to look at certain constellations or clusters of elements in the concrete world. Each major
complex of questions demanding solution led to the scrutiny of a
special coherence or system of these elements which later came to
be called by the names of each of the social sciences. And this

process continues today. As new urgent questions arise new social sciences emerge or old ones are fused together in a new synthesis.

One kind of major set of questions which men have asked from time immemorial leads to the emergence of the body of potentially systemic knowledge we call psychology. What influence have the motivations of men on the emergence of social problems? This is the key question. It is purely an abstraction because it does not lead the interrogator to seek a solution to all the complications of social life at once. He is putting only a limited question. He hopes that when others who put limited questions from other points of view get together with him or when he acquaints himself with their knowledge, he will be in a superior position to examine the problems of his world in their total complexity. From this desire, therefore, to know the extent to which human nature influences social events, men were prompted to turn to a detailed study of the way human beings behave individually.

Ultimately inquiry of this sort became the field of psychology; it gradually became apparent through the ages that to know something about individual human behavior certain kinds of data were very relevant, other kinds less relevant. The relevant kinds ultimately tended toward a coherent and organized body of facts, a system isolated from other social facts, which we know as psychology. Certain kinds of knowledge had to cluster together into this social science if its original question, dealing with individual behavior, was to be answered. Through the process of research it was discovered that knowledge about prices or political authority was not directly relevant to this question and such data was set aside. Through a long process of selection, ultimately the psychological cluster alone remained. This process was not of a decade or two; it took centuries for the discipline to emerge as a relatively cohesive body of knowledge. But the questions which led to this discipline were asked by the earliest social philosophers and that is why it is impossible to return to Aristotle or

Plato, and even the Biblical literature, without obtaining some insights into what we identify today as a psychological matter.

A similar process took place for each of the other social sciences. Each is a body of knowledge relating to a set of key issues in which society has shown a vital concern. The view here presented means, therefore, that any social science emerges for a deeper reason than mere historical accident or the need to divide the burden of research. It is in the logic of the situation that each separate, distinct, and vital set of questions posed, leads to the discovery that the answer involves the pursuit of ramifying paths of related knowledge. All the social sciences may well have a common body of theory,[7] and the paths of the social sciences may cross and may be the same at some points for short distances. But each social discipline works out its own pattern or system since its motivating questions lead it to a different proximate goal, although the ultimate purposes to serve human needs are the same.

Political science, too, arose in this way. The body of data which compose it grew up in response to some key questions, the answers to which men thought would help in the amelioration of their collective lives. These key questions set the initial orientation of political research. The knowledge, therefore, that it is the motivating questions that distinguish the social sciences helps us to understand the subject matter of political science itself. It leads us to search for these questions, which, strangely enough, are not easily discovered. Although men who are political scientists have no doubt about the fact that they are political scientists— after all, they were trained as political scientists or they are paid by political science departments, a matter of no small importance —there is some doubt about why the congeries of subjects they discuss properly fall within the scope of politics or constitute variables within a concrete political system.

Lack of awareness, and where awareness does exist, of agreement, about the major orienting concepts of political re-

[7] T. Parsons, *Essays in Sociological Theory Pure and Applied,* chapter 3.

search is an index of the fact that this discipline is coming late into the field as a social science. Men will always differ about the reasons for their activity, but there does seem to be less agreement in political science than in most of the other social sciences. The task of the rest of this chapter and the next will be to identify the basic questions in search of an answer to which men have turned to the study of the distinctively political aspects of human activity. In this way we may be able to unearth a few integrative concepts that serve to identify the major characteristics of the political system.

4. The Concept of the State

Although there is little agreement on the key questions which orient political research, in the course of history two main schools of thought have developed. One directs itself to the study of political life by asking what are the nature and characteristics of the state; the other, by asking what can be understood about the distribution and use of power. We must examine the extent to which the question of either school leads to a gross frame of reference revealing the most general and characteristic properties of political life.

The weight of the discussion here will be that neither the state nor power is a concept that serves to bind together political research. Each has some merit but also has distinct shortcomings. It could be argued, of course, that political science ought to confine itself to something called the state or it ought to display an exclusive interest in power. To do this, however, would be to attempt to create a new field in the pattern of its designer. No such attempt will be made here since there is no evidence that political science shows any inherent limitations in its present focus to prevent it from answering the kind of questions it really asks. In the next chapter I shall suggest that this question is: How are values authoritatively allocated for a society? Hence, an attempt at total revision would be needless and gratuitous. Here the objective is simply to describe for purposes of clarification the major kinds of variables that scholars who deal with politics, whatever their personal inclinations, have been compelled to scrutinize in order to solve the questions they posed. The conclusion will be that we must reconstruct prevailing conceptions of the subject matter of political science if we are to understand what has given political research its minimal coherence over the centuries.

The opinion is broadly held that what draws the various divisions of political science together is the fact that they all deal with the state. "The phenomena of the state," reads an elementary text, "in its varied aspects and relationships, as distinct from the family, the tribe, the nation, and from all private associations or groups, though not unconnected with them, constitute the subject of political science. In short, political science begins and ends with the state." [8]

This description is deceptively simple. The truth is that it achieves greater success in confusing than in clarifying since it immediately begs the question as to the characteristics of the state. And to anyone who is familiar with the infinite diversity of responses to this question, the suspicion must indubitably arise that it succeeds in substituting one unknown for another; for the unknown of "political science" we now have the unknown of the "state."

What is the state? One author claims to have collected one hundred and forty-five separate definitions. [9] Seldom have men disagreed so markedly about a term. The confusion and variety of meanings is so vast that it is almost unbelievable that over the last twenty-five hundred years in which the question has recurringly been discussed in one form or another, some kind of uniformity

[8] J. W. Garner, *Political Science and Government* (New York: American Book, 1928), p. 9. See also R. G. Gettell, *Political Science* (rev. ed., New York: Ginn, 1949), p. 19: "Since political science is the science of the state, a clear understanding of what is meant by the term 'state' is important."

[9] C. H. Titus, "A Nomenclature in Political Science," 25 *American Political Science Review* (1931), 45-60, on p. 45.

has not been achieved. One person sees the state as the embodiment of the moral spirit, its concrete expression; another, as the instrument of exploitation used by one class against others. One author defines it as simply an aspect of society, distinguishable from it only analytically; another, as simply a synonym for government; and still another, as a separate and unique association among a large number of other associations such as the church, trade unions, and similar voluntary groups. For those who ascribe to the state ultimate power or sovereignty within constitutional or customary limits there are corresponding thinkers who insist upon the limited authority of the state whenever a conflict of allegiance to it and to other associations arises. There is clearly little hope that out of this welter of differences anyone today can hammer out a meaning upon which the majority of men will genuinely, consistently, and constantly agree. When general agreement has sometimes arisen, small differences have usually become magnified and have laid the basis for new and forbidding disagreement. Hence it seems pointless to add a favored definition of my own to those already listed.

After the examination of the variety of meanings a critical mind might conclude that the word ought to be abandoned entirely. If the argument is raised that it would be impossible to find a substitute to convey the meaning of this term, intangible and imprecise as it is, the reply can be offered that after this chapter the word will be avoided scrupulously and no severe hardship in expression will result. In fact, clarity of expression demands this abstinence. There is a good reason for this. At this stage of our discussion we are interested in concepts that pick out the major properties of the concrete political system. If we were to use the concept of the state with its most widely adopted meaning today, we would find that it has a number of obvious shortcomings for an understanding of the political system. It describes the properties not of all political phenomena but of only certain kinds, excluding, for example, the study of pre-state societies; it stands overshadowed as a tool of analysis by its social utility as a myth; and it constitutes at best a poor formal definition. Let us look at these three defects in this order.

If political science is defined as the study of the state, can there be said to be any political life to understand in those communities in which the state has not yet appeared? Among the varied conceptions of the state today, the most generally acceptable view accords most closely with that offered by R. M. MacIver. In *The Modern State*[10] he sees the state, in modified pluralist vein, as one association among many with the special characteristic that it acts *"through law as promulgated by a government endowed to this end with coercive power, [and] maintains within a community territorially demarcated the universal external conditions of social order."* [11] The state is different, then, from other kinds of associations in that it embraces the whole of the people on a specific territory and it has the special function of maintaining social order. This it does through its agent, the government, which speaks with the voice of law. Expressed in most general terms, the state comes into existence when there is a fixed territory, a stable government, and a settled population. In the United States this view, with incidental modifications, prevails in a major part of empirical political research that turns to the state as its focus of attention. The territorial state as we have known it since the Treaty of Westphalia has thus become the prototype from which the criteria for all political systems are derived.

But prior to the seventeenth century, for the vast span of time in which men lived and governed one another, according to this interpretation of the state at least, no state was in existence. At most there was a truncated form of political life. Greece had its city-community, mistranslated today as the city-state; the Middle Ages had its system of feudalities; contemporary exotic communities have their councils, leaders, and headmen. But, by definition, this modified pluralism denies that in these communities there is a fully-formed political system. These are transitional political

[10] (London: Oxford University Press, 1926).
[11] Ibid., p. 22. Italics in original.

forms, pre-states, or nascent states, and therefore of only passing interest to political scientists since their main concern is presumably with states fully developed.[12]

Not all scholars would agree when or where the state in this sense appears. But whatever the time and place, all preceding kinds of social life are considered to have been devoid of identifiable political aspects. One student, for example, pushes back the appearance of the state to a very early period in human history. "The shift to agriculture," he writes, "may have taken place first in the alluvial valleys of the Nile and Euphrates, or of the Chinese rivers. While these rich river-bottoms were enormously productive when cultivated, the surrounding regions afforded meager pasturage. When a pastoral kinship group settled on the land, the State began. The group had already set up a government; it now acquired territoriality." [13] In this view, clearly, it took the establishment of a fixed territory to convert mere social life into political life. Not even the existence of government could inform the social existence of the pastoral kinship group with a political quality. The state being non-existent in pastoral groups, there could be little subject matter for political research.

Common sense alone, however, would compel us to deny this restriction upon political inquiry. The literature on contemporary nomadic groups, for example, suggests that the strife within

[12] "Of all the multifarious projects for fixing the boundary which marks off political from the more general social science, that seems most satisfactory which bases the distinction on the existence of a political consciousness. Without stopping to inquire too curiously into the precise connotation of this term, it may safely be laid down that as a rule primitive communities do not and advanced communities do manifest the political consciousness. Hence, the opportunity to leave to sociology the entire field of primitive institutions, and to regard as truly political only those institutions and those theories which are closely associated with such manifestation. A history of political theories, then, would begin at the point at which the idea of the state, as distinct from the family and the clan, becomes a determining factor in the life of the community." W. A. Dunning, *A History of Political Theories* (New York: Macmillan, 1902), pp. xvi-xvii. See also R. M. MacIver, op. cit., p. 338.

[13] E. M. Sait, *Political Institutions* (New York: Appleton-Century, 1938), p. 131.

a migratory tribe for control of its movement and resources is exactly similar to what we would consider political struggle. Similarly, the investiture conflict in the Middle Ages was as highly charged with politics as any dispute today. And there is also a growing awareness that too little attention has been paid to the anthropological data about political life among primitive and non-literate peoples. Where there is any kind of organized activity, incipient as it may be, there, what we would normally call political situations, abound. Thus even if we could reach agreement to adopt as our meaning for empirical research the most general definition today given to the concept of the state, it must still fall short of providing an adequate description of the limits of political research. By definition it excludes social systems in which there can be no question that political interaction is an essential aspect.

The historical origins of the term further help to explain both the difficulties we have with its meaning today and its unsatisfactory nature as an orienting concept. The truth is that the concept was originally less an analytical tool than a symbol for unity. It offered a myth which could offset the emotional attractiveness of the church and which later could counteract the myths of internationalism and of opposing national units.[14]

As a concept the state came into frequent use during the sixteenth and seventeenth centuries. It appears in Machiavelli's *The Prince* although at that time it usually referred to officials of government or to the government itself, not to the political aspects of the whole community. Although it was not until the nineteenth century that the term developed its full mythical qualities, in the interval it served the growing needs of nationalism as against the universal claims of the medieval church and the particularistic com-

[14] Ibid., pp. 88-9; George H. Sabine, "State," *Encyclopaedia of the Social Sciences* (New York: Macmillan, 1930), Vol. 14, pp. 328-32; R. Kranenburg (transl. by R. Borregaard), *Political Theory* (London: Oxford University Press, 1939), pp. 76-7; C. J. Friedrich, *Constitutional Government and Democracy* (Boston: Little, Brown, 1941), chapter 1; F. Watkins, *The State as a Concept of Political Science* (New York: Harper, 1934); H. Finer, *The Theory and Practice of Modern Government* (London: Methuen, 1932), 2 vols., Vol I, chapter 1.

petition of the local feudal powers. It was especially vital as a symbol to combat the emotional appeal of the church. The varied ecclesiastical institutions, officials, and governing bodies could be personified and crystalized in two words, the church. The growing national territorial governments required a similar emotionally imbued concept, and they found it in the happy notion of the state. Men need not serve a government, a king, or an oligarchy; they could pledge their loyalties to a unity as transcendental and eternal as the church itself. Leaders and rulers may come and go, but the state is everlasting and above mundane dispute. Secular authority could thus hope to draw men's allegiance with all the force of religion without depending wholly upon religion for its emotional appeal.

The state concept became a crucial myth in the struggle for national unity and sovereignty. Its very vagueness and imprecision allowed it to serve its purposes well. Each man, each group, and each age could fill the myth with its own content; the state stood for whatever one wanted from life. But however diverse the purposes imputed to the state, it symbolized the inescapable unity of one people on one soil. By the nineteenth century the struggle of nation against church had been largely resolved in favor of the former, but new problems in the form of international conflict arose. In giving an ideological basis for the kind of national sovereignty with which we are familiar, the concept of the state now reaches the height of its political utility. Each state can claim the ultimate loyalty of its members as against a class or an international society because it, the state, in some mystical way now represents the supreme virtues.[15]

Bearing in mind the actual history of the political use of the concept, it is difficult to understand how it could ever prove to be fruitful for empirical work; its importance lies largely in the field of practical politics as an instrument to achieve national cohesion rather than in the area of thoughtful analysis. We can,

[15] C. J. Friedrich, "Deification of the State," 1 *Review of Politics* (1939), 18-30.

therefore, appreciate the difficulty into which we must fall if we attempt to treat the concept as a serious theoretical tool. And yet, for want of a superior set of guiding concepts, this is exactly what large numbers of practicing political scientists do attempt.

This brings us to the last of the three shortcomings mentioned earlier: the inadequacy of the state concept for depicting in general terms what it is the political scientist studies that distinguishes him from other social scientists. The concept falls short of a satisfactory kind of definition. It defines by specifying instances of political phenomena rather than by describing their general properties.

Basically the inadequacy of the state concept as a definition of subject matter stems from the fact that it implies that political science is interested in studying a particular kind of institution or organization of life, not a kind of activity that may express itself through a variety of institutions. For this reason, the use of the state concept, as we saw, could not explain why political scientists ought to be interested in forms of social life, such as nonliterate and exotic societies, in which the state, at least as defined by modified pluralism, does not exist. No one could deny that political science is indeed interested in the state, as defined here, as one type of political institution. But it is equally apparent that political research today, stimulated by the knowledge made available by social anthropology, has begun to accept the fact that societies in which the so-called state institution is nonexistent afford excellent material for a general understanding of political life.

The major drawback of the state concept is thus revealed. It does not serve to identify the properties of a phenomenon that give the latter a political quality. At most, the state concept is usually just an illustration of one kind of political phenomenon, a comprehensive political institution. However, since there are periods in history when such states did not exist, and perhaps the same may be true in the unknown future, the state is revealed as a political institution peculiar to certain historical conditions. Pre-

sumably in order to understand the full scope of political research, it would be necessary to specify in equal detail the kind of
institutions to be studied in social systems from which the state is
absent. The point here is that in practice the field of political science
is usually described by the least desirable and least meaningful
kind of definition, denotation.

There are two substantially different ways of defining an
object—by denotation and by connotation. You can say that a
table belongs to the same class of objects as a desk, a work bench, a
sideboard, and so on, enumerating a list of objects exhaustive at
the time, which are considered to be part of the class in which
table falls. But as time goes on, in all likelihood some new object
would be constructed or discovered which would have to be added
to the list. One would never really know why the new item fell in
that class except for the vague feeling that it has something in
common with other known members of the class. This is a denotative description of a class.

Now, very often in the exploratory phases of research such
a denotative definition is necessary simply because the general
characteristics of a class are at first unknown. But as time passes
attempts are always made to get at the general reason for establishing the class—the properties that the things which fall into this
class must have in common. Here the definition is by connotation.
In the case of tables it is obvious that all these objects have in
common legs or other supports topped by a flat surface. A rough
connotative definition of a table might therefore be "an object
with upright supports upon which rests a flat surface." This would
be a sufficiently general description of its properties to allow any
person to tell clearly whether or not a new object falls into the
class.

The same standards of reasoning apply to the description
of political science. As long as it is characterized as the study of the
state, it must remain at the level of enumerating or denoting the
various kinds of institutions which it examines. Once we ask,

however, just why political science studies the kind of institution often called the state together with other institutions in societies where states are acknowledged to be non-existent, we have a means of discovering the connotative meaning, that is, the general properties of any political phenomenon. We find that we are looking for a kind of activity which can express itself through a variety of institutional patterns. Since new social conditions call forth new kinds of structures and practices for the expression of this activity, the precise mechanism, whether it be an organizational pattern called a state or some other kind, is always a matter for empirical investigation. A general description of this activity, for the moment indifferent to its particular institutional pattern, would indicate the properties that an event must have to make it relevant for political science. To say, therefore, that in asking "what is the nature of the state?" political science is drawing attention to the core of its subject matter, is at best to mistake a part for the whole and to attempt to describe the properties of an activity by a single, even if important, instance.

5. The Concept of Power

Although the state concept as such has seldom been directly attacked or rejected, it has come in for oblique criticism from a long line of writers who see that the characteristic of political activity, the property that distinguishes the political from the economic or other aspect of a situation, is the attempt to control others. In this view the motivating question behind political research is "who holds power and how is it used?" It is true that most political scientists who adopt the power concept continue to speak of the state and seldom go so far as to argue that there is an intrinsic hostility between the two ideas in an empirical context. Nevertheless, the idea of the state usually recedes into the shadows of their empirical research and plays little part in their conclusions.

The obvious merit of the power approach is that it identifies an activity, the effort to influence others. *Prima facie* this makes it superior to the institutional description of political life as the state. Any activity that is characterized by the general property of being able to influence others immediately acquires political relevance. Therefore, we have here at least a connotative definition. In spite of this and in spite of the prevalence today of the conviction that power lies at the heart of political research, my conclusion will nevertheless be that the idea of power, as it has been employed until quite recently, has failed to provide a rounded description of the gross subject matter of political science.

Because the power concept has in the past been associated with doctrines that asserted the limitless power of government, students have traditionally adopted a deep suspicion towards this approach. Where a social philosopher has adopted the idea of power as central to his thinking, as in the case of Machiavelli or Hobbes, it has usually seemed to imply abusive coercion on behalf of the coercer. It has therefore appeared that this view of the central problem of politics must always carry with it a certain misanthropy towards life. Where political life seemed to be reduced to a mere struggle for power, all the noble aims which the philosophers have depicted as the matrix of life seemed to crumble.

In spite of these unhappy associations of the power approach, however, some contemporary students of political science have succeeded in rehabilitating it as an orienting concept. They have discerned in it an activity which would lend itself to scientific study and which might cover the whole field of political life. Their great merit has been that they have made the power approach more respectable in the United States than it ever had been. They have converted it from a street urchin to an irreproachable child of the age. Indeed, it has become respectable enough today for courses on power to be offered in the universities and for widely used texts, such as *Politics Among Nations* by H. J. Morgenthau,[16] *American Politics* by P. H. Odegard and E. A. Helms[17] and *Politics Parties and Pressure Groups* by V. O. Key[18] to use power as the central theme around which to weave their facts about political life.

Despite this latter-day, hard-earned popularity, however, for a reason not difficult to find, the power approach must fail to convince us of its merits as an adequate, initial identification of the boundaries of political research. The reason for this is that power is only one of the significant variables. It omits an equally vital aspect of political life, its orientation towards goals other than power itself. Political life does not consist exclusively of a struggle for control; this struggle stems from and relates to conflict over the direction of social life, over public policy, as we say today in a somewhat legal formulation. Some attention to the work of George Catlin[19] and Harold D. Lasswell,[20] two of the most articulate architects of power theories, will point up the merits, inadequacies, and necessary modifications of an attempt to describe the limits of political science predominantly in terms of power relations.

The work of Catlin represents one of the few deliberate and serious efforts to build a systematic theory for the study of political life. In its attempt to construct an abstract analytical framework, his work blazes a trail, however rough, along which political science must ultimately follow. At the same time, however, it is a lesson of the pitfalls encountered in premature systematization, especially before the problems of theory formulation, basic concepts, and essential types of data[21] have been thoroughly aired

[16] (New York: Knopf, 1948), p. 13: "International politics, like all politics, is a struggle for power."

[17] (New York: Harper, 1947, 2nd ed.). See p. 1 where the authors quote with approval H. Lasswell's and M. Weber's descriptions of politics as power.

[18] See p. 3: "The sphere of politics . . . may be restricted primarily to an examination of those power or control relationships having to do with the machinery of government."

[19] See especially *A Study of the Principles of Politics* and *The Science and Method of Politics*.

[20] Particularly in *Politics: Who Gets What, When, How* (New York: McGraw-Hill, 1936) and with A. Kaplan in *Power and Society*.

[21] See chapters 6, 7, and 8.

and understood. We shall be concerned at this point only with Catlin's isolation of power as the primary and most inclusive variable of political life.

Catlin voices a common complaint against traditional political science. It is largely interested in political institutions, but unfortunately these appear with relative rarity in the world. If we study the so-called state, there are less than seventy in all. How can one hope to discover highly probable generalizations about them when they are so few. The physical scientists would have little knowledge about their data if they had to confine themselves to less than a hundred atoms. In the same way, even if one takes political parties, legislatures, or any other political organization, the number available for study are so limited that comprehensive and stimulating comparison is almost impossible. Catlin contends, therefore, that the reason for the relative backwardness of the study of politics as a science lies largely in its failure to isolate a political phenomenon which is repeated with a frequency sufficient for it to be studied exhaustively. Political data must be so repetitive that their functioning can be understood from the unlimited variety of available cases.

Unconsciously emulating Cornewall Lewis, who a hundred years earlier had unsuccessfully attempted to lay the foundations for a science of politics, Catlin in effect contends that "all political conduct is resolvable into a series of political acts." [22] Only through the discovery of the distinctly political act will political science be able to find a datum as fundamental as that of the atom. Catlin claims to have located this datum. It is the act of will, that is, the desire to execute one's desires. Here, he says, in the act of will, is a fact which appears constantly in all human activity. Whether we wish it or not, whether we are aware or totally ignorant of it, all people seek to assert themselves, if only to retire from the society of men to seek nirvana. The act of withdrawal itself requires sufficient influence over other wills so that this desire

[22] G. C. Lewis, *A Treatise on the Methods of Observation and Reasoning in Politics,* Vol. II, p. 310.

for solitude can be realized. This desire to fulfill one's desire is the prime psychological fact upon which a science of politics can be built.

But to assert the will, control over the will of others is required and accordingly the political fact at the second level is, in Hobbesian vein, a conflict of wills, in which each seeks to dominate by force, cajolery, persuasion, tradition, or law over the wills of others. This is the essence of the struggle for power. The study of power does not involve solely the way in which government dominates society and maintains order, although that is important, but it embraces the far broader problem of the way in which one person or group influences the activity of another. The securing of the adjustment of the will of another to one's own is the essence of the political act.

With the struggle of wills as the foundation of politics and as the core around which causal political theory in the strict sense must be built, for Catlin the rest of the subject matter of political science is clear. It deals with all the institutions, conventions, and mores which give free rein to or balk the will of individuals, with the character of those who control others, and, finally, with the nature, degree, and intensity of this power.

The merit of Catlin's conceptualization is that it does recognize the need to focus on a property, a kind of activity that converts a situation into a proper datum for political research. But the selection of the power aspect alone as the exclusive property of that datum leaves much to be desired. This lacuna will be examined after we look at the theory of Lasswell.

Lasswell is a second serious student of power relations, and perhaps in recent times, together with other members of the so-called Chicago School, he has contributed more than any other individual to the popular diffusion of this approach in the United States. He approaches the study of politics from a point of view slightly broader than that of Catlin and consequently differs from the latter considerably in his conclusions. They both agree, however, in their emphasis on power. Lasswell sees political science as an "autonomous" discipline and "not merely applied psychology or applied economics." [23] He describes it initially, not as the power process, but as "the study of changes in the shape and composition of the value patterns of society." [24] However, since the distribution of values must depend upon the influence of the members of society, political science must deal with influence and the influential. Integral to his thinking, therefore, is the conclusion that the major concepts guiding political research must be values and power. In its broadest perspective the task of political research is to show the interdependence between the two: how our values affect the distribution and use of power and how our location and use of power act on the distribution of values. Or as he phrased it in the happy title of his well-read little book, political science concerns *Politics: Who Gets What, When, How.*

The title of this book represents his most general conception of the subject matter of political science and was offered as such by the author himself. "Those who accept the frame of reference here proposed," he wrote in his preface to this book, "will share common standards to guide future intellectual effort." In terms of the actual problems that were explored in this work, however, the title appears somewhat overambitious. It does not really mirror the contents lying between its covers. It bears the promise that the author will discuss how social values are distributed in society—when it is and how it is that certain groups get more or less of socially valuable things. In fact, however, it is devoted to exploring the sources of power held by a political elite. Its focus therefore is not on the way values are distributed but on the way the elite, which has power, uses it to acquire the desirable things of society, such as safety, income, and deference. The book is primarily an inquiry into the means the elite uses to arrive at and survive in the seat of power. If political science is devoted to the study of changing value patterns, as Lasswell maintains, this study

[23] *Power and Society,* p. xviii.
[24] *World Politics and Personal Insecurity* (New York: McGraw-Hill, 1935), p. 3; see also *Politics: Who Gets What, When, How* chapter 1; *Power and Society,* pp. xii and 240.

must be interpreted as describing only a small part of the whole process. It is restricted to revealing the role of the minority that holds power.

Contrary to general belief, therefore, this work on *Politics: Who Gets What, When, How* does not in itself provide a general framework for the study of political life. It is a vehicle not for the investigation of the whole political system but only for determining the power and characteristics of one social formation, the elite. The book is devoted, therefore, to an examination of the composition of the elite and the conditions and techniques of its existence. The fact is that under exactly the same title one could write a volume making the antithetical assumption—that the masses dominate over policy—and then go on to explore historically the composition of the various masses and the conditions and techniques surrounding their survival and change. Such a work would provide no more comprehensive a framework than a study of the variables influencing the power of the elite.

In short, the elitist theory is only a partial scheme of analysis helping us to discern the sources of power over values of certain groups but presenting us with little data about the power of others. It centers only on one problem, however crucial it is today: the tendency in mass societies for power to concentrate in the hands of a minority. It assumes that this oligarchic tendency in the political system eternally prevents the diffusion of power beyond the governing group. Aside from the validity of such a theory and its insight, the point here is that all it provides is a synthetic theory.[25]

This narrow-gauge theory, however, has been interpreted by most political scientists to mean that Lasswell conceived the whole subject matter of political science to be the struggle for power. And, in fact, until the publication of *Power and Society,* the emphasis of Lasswell's research was weighted so heavily on the power side, that it was justifiable to draw the inference that he thought power stood alone at the heart of political research. In

[25] See chapter 2 for this term.

Power and Society, however, Lasswell and his collaborator under-take the broader task suggested in *Politics: Who Gets What, When, How* of exploring the total configuration of power in relation to values. The authors write that "the political act takes its origin in a situation in which the actor strives for the attainment of various values for which power is a necessary (and perhaps also sufficient) condition." [26]

We shall see in the next chapter that even this attempt, unique with Lasswell, to describe political science as the study of the distribution of values is unsatisfactory. It describes all social science rather than political science alone; this helps to explain why in recent years he has broadened the scope of his own research to cover all the social sciences, the policy sciences as he is fond of calling them.[27] However, from the nature of his early work and of his influence as a teacher and author, power appeared to be the central datum of political science. In retrospect we can see this to be a misconstruction of his conception of the nature of political life, but in terms of his impact on American political research, we can say that until recently, with Catlin, he appeared to have adopted an exclusively power orientation.

In contrast to Catlin's use of the power concept, Lasswell's yielded immediate and promising results within the limits of his elitist interpretation of the location of power. It offered greater opportunity for fruitful empirical research largely because, unlike Catlin, Lasswell consciously defined the field so as to invite concrete investigations. It stimulated an interest in the characteristics of governing groups, their skills, class origin, subjective attitudes and personality traits, and the instruments, such as goods, practices, violence and symbols, that they use in arriving at and surviving in the seat of power. It led Lasswell to inquire, from a concurrent interest in psychoanalysis, into the personality types that arrive, an inquiry that brings out sharply the emphasis in our

[26] *Power and Society,* p. 240.
[27] See, for example, his *Power and Personality* (New York: Norton, 1948), esp. chapter 6; and D. Lerner and H. D. Lasswell, *The Policy Sciences* (Stanford: Stanford University Press, 1951), esp. chapter 1.

culture on power as a driving motive. It thereby broke new ground in the study of political leadership. The use of the power concept helped to tie together what seemed like miscellaneous data about the operation of various political pressure groups and about the tactics of politicians. These data could now be viewed as contributing towards a theory of power.

But in spite of these obvious merits, neither Lasswell nor Catlin do provide us with a satisfactory minimal orientation to political phenomena. Both writers argue that all power relations, wherever they may exist, are automatically an index of the presence of a political situation. For these writers the hierarchical arrangement of relationships within a criminal band or in a respectable fraternal club both testify to the existence of political life there. The realization of this implication when politics is described as power, pure and simple, reveals the excessive breadth of the definition. Not that Catlin and Lasswell were wrong in maintaining that political science is and ought to be interested in these phenomena, but they were misleading when they failed to point out that political scientists are not concerned with them for their own sake. The definition is too broad, for political science is not interested in the power relations of a gang or a family or church group simply because in them one man or group controls the actions of another. It might be necessary, to be sure, to devote time to such a comprehensive examination of power situations in order to develop a generalized theory of power. This theory would be very helpful to the political scientist, but by the nature of his task he directs his attention not to power in general but to political power.

What Catlin and Lasswell, and in fact many power theorists, neglect to clarify is the distinction between power in general and power in a political context.[28] In fact, even though they do not distinguish verbally between these two different aspects of power and insist upon power in general as the central phenomenon of

[28] For examples of political scientists who do make this distinction in practice see V. O. Key, op. cit., p. 3, and P. H. Odegard and E. A. Helms, op. cit.

politics, in their practical research their natural predisposition toward political questions quite logically leads them to emphasize the political aspects of power. An inquiry into the characteristics of this aspect will compel us to modify their conception of the limits of political science.

Neither the concept of the state nor that of power in general offers a useful gross description of the central theme of political research. The task of the next chapter, therefore, will be to explore suitable concepts for identifying in broad outline the major political variables.

Chapter **5**

A Convenient Guide for Political Inquiry

> The notion of "The State" draws us
> imperceptibly into a consideration of the
> logical relationship of various ideas to one
> another, and away from facts of human
> activity. It is better, if possible, to start from
> the latter and see if we are not led thereby
> into an idea of something which will turn
> out to implicate the marks and signs which
> characterize political behavior.
>
> John Dewey

LET us recall for a moment what our task is at this point. We are trying to find a convenient way of describing very roughly the limits of political research, trying to identify the major properties of the political aspects of social life. Not that we ought to expect to arrive at a definitive description of political science valid for all time. As I have observed, this would be the task of a final and eternally valid conceptual framework, a goal that in principle lies beyond the realm of possibility. Nevertheless, each age is called upon to reformulate its own views of the limits of political research, and of necessity such views will reflect the level of the prevailing knowledge. The least that can be said today, therefore, is that from the perspective and knowledge available to students of political life, neither the concept of the state nor that of power is satisfactory even as a rough approximation. This chapter will inquire into a possible alternative way of depicting in gross outline the kind of things usually called political.

1. The Common Sense Idea of Political Life

The question that over the centuries has inspired the research of those interested in the political side of life, even though they themselves did not always take the trouble to verbalize it, is this: First and foremost, what is the nature of the good life, that is, what kind of goals ought men to seek?;[1] and once they are articulated, what steps ought the society to take to put them into effect as an authoritative statement of policy? From this initial inquiry there flows a series of questions out of which empirical political research has stemmed. To find out how a society can realize its goals, we must immediately seek answers to such questions as these: What are the actual authoritative policies adopted by a society? How are they determined and how are they put into effect? These are the lead or orienting questions around which the study of political life revolves. In a moment we shall refine these questions and explore the meaning of the constituent terms. Here, however, we need first, by an appeal to common sense, to test the validity of thus identifying the central problems of political research. If our orienting concepts do not appeal initially to common sense, there is little likelihood that they could be made more attractive simply by incorporating them in a technical vocabulary.

Let us for a moment retrace our steps as social scientists and return to the outlook of the ordinary person who has not re-

[1] See L. Strauss "On Classical Political Philosophy," 12 *Social Research* (1945), 98-117.

ceived technical training in either political or social science. If we can recapture for a moment our original and unembellished naïvete about matters political, it will help us to perceive their primary characteristics. In the mind unburdened with professional learning two things immediately associate themselves with the political aspect of life. In the first place, there is an immediate awareness of the pervasiveness of a kind of activity that in our idiom we call politicking. Wherever we find a group of people, whatever their purposes or form of organization, there we usually encounter maneuvering for position and power. We speak in this sense about the politicking within a group, and if we have not had very much experience with social groups we might be inclined to deplore this kind of activity. We might join Emerson in speculating on "what satire on government can equal the severity of censure conveyed in the word *politic,* which now for ages has signified *cunning,* intimating that the State is a trick?" [2] Experience, however, quickly leads us to the conclusion that there is seldom a group, however noble and even sacred its purposes, in which such practices do not occur. When these practices are detected in large social groups such as trade unions, or among nations, we call them the struggle for power.

Upon pressing our inquiry further we find that, if freed of special knowledge, when we speak about a political problem we also use the term "political" in a second typical sense which includes politicking and yet goes beyond it. In this second sense, the word normally refers to an activity related in some vague way to problems of government or the making of policy for the whole society in which we live. We have in mind some dispute over the policies accepted as authoritative for the society; what we mean by authoritative can be set aside for the moment. What is certain is that we know quite naturally that not all policies made in a society are of the same scope. Some, adopted by private groups such

[2] R. W. Emerson, "Politics" in *Essays and Other Writings* (London: Cassell, 1927), p. 343.

as a family, an association, or the like, are expected to apply only to the members of these groups or to others who wish to abide by them. But other policies apply to members of the whole society by virtue of their presence in or ties with the society. Such policies are considered to be authoritative for the society. There is politicking or a struggle among various groups to influence the kind of policy adopted as authoritative for the society of which they are part.

In this quite natural and unstrained kind of reasoning we can see that in its most comprehensive aspect and in the sense normally used when referring to public affairs, the central theme of a political problem is as much the kind of policy at stake as the means used to influence that policy. In ordinary conversation when we engage in political dispute, the point at issue is usually the kind of program we approve, the kind of policy we would like to see adopted for our society. We may deplore the kind or amount of politicking that may exist in relation to political issues but we consider ourselves embroiled in a political situation when we differ about the ends to be adopted in the name of the broadest group to which we belong.

Normally, therefore, we may speak of the power struggle in a fraternal organization as politics in a narrow sense; but we do not speak of dispute over the kind of decisions this group ought to make with regard to its internal matters as a political issue. We reserve the term "political" in this sense for public or social matters. Although inescapable, our interest in politicking or the struggle for power is only derivative; it helps us to understand the kind of policy finally adopted for the society and the way in which such a policy has been put into effect. If we were to sum up our common sense conception of politics it might conceivably take the following form: Political life concerns all those varieties of activity that influence significantly the kind of authoritative policy adopted for a society and the way it is put into practice. We are said to be participating in political life when our activity relates in some way to the making and execution of policy for a society.

2. The Authoritative Allocation of Values for a Society

Let us examine more closely, within the framework of our discussion to this point, what is implied in these conclusions derived from just ordinary knowledge about politics. In effect, what we have here described in the crude terms of common sense is the empirical or concrete political system. We are in effect saying that all those kinds of activities involved in the formulation and execution of social policy, in what has come to be called elliptically in political science, the policy-making process, constitute the political system. The principle upon which these activities can be said to cohere or provide a minimum of relatedness is the fact that they all bear some relevance to the way in which policy for a society is created and effectuated. It is this, consequently, that must give the political system a quality distinguishing it, for example, from the economic system. And because political science has historically set for itself the task of understanding what social policy ought to be, how it is set and put into effect, its general objective must be to understand the functioning of the political system. We have in the concept of authoritative policy for a society a convenient and rough approximation to a set of orienting concepts for political research. It provides us with the essential property of that complex of activity, called political, that over the years men have sought to understand.

But this is only the first step on the way to discovering the focus of political research. We must inquire into the meaning of the three concepts used in this description: policy, authority, and society. We shall examine them in this order and in the process we shall be led to rephrase the description slightly. In the end, I shall suggest, convenience for purposes of actual research dictates that political science be described as the study of the authoritative allocation of values for a society.

To look at the first of the three concepts just mentioned, what do we mean when we talk about policy? The essence of a policy lies in the fact that through it certain things are denied to some people and made accessible to others. A policy, in other words, whether for a society, for a narrow association, or for any other group, consists of a web of decisions and actions that allocates values. A decision alone is of course not a policy; to decide what to do does not mean that the thing is done. A decision is only a selection among alternatives that expresses the intention of the person or group making the choice. Arriving at a decision is the formal phase of establishing a policy; it is not the whole policy in relation to a particular problem. A legislature can decide to punish monopolists; this is the intention. But an administrator can destroy or reformulate the decision by failing either to discover offenders or to prosecute them vigorously. The failure is as much a part of the policy with regard to monopoly as the formal law. When we act to implement a decision, therefore, we enter the second or effective phase of a policy. In this phase the decision is expressed or interpreted in a series of actions and narrower decisions which may in effect establish new policy.[3]

If the law directs that all prices shall be subject to a specified form of control but black markets take root and the appropriate officials and the society as a whole accept their existence, the actual policy is not one of price control alone. It also includes the acceptance of black markets. The study of policy here includes an examination of the functioning and the determinants of both the legal and the actual policy practices. Similarly, if the formal policy of an educational system forbids discrimination against Negroes but local school boards or administrators so zone school attendance that Negroes are segregated in a few schools, both the impartial law and the discriminatory practices must be considered part of the policy.

If we are to orient ourselves properly to the subject matter

[3] H. Simon, D. Smithburg, and V. Thompson, in their *Public Administration*, elevate administrative practices to a central place in political research. See also F. M. Marx (ed.), *Elements of Public Administration* (New York: Prentice-Hall, 1946), *ad hoc*.

of political research, therefore, it is important that we do not narrowly construe social policy by viewing it only as a formal, that is, legal, decision. It is possible, of course, to interpret policy as the "apportionment of rights and privileges" [4] by law. But this is only one of the ways in which a policy expresses itself, and from the point of view of empirical research, the legal description of policy cannot be allowed to consume the whole meaning. Therefore, in suggesting that political science is oriented to the study of policy, there is no intention to mistake its subject matter for the kind of legal construction prominent until quite recently. I am suggesting rather that political science is concerned with every way in which values are allocated for a society, whether formally enunciated in a law or lodged in the consequences of a practice.

It would be manifestly erroneous to urge, however, that political science attempts to understand the way in which society allocates all its values. Political science is concerned only with authoritative allocations or policies. This is the reason why Lasswell's intention, as we saw in the preceding chapter, to describe political science as the study of the distribution and composition of value patterns in society must be considered far too broad. We set this matter aside at the time, but we are now ready to return to it. We can see now that political scientists have never been concerned with so extensive a problem, nor for that matter is Lasswell himself in most of his own practical research.

If political science sought to explore the total value pattern of society it would have to embrace all social science. The reason for this is that all social mechanisms are means for allocating values. The structure and processes of society determine the social statuses that we have and the roles that we perform; these in turn enable us to acquire certain benefits or rewards not available to others. Our economic statuses and roles, for example, help to determine the economic benefits that we get in the processes of production and exchange. Similarly our class, educational, religious,

[4] P. H. Odegard and A. E. Helms, op. cit., p. 2.

and other institutions help to distribute unequally other advantages available in a society.[5] Every other set of institutions helps in one way or another to distribute the values in a society.

But none of these modes for allocating desirable or undesirable things need be authoritative. Political science can learn much from the other social sciences because they are all interested to some degree in how institutions distribute what we consider to be advantages or disadvantages. I am suggesting, however, that political research is distinctive because it has been trying to reveal the way in which values are affected by authoritative allocation. We must inquire, therefore, into the characteristics that lend the color of authority to policies. This brings us to the second of the three concepts just mentioned.

Although the literature is replete with discussions about the nature of authority,[6] the meaning of this term can be resolved quickly for our purposes. A policy is authoritative when the people to whom it is intended to apply or who are affected by it consider that they must or ought to obey it. It is obvious that this is a psychological rather than a moral explanation of the term. We can justify its use in this way because it gives to the term a meaning that enables us to determine factually whether a group of people do in practice consider a policy to be authoritative.

I do not, of course, intend to argue that political science ought to or does ignore the moral aspect of authority; a later chapter will deal with the necessary moral foundations of all political research. However, my point here is that the grounds upon which a person accepts a policy as authoritative can be distinguished from the actual acceptance of the authority of the policy. Acceptance of a policy may flow from a number of sources: moral, traditional or customary, or purely from fear of the consequences. Thus when Congress passes a law, we may consider this formal expression of policy to be authoritative because we agree with its

[5] P. Sorokin, *Social Mobility* (New York: Harper, 1927).
[6] For a discriminating bibliography see H. Simon, D. Smithburg, V. Thompson, op. cit., pp. 571-2.

immediate desirability or even with the moral premises out of which it stems. Normally, of course, if we accept a law that we dislike, we do so because in our hierarchy of values the maintenance of a constitutional system may take priority over disobedience to any one policy. Conceivably, however, we could reject this moral premise as the reason for agreeing to the authority of the policy; acceptance might flow simply from a desire to conform, fear of coercion, or total indifference and apathy.

For many purposes, examination of the grounds for accepting the authority of policy might be vital. For purposes of identifying the subject matter of political research, however, whatever the motivations, a policy is clearly authoritative when the feeling prevails that it must or ought to be obeyed. In the present context, therefore, authoritative will be used to mean only that policies, whether formal or effective, are accepted as binding.[7]

As we shall shortly see, it is a necessary condition for the existence of a viable society that some policies appearing in a society be considered authoritative. But a moment's reflection will reveal that political science is not initially and centrally interested in all authoritative policies found in a society. For example, the members of any association, such as a trade union or a church, obviously consider the policies adopted by their organization authoritative for themselves. The constitution and by-laws of an association constitute the broad formal policy within the context of which members of the organization will accept lesser policies as authoritative. Minorities within the group, while they remain as members, will accept the decisions and practices of the group as binding, or authoritative, for the whole membership.

[7] In one of his penetrating asides, Max Weber has expressed this idea neatly. "When we inquire as to what corresponds to the idea of the 'state' in empirical reality," he observes, "we find an infinity of diffuse and discrete human actions, both active and passive, factually and legally regulated relationships, partly unique and partly recurrent in character, all bound together by an idea, namely, the belief in the actual or normative validity of rules and of the authority-relationships of some human beings towards others." E. A. Shils and H. A. Finch, *Max Weber on the Methodology of Social Sciences* (Glencoe, Ill.: Free Press, 1949), p. 99.

In organizations that are less than society-wide we have, therefore, the existence of a variety of authoritative policies. And yet, in spite of the fact that for the members of the organization these policies carry the weight of authority, it is at once apparent that political science does not undertake to study these policies for their own sake. Political science is concerned rather with the relation of the authoritative policies, made in such groups as associations, to other kinds of policies, those that are considered authoritative for the whole society. In other words, political research seeks first and foremost to understand the way in which values are authoritatively allocated, not for a group within society, but for the whole society.

The societal nature of policy is therefore the third conception helpful in isolating the subject matter of political research. We must, however, clarify the meaning of this a little further. In suggesting that policy is of central interest when it relates to a whole society, I do not intend to imply that every policy, to be societal in character, must apply in its immediate consequences to each member of a society. Clearly, policy is selective in its effects, however generally it may be stated. The point is that even though a policy, such as an income-tax law or regional legislation like the TVA Act, may take away or give to only a part of the people in a society, in fact the policy is considered to be authoritative for all. To put this in its legal form, a law as executed may affect the activity of only a few persons in a society, yet in a constitutional political system it will be considered legal and binding by all. This is simply a particular way of saying that where a society exists there will always be a kind of allocation of values that will be authoritative for all or most members of a society even though the allocation affects only on a few.

My point is, in summary, that the property of a social act that informs it with a political aspect is the act's relation to the authoritative allocation of values for a society. In seeking to understand all social activites influencing this kind of allocation, political science achieves its minimal homogeneity and cohesion.

3. The Need for Authoritative Allocations in Society

If it is true, as I have maintained, that from time immemorial men have been asking questions that lead them to seek an understanding of the way values are authoritatively allocated, this has not been just a matter of accident. A minimum condition for the existence of any society is the establishment of some mechanisms, however crude or inchoate, for arriving at authoritative social decisions about how goods, both spiritual and material, are to be distributed, where custom fails to create other patterns. Because every society must fulfill this task there has recurred in every literate society the kind of question political scientists ask today. Let us examine for a moment why this need arises; we will then be in a position to probe more fully into just what is meant by the phrase authoritative allocation of values for a society, and therefore into what gives coherence to political research.

The need for social policy stems from the very character of a society.[8] As a social system, a society is a special kind of human grouping the members of which continually interact with one another and in the process develop a sense of belonging together. This common consciousness, as it is often called, reflects the fact that the members of the social system have a basic similarity in their culture and social structure. But a society consists of more than these characteristics. Dependent nationality groups, for example, experience this feeling of togetherness induced by a common culture and social structure. The societal group, however, is further distinguished by the fact that it seeks to solve all the problems usually associated with the survival and perpetuation of a group of people. The activities of a society, in other words, are broader than those of any of its component groups. Briefly, the broadest grouping of human beings who live together and collectively undertake to satisfy all the minimum prerequisites of group life is what we refer to when we speak of a society.

[8] See a suggestive analysis of the characteristics of a society in J. W. Bennett and M. M. Tumin, *Social Life* (New York: Knopf, 1949).

Various groups may be devoted to special tasks important for the continuity of any society. Groups may devote themselves to tasks such as those of production and exchange for purposes of physical sustenance, the dissemination and communication of knowledge, the maintenance of order, the inculcation of a sense of common purpose and destiny, or provision for the common defense. It is however the peculiar task of no one group within a society to undertake to fulfill all these conditions for existence. Any one group may help to meet some of the conditions; no group aside from society meets them all. The religious and philosophical institutions, for instance, help to instill purpose; the army and foreign policy associations devote themselves to defense; trade unions, business, and consumers' organizations are involved with problems of exchange and distribution of wealth. Each group has sets of tasks, the scope of which embraces something less than all those conditions demanded for the survival of society as a whole. Only a society casts its net over all these tasks.

As I have suggested, wherever we have such a grouping of people who seek to satisfy all these conditions for collective existence, there we find that one of these conditions calls for authoritative allocation of values. The reason for this is elementary. In spite of the glowing early liberal picture of a future when all social relations would be automatically adjusted without intervention in the name of the collectivity, in no society that has yet existed has this occurred. The grain of truth in the late eighteenth-century liberal view lies in the fact that in every society custom does provide for the private solution of a vast variety of differences and conflicts among individuals with regard to their share of the values. But the greater the size and complexity of a society, the narrower does the scope of private negotiation become; and conversely, even in the smallest and simplest society someone must intervene in the name of society, with its authority behind him, to decide how differences over valued things are to be resolved.

This authoritative allocation of values is a minimum prerequisite of any society, even though it is not the only prerequisite. When individuals or groups dispute about the distribution of things considered valuable, whether they be spiritual or material, and when these disputes are not resolved to the satisfaction of the parties through some customary process of private negotiation, then a policy is enunciated with the authority of society behind it and with its acceptance by society as authoritative. It is patent that without the provision for some means of deciding among competing claims to limited values, society would be rent by constant strife; the regularized interaction which distinguishes a society from a random mob of individuals could not exist. Every society provides some mechanisms, however rudimentary they may be, for authoritatively resolving differences about the ends that are to be pursued, that is, for deciding who is to get what there is of the desirable things. An authoritative allocation of some values is unavoidable.

This conclusion may appear to be at odds with the undeniable facts about our international society today or about nonliterate societies where there are no central organs, the policies of which are recognized as authoritative for the whole group. This does appear to raise a difficulty. The trouble flows, however, from an assumption that I have not intended, namely, that authoritative allocations require the existence of a well-defined organization called government.

The question we must ask is this: To what extent does government as we know it today in any unified nation need to exist in order to be able to say that social life has a political aspect? To this point I have said little about the kind of institutional mechanisms necessary for the translation of social power into social policy. The fact that policies recognized as authoritative for the whole society must exist does not imply or assume that a central governmental organization is required in order to make decisions and effectuate them. Institutional devices for making and executing policy may take an infinite variety of forms. The clarity and precision with which the statuses and roles of legislators and administrators are defined will depend upon the level of development of a particular society. Societies could be placed on a continuum with regard to the degree of definition of such roles. Well-defined organizations, which we call government, exist in the national societies of western Europe; scarcely discernible statuses and roles of which a governmental organization is constituted exist in international society and in non-literate societies.

In the interaction among nations today, for example, when they are viewed as units, we have a genuine society even though it is at a less integrated and less rationalized stage of development than in national societies. Nevertheless, it is a separate society. The fact of the continuing contact that we associate with a society, a minimum feeling of similarity which has been growing with the increase in the material and cultural exchanges of a shrinking world, and the obvious need to solve the basic conditions of social coexistence among national units all require that some mechanisms be established for the solution of differences. This is demanded by virtue of the fact that not all disputes are automatically settled through the efforts of individual nations along customary lines. As in the domestic sphere, the solution of differences is in large measure left to the individual national units through bilateral or wider negotiations. Private negotiation is a major mechanism, just as within any national unit there are far more differences over the distribution of values solved by the interacting parties alone than by any authoritative agency acting in the name of society.

But without an explicit statement to the effect, it is patent that the general atmosphere or set of relations within which the individual national units are able to conduct their private negotiations about the distribution of values is dominated and supervised by the great powers. In the last resort, if any specific pattern of distribution of values, or if the general pattern emerging from individual private negotiations over time, does not accord with their conception of a desirable disposition of resources internationally, it has been normal for the great powers to step in to speak with the voice of the international society. We generally associate the collective action of the great powers with crisis situations such as the historic conferences at Westphalia, Vienna, The Hague, Versailles, Teheran, or Potsdam. But between crises it is obvious that the international allocation of values is closely scrutinized by the great powers; therefore, the political matrix within which international activity takes place reflects their outlook.

Within the last fifty years periodic attempts have been made, especially through the structures of the League of Nations and the United Nations, to broaden the base of the organs responsible for speaking with the authoritative voice of the international society. To this extent we have been seeking to rationalize or define more clearly the institutional mechanism for making authoritative allocations of values. These new organizations do not introduce for the first time the idea of providing a formal policy-making and policy-executing mechanism for the international society. The great powers, with lesser powers at the fringe, have always themselves assumed the obligation of fulfilling an obvious condition for the existence of any international contact. The new organizations were designed only to take the place of the earlier device of periodic meetings among the great powers. No less than within national units themselves, the fact of persisting international contact lays down as one of the conditions for its continuation the creation of means for the authoritative settling of differences. For this reason the study of international politics is integral with the study of politics in general; it concerns the same genus of subject matter. It deals with the functioning and determinants of those policies, both formal, legal decisions as well as practices, which have most influenced the allocation of social goods—or we might say analogically, with the functioning and the determinants of authoritative policy in the international society. It differs from political research in domestic matters only with regard to the society to which it refers.

A glance at non-literate societies indicates even more clearly that the kind of institutional mechanisms for making authoritative policies or the clarity with which the roles of policy-makers are defined is irrelevant to the fact of the existence of such policies. Consider the case of two Bantu tribes living in western Kenya, the Logoli and the Vugusu[9] of approximately 45,000 inhabitants each, as they functioned before the intrusion of Western civilization. Each tribe is divided into clans, subclans, and lineages. Neither of these tribes has a formal political organization, either for the resolution of disputes among the members of the tribe or between the tribe and some outsider. To the casual observer it might appear that no political activity goes on here at all since there is clearly no central body to make authoritative policy. Political statuses and roles are hardly distinguishable; there is no institution that at first glance seems to undertake the tasks of government as we know it. Interpersonal private negotiation, dominated by custom, regulates the largest part of the life of the tribes, so that where differences arise they are automatically resolved without recourse to the kind of special deliberation we associate with government.

But as is usual in these circumstances, custom is never strong enough to bind all men equally; and, in addition, novel situations arise where the rule to be invoked is in doubt. The political function is here taken over by the elders of a subclan when the dispute is confined to members of the same subclan; and when it involves members of different subclans, by the elders of the clan as a whole. There is normally no formal meeting of the elders in the subclan, who can be found talking over local problems in the pasture every morning. Only when the elders of the entire clan are required, is a special meeting called. If these individuals agree on a policy, means are available through their prestige to enforce it; but if the elders are divided on the solution, then it is possible that the minority may secede from the clan and join another. In

---

[9] See the account of the political organization of these tribes in M. Fortes and E. E. Evans-Pritchard (eds.) *African Political Systems,* pp. 197-238; K. Davis, *Human Society* (New York: Macmillan, 1950), pp. 481 ff., draws on this material in his discussion of political institutions. The whole of *African Political Systems* is of exceptional value to political scientists because of the theoretical problems it raises in an empirical context.

cases of inter-clan friction, it is the elders of the offender's clan who are expected to settle the policy; if they fail to produce a satisfactory solution then the clans may enter into violent conflict. This sets in motion attempts by the elders of neutral clans to arbitrate and seek a reconciliation.

It is clear that in all these procedures we have a mechanism, at times peaceful, at others violent, for arriving at authoritative policy, a condition for the continuation of the society. We are accustomed to associate the mechanisms for deciding political issues with peaceful, even perhaps rational, procedures; but there is no prior reason why this must be the case. As we know from our own strife, industrial, civil, and international, violence itself is a recognized, even though usually a deplored, procedure for arriving at authoritative policy. It is, however, as much a part of the political process as peaceful means; hence, it has become a significant part of political research. Among these Bantu tribes, as in contemporary international society, the decisions may not meet with the approval of all parties, but what is accepted is the fact that in the elders, as in the great powers, there is a group which normally undertakes the task of dealing authoritatively with policy when other means of solving differences over values fail.

It is clear, therefore, that even in societies peripheral to ours, a process that corresponds to what in our own society we call the making and execution of policy for society must take place, even though the devices may be less formal and even though there may be few, if any, legally recognized means for enforcing decisions. The form of the mechanism and the kind of sanctions are, however, matters for empirical investigation; they do not invalidate the conclusion that there is discernible a process whereby values are authoritatively allocated for the whole society.

4. Consequences of an Orientation Toward Policy Activities

As I have suggested, historically political research has its origins in a moral context; it arises from the desire to find criteria for evaluating the moral worth of social policy. On its empirical side, however, political science has displayed an initial coherence because it has attempted to understand the functioning and determinants of policy. Acceptance of this interpretation further helps to clear up certain difficulties that flow from the conception of political science as the study of the state or of power.

In identifying the political aspect of life as the state, modified pluralism, for example, ran into considerable trouble in explaining the interest of political science in the city-community of ancient Greece or in any other of the so-called prestate forms of political life. This became evident in the preceding chapter, but we can now see the reason for this difficulty somewhat more clearly. At most, the state in a pluralist sense is a particular institutional form that political life takes at some historical moments. This form is distinguished by the existence of a stable population, fixed boundaries, and the differentiation of statuses and roles that we associate with government. Where the structure of political life is the focus of attention, this view of the state may serve important purposes; it defines in a preliminary way the outlines of the broadest institution within which political activity may take place at a given time and place. It describes one institutional or structural variant of a political system. But since there is no general agreement on the meaning of the term, state, its usefulness in this respect declines considerably.

If we continue to consider the term in its modified pluralist interpretation, however, we can now see that even though it identifies the institutional pattern of political activity under certain historical conditions, the concept fails to provide us with a clue to the kind of activity expressed through this kind of structure. If we could understand the kind of activity, then we would be able to recognize its presence even when institutions other than the state served as a vehicle for expression. We would have a connotative definition. The idea of the authoritative allocation of values fulfills this need. It indicates that even where the state as here conceived does not exist (as among nomadic tribes or non-literate societies), as long as something we can call social policy appears, then there are data for political research. The concept of the state as here interpreted refers to special political circumstances; the idea of authoritative allocation of values characterizes a function or web of interrelated activity present in every viable society.

We are now also in a position to complete the discussion begun in the preceding chapter concerning the adequacy of the power concept. The struggle for power does not describe the central phenomenon of political life; rather, it refers only to a secondary even if crucial aspect. In fact, in our first approach to political phenomena, as we seek the minimal and widest orientation, we can for the moment omit all specific reference to problems of power. We need merely recognize that political life consists of those actions related to the authoritative allocation of values. Only upon closer inspection does it become evident that power is of derivative interest to political science; an understanding of who has power and how it is used helps us to understand how social policy is formed and executed.

Power, it has long been recognized, is a relational phenomenon, not a thing someone possesses.[10] It is based on the ability to influence the actions of others. But not all influence needs to be considered power. Any reciprocal contact between human beings leads to the modification of the actions of each of the participants. If power is so broadly conceived, then every relation is an illustration of a power situation and all social science must be considered the study of power. To give power any differentiated meaning we must view it as a relationship in which

[10] C. J. Friedrich, op. cit., chapter 1; C. E. Merriam, *Political Power* (New York: McGraw-Hill, 1934), esp. Introduction; H. D. Lasswell and A. Kaplan, op. cit., p. 75; W. H. Hollister, *Government and the Arts of Obedience* (New York: King's Crown Press, 1948), Introduction.

one person or group is able to determine the actions of another in the direction of the former's own ends. Furthermore, and this is the aspect that distinguishes power from broad influence, this person or group must also be able to impose some sanction for the failure of the influenced person to act in the desired way. Power, therefore, is present to the extent to which one person controls by sanction the decisions and actions of another.[11] For this reason concern about authoritative policy for a society leads us to inquire derivatively into power relations. To understand how policy is made and put into effect we must know how people are able to control the way in which others make and execute decisions.

This interweaving of power and the authoritative allocation of values explains why we must amend the view of Catlin and numerous others that the central unifying variable of political research is power. The interest of political science in power is only educed from its preoccupation with how policy is made and executed.[12] Hence its ultimate goal as an empirically oriented science is not the discovery of a general theory of power as Catlin presupposed and as Lasswell has often been misconstrued to mean. Such a theory would be most helpful, of course, in discovering how our ability to set and sanction the value and factual premises for the decisions and actions of others, the essence of a control relationship, influences the formulation and execution of authoritative policy.

Conceiving political science in this way explains why the oft-repeated lament among empirical political scientists that the

[11] See H. D. Lasswell and A. Kaplan, op. cit., chapter 5.
[12] With his usual feel for politics, V. O. Key expresses doubt about an unlimited power description of political science. "To say that the study of politics is the study of control, or of influence and the influential, states a characteristic of the nature of the human relationships involved, but it does not fix the outer boundaries of the subject. Does the study of politics include all relationships of influence, control, power? . . . It is not essential for the purposes of this volume to decide this issue. In order that the study may be kept within manageable limits, it may be restricted primarily to an examination of those power or control relationships having to do with the machinery of government." Op. cit., p. 3.

sociologist and the psychologist are invading their field, that politics is being taught all over the campus, is in most cases largely unjustified and reveals conceptual confusion. The fact that the sociologist applies his skills to political institutions does not in itself make him a political scientist. Normally he is interested in different aspects of these institutions. For example, although F. S. Chapin devotes several chapters of his *Contemporary American Institutions*[13] to a discussion of political institutions, it is clear that helpful as his work may be to political science he has undertaken his study with a different end in mind. He seeks to develop a theory of institutions in general and whatever interest he shows in politics must be referred back to this initial task. What he definitely does not seek or wish to do is to relate these institutions directly to an understanding of authoritative policy. Similarly, although sociologists or other social scientists investigate power relationships, in itself this does not necessarily indicate their preoccupation with political issues.

Alone, a theory of power provides too broad a frame of reference for political research. The latter is devoted to the study only of the political aspect of power relations, not with their totality. If it turns to the internal division and location of power in a trade union, a business corporation, a church, or a fraternal organization, the interest, even if it be in a general theory of power, stems from a desire ultimately to reveal the connection between the power pattern in the group and the policy in the society. We find out how power is used anywhere only the better to know how it is used in relation to social policy. As it has been formulated by Catlin and others, power would become the exclusive preoccupation of political research. In the light of our discussion this is a truncated and at the same time overambitious interpretation of the central political variable. The very most that we could say is that there is a close tie between the pattern of values stemming from any authoritative allocation and the dis-

---

[13] (New York: Harper, 1935).

tribution and use of power. Political science is the study of the authoritative allocation of values as it is influenced by the distribution and use of power.

5. Validity of This Orientation

Before closing, the question might be raised here as to why the political scientist should be interested initially in the authoritative allocation of values and derivatively in power. Is it not arbitrary to confine him largely to these two major areas of research? In reply it might be argued that this description of the field of political research is simply a matter for definition, and any one definition is as good as another. In a sense this is quite true. Each person could describe the field to suit his own convenience, interests, and tastes. But this would be doing violence to the function of definition. To define is not arbitrarily to set up a class of objects or to carve out a part of reality at random and apply a label to it. A definition takes its strength from the purposes for which it is created. A useful definition of a discipline must indicate that aspect of reality about which a group of specialists have been talking. Presumably experience has taught them that by exploring certain kinds of activities they are better able to understand that part of human life to which they are devoted. A useful definition would identify the system in society in which they have become interested. In looking at the limits of political science, I am simply trying to make explicit the kind of subject matter about which, it is now apparent, students of political life have all along been speaking implicitly.

To put the matter in another way, interpretation of the nature of political research must ultimately rest, within certain limits, upon a value judgment. There is nothing unalterable about the view that political science should study one set of phenomena as contrasted with another. If the study of the part of society in which political scientists are interested is to lead to scientific understanding, the only limits are that a sufficiently broad and related subject matter must be chosen so that it can be treated as a conceptually coherent body of phenomena. Within these limits we could convert political science into a pure science of power, of the state, of decision-making, of public and private government, and so on.

But the fact is that sciences do not arise capriciously. They become areas for special research, within the limits of requirements for systematic knowledge, because of the cultural and ethical demands of society. Western society has required that certain kinds of questions central to the kind of civilization that has been growing up, be answered. For these answers, as I observed earlier, it has been necessary to inquire into the way in which social policy is formed and put into practice. Society is not especially concerned with power as a phenomenon in and of itself or with government as such. Its interest is always derived from a prior concern with policy.

Once men began to ask questions about the nature of social policy there was no alternative but to examine the contest over the shaping and execution of such policy. The contemporary interest in political philosophy, for example, reflects an attempt to work out the goals within the terms of which social policy ought to be formulated; the study of political institutions shows an interest in the structural devices which will best enable us to reach the kind of formal and effective policies we desire; the manuals for rulers that we find in Machiavelli, in the wisdom literature of the East, and in many of our texts today are suggested techniques whereby the aims of a group with a particular policy can be realized; analyses of the law, statutory, judicial, and administrative, are precise logical inspections of the relationship between formal expressions of policy and the policy as it is put into effect; research into the operations of interest groups and parties are attempts to reveal forces ultimately cast into formal and effective policy; and each problem, if it has significance for political science, will show a relation, more or less direct, to the problem of the use and distribution of power in the shaping and execution of authoritative policies for a society. It is this interest that draws together apparently diverse and isolated social data into a political system.

The purpose of this and the preceding chapter has been to explore the kind of limits that political research ought to set for itself. As I have indicated, all that we can expect to do is to set some convenient limits suggested by the level of development of political knowledge today. Each generation redefines its own image of political science, with greater insight, one might hope, as our understanding of political life increases. But however incomplete a description may be at any stage, satisfactory inquiry is impossible without some minimal guidance to keep all research within a roughly similar realm. This must be the initial and irreducible prerequisite for the construction of any systematic theory upon which succeeding research might build.

Chapter 6

Situational Data

> We are forcibly reminded that the governing
> body has no value in itself, except as one
> aspect of the process, and cannot even be
> adequately described except in terms
> of the deep-lying interests which function
> through it.
>
> Arthur F. Bentley

1. Theory and Types of Data

A theoretical perspective towards research calls upon us to go beyond the major orienting concepts and the variables to which they refer. It leads us into the further unavoidable task of inquiring into the major classes of data that ought to be incorporated into a theory. The construction of theory presupposes an awareness both of the variety of data which must be examined in order to analyze a problem exhaustively and of the relative weight and position of each kind of data in the analysis. Knowing what the possible kinds of data relevant to political activity are, we would then have considerable guidance in empirical research.

A student of the political system undertakes a piece of

research because of the existence of a difficulty in explaining a political phenomenon. He can approach this problem in a hit-or-miss manner, based upon a prudence developed from experience, hoping that he will exhaust all the relevant types of data. Or he can bear in mind some schema, the product of prior, general inquiry, which describes the possible varieties of data. This analytical schema would then help him to test whether he had included all relevant kinds of data in his investigation or whether an important variety had been omitted.

For example, if a political scientist is interested in the role of interest groups in the political system, it is not enough to know that certain kinds of phenomena are more directly relevant than others, such as propaganda, organizational cohesion, leadership, and techniques of persuasion. These are all vitally related. But from the point of view of theoretical analysis, what ought to be established in advance are the various classes of data into which these phenomena might fall. Are they part of the physical environment which influences the growth and functioning of interest groups? Are they related to the feelings and attitudes of the participants? Do they refer to the structure in which the activity takes place? It is possible that without some prior well-founded classification as a guide, a research worker through habit might be seeking only certain types of data and omitting other highly significant kinds which a careful general analysis might reveal.

To cite an obvious case, we might be looking at leadership and viewing its activity solely as the result of the personalities of the leaders. We should thereby be neglecting such clearly relevant data as the impact of the organizational structure within which the activity takes place or the conditioning of the physical environment itself. The task of this and the succeeding two chapters will be to explore further the matter of kinds of data, to see just what kind American political science has been examining, and to suggest, as a practical illustration rather than as a definitive solution, a tentative classification. A satisfactory classification would be an integral part of any general theory.

Some knowledge of the kinds of data to which political science has been and is at present committed compels us to survey in a brief and broad way the course that American political research has traveled from late in the nineteenth century to the present. The historical context will be introduced, however, only to the extent necessary for analytical purposes. For this reason, what follows in no way aspires to be a history of empirical research, a document still lacking for political science not only in the United States, but in all other countries.[1]

In the history of American political science over the last seventy-five years, two kinds of answers have been given. Neither of these has been explicit, but each is nonetheless present in strength. In effect, one group has maintained that political life can be understood and explained if we try to discern the effect of institutionalized activity on policy. This answer was the first to appear. It has been traditional to locate the source of policy, and the influences molding it, in the institutional mechanisms of the times. For this reason, members of this school can be called the traditionalists or, less appropriately, the institutionalists.

The second group has in effect been arguing that the most significant kind of data is psychological. Policy is to be understood in the light of the kind of people who act in political life, not as a result of the kind of institutions or structures through which they act. Those committed to psychology have insisted that to explain political activity, even the institutional patterns, political science must turn to the motivations and feelings that individuals bring to political life or acquire through the political process itself. This group has stressed the study of what is often loosely called political behavior in contrast to political institutions. For this reason, we can call the group behavioralists, so long as we do not confuse their views with that of strict, and now antiquated, behaviorism.

[1] The closest thing to such a history for American political science is the work of A. Haddow, op. cit. and occasional references to political science in histories of the social sciences, such as in the *Encyclopaedia of the Social Sciences,* Vol. I, "The Social Sciences as Disciplines," pp. 324-49.

To this stage in the development of political science, there has existed only latent recognition of the fact that there are different kinds of data relevant to the understanding of a political problem. For the most part, each political scientist has been inclined to insist upon the priority, if not the exclusiveness, of the kind of data to which he happens to be committed and to neglect almost entirely other kinds. And yet, unawareness of the kinds of data typically used as the basis of contemporary research must leave us incapable even of discussing the issues involved in the formulation of systematic theory, let alone making a start at the substantive task of formulating such a theory.

2. Prescribed or Legal Aspect of the Situation

It can be said that students in traditional research have quite unwittingly been trying to establish the influence of the *situation* upon authoritative policy. In effect, they have been suggesting that what we must look at to understand the variables influencing policy is the impact of the situation created by individuals out of their structured relations. Although few in political science use the notion of situation deliberately and clearly, the ideas underlying it constantly appear. Traditional political science has been preoccupied with the role of institutions in the political process. It has been so because instinctively it has felt that the political situation or pattern of power created by the existence of various institutions has been a factor shaping policy. As a determinant of policy, the situation by implication has been conceived to be quite distinct from and more significant than the kind of people who acted in the situation. What is thus meant by situational as contrasted with psychological data will become apparent in due course.

A superficial glance over the history of traditional political science in the last fifty to seventy-five years would leave a contrary impression; namely, that it has dealt not with one kind of data, called situational, but with at least two different kinds of data. This conclusion would, however, be true only superficially. Closer scrutiny would reveal that although traditional research has been concerned with varying classes of phenomena, at least two, to be specific, the generic quality of these phenomena as data for research has in fact remained constant. This remark may seem puzzling at first, but it will become clear if we turn briefly to the evolution of political research.

If we take the Civil War as a starting point, we can see that research has passed through two important phases, each marked off by the kind of phenomena used to understand political activity. Each phase turned to different kinds of institutions to describe political life. In the first, research was concerned with governmental institutions, those organizations recognized as legally performing for society the special tasks of deciding and executing formal policy.[2] These institutions are described, at first, in purely legal terms and later, in "realistic" terms, as an aspect of human activity. In the second phase, traditional research seeks to explain the political process, on the one hand primarily through the study of non-governmental organizations, such as the organized pressure or interest group, and on the other, through the description of the influence of stable, enduring social aggregates of an unorganized nature such as social classes, regional, religious, ethnic, and similar social classifications.

My point here will be that the movement of traditional research through these two phases did not lead to a change in the general nature of the data being investigated. The kind of phenomena, it is true, did change. Interest in the legal aspect of governmental institutions yielded to concern for the activity of the human beings in the government. The latter, in turn, gave way

[2] Governmental institutions can no longer be differentiated from others merely by virtue of the sanctions that they are able to impose. Essentially these sanctions are little different from those of other organizations such as the church, trade unions, and the like. At one time or another all have used both violent and non-violent means of persuasion with varying degrees of legitimacy attached to this use.

to an interest in the activity of the social groups whose influence government tends to reflect. The generic quality of the research data, however, remained the same. All changing phenomena were ways whereby traditional research sought to illuminate the various institutional elements in the political situation. The data, therefore, remained situational throughout the whole period. A few words and illustrations about the historical development of empirical research will clarify this point and at the same time elaborate on the meaning of situational data.

Sometime after the Civil War, as political science begins to evolve into a discipline separate from economics, sociology, philosophy, and other branches of knowledge, the character of research typical to this new discipline becomes clear. Wherever they are not just political history, political data are composed of legal descriptions of the governmental structure or of the activities going on within the governmental and near-governmental structures. In its historical development, interest in the legal aspect of governmental institutions arose first, preceding the kind of research which, for reasons soon to be evident, I shall call political realism. Let us look first at the legal interest in structure.

Although the great constitutional, that is, legal, debates of the late eighteenth century in the United States stimulated an interest in and esteem for legal description of political life, in the last analysis this interest reflected and at the same time contributed to a typically European way of looking at politics. Utilitarianism is the classic theoretical expression of the legal outlook. The English utilitarians, deriving their inspiration from Bentham, presupposed that men were rational in their activity. To achieve political change, they need simply select the kind of political relations they consider preferable, issue laws formally establishing these relations, and men will automatically adjust to the prescribed structure. The rationalistic aphorism implicit in political studies was "change the institutions and men will follow."

Obviously what was meant by a change of institutions was

that legal injunctions establishing new political relations would automatically produce the anticipated results. The founders of a constitution might conceivably have made some error because of ignorance of what was actually desired or inadequate wisdom as to the kind of structure that would make the attainment of a particular goal possible. But within the terms of the structural rationalism of utilitarian premises, the lessons of trial and error need only be incorporated into subsequent modifications of the original institutions to lead men to conform to one's objectives. Bentham had expressed this well when he had argued for the establishment of an artificial harmony in men's political relations by the simple device of wiping out by law the old social and commercial customs and substituting for them a new political structure based on popular suffrage and a rationalized legislature. It led Bentham and James Mill to assume that the extension and architecture of the franchise would go a long way towards controlling the actions of political representatives.

In the United States, the juristic premises with regard to political institutions merged with the historical circumstances to entrench them even more firmly than in Europe. It seemed almost inevitable for the dispute over the Constitution to take legal shape. By its very nature, the Constitution had been the product of legal decisions formally taken at one moment in history. The dominant note of *The Federalist,* which early became a prominent political text in the universities, was legal simply because the new political structure discussed in these essays was still only a piece of paper, a set of legal injunctions calculated to organize or structure the activities of men. The authors of the Constitution were compelled by the circumstances to stress the structure of political life rather than the process. They could not describe the actual activity of those in authority towards one another; they could only prescribe the desired relations of authority. The example of the founding fathers prevailed for almost a century and merged with European legal rationalism, the influence of which America did not escape.

With some notable exceptions, until the eighties, the Constitution was studied as though men acted out their political life in close conformity with its directives.

Not all research that dealt with political data was legal in nature. What we know as political science drew the attention of historians, theologians, and philosophers, among others. But as the separate discipline of political science began to emerge, where research sought to be primarily empirical rather than moral, its legal nature became paramount; it consisted largely of an examination of the legal provisions of the Constitution. It sought to determine the ways in which authority was distributed, without seriously examining political relations to see whether they accorded with legal prescription.

A glance at one of the basic texts in use as late as the turn of the century illustrates this concern for legal structure. Burgess in his *Political Science and Comparative Constitutional Law* (1890) draws what appears to be a sharp distinction between law and political science or the political and the legal approaches to research. Political research, he writes, treats of the origins of states and constitutions. It describes the way in which particular political organizations have arisen and the social forces behind them. Legal description, on the other hand, explains the legal provisions for the organization of the state and government (such as the laws providing for liberty), for the organization of the state for change through amendment, for the constitution of government or distribution of authority in various bodies. It is clear here, in the light of the subsequent development of American political science, that what Burgess called political science in his day was, in fact, political history and that the emerging political discipline was already distinguished by an interest in the legal analysis rather than in the evolution of political institutions. Their analysis, Burgess felt, was the appropriate domain for legal research. Political institutions, it was thought, could be understood by describing the legal code.

What prompted students to turn to the legal code was not

only the rationalistic assumptions concerning the relation between the individual and the political structure, but also the utilitarian pre-occupation with the locus of formal political authority, that is, with sovereignty. Since Bodin, a large part of modern political science has turned on the search for the nature and locus of sovereignty. By the very nature of the formulation of the problem this quest for sovereignty led men to seek the seat of authority, the position of those who by law had the right to establish formal policy. Although not everyone conceived of sovereignty in the same terms, the matter always resolved itself either into a search for those who had the legal right to make policy or who ought to have this right. For Rousseau, it was a moral problem as to where the right ought to lie. For the utilitarians, such as Austin or Pollock, it was a factual problem as to who actually had the legal right to create policy. With the later utilitarians who sought scrupulously to separate the moral from the factual problems, empirical research therefore restricted itself largely to describing the legal organs that had this sovereign right together with the various subsidiary organs utilized in its exercise.

Succeeding students of political science rejected the legal interpretation because they felt that it did not describe the active variables which influenced the making of social policy. Strict legalistic, amoral utilitarianism had not, of course, intended to deal with the question of the real source or determinants of power. It was still under the influence of Bodin in a sense; it was striving to indicate the legal basis of independence for a nation and hence was wrapped up in the problem of nationalism rather than in the search for the determinants of the political process. One of the characteristics of the independent political unit was the fact that somewhere within it there was an authority which had the supreme legal right to make policy. Quite consciously it was dealing with the legal code rather than the actual political practices.

After the eighties when students in increasing numbers began to challenge the value of this kind of political data, in their haste to get down to so-called realities they lost sight of the value of legal analysis. They did not realize that it had actually been defining an element of the situation which helps to determine policy. The legal aspect of political structure may in fact play an important role in limiting the alternative uses to which political power is put. However, in this period since those students who were attached to legal data had not conceived of political life as a complex web of interacting political activities, it was impossible for them to recognize the effective role of legal prescriptions in helping to determine the authoritative allocation of values. Instead, they centered their attention in large measure on the problem of locating and explaining the competence of the supreme legal authority of a society. The question to which they sought an answer was: Who has legal authority (not who has real power), and how is it brought to bear on authoritative policy? Failing to seek out the sources of effective power, they neglected to visualize their own data as one element in a political situation.

To see the role of the legal aspect of structure in the situation, we must begin with the fact that a political situation occurs whenever two or more individuals interact in relation to social policy. The situation is structured when these persons stand in a relatively stable relation to each other. The situation has a legal structure when there is a code or set of imperatives that prescribes the legitimate rights and duties of each group of actors as compared with any other group.

When the legal aspect of a political situation is viewed in this way, it immediately becomes apparent that the structuring by law helps to influence policy. A person seeking to influence policy must take into consideration the following facts: first, that the law consists of rules of conduct which people normally consider to be legitimate; and second, that if the law prescribes a formal structure allocating powers of making legitimate rules to various parts of that structure, then this formal authority can be neglected only at one's peril. "The legal is likely to emerge with the crown of victory, other things being equal." [3]

[3] C. E. Merriam, *Political Power*, p. 13.

A simple example will illustrate this point. If for the moment we describe the separation of powers in the purely legal language of the Constitution (as amended by decisions of the Supreme Court), there is one fact no reasonable person could neglect. Whether or not the President uses his power, say, to veto legislation, he at least has the legitimate or legally recognized power to do so. In other words, the President's relation to Congress is such that he has the legitimate[4] power to influence in this way the outcome of policy discussion. The structure of the particular situation here, that is, the relation of the President to Congress, leaves an impact on the activity within the situation which if ignored would omit one of the determinants of policy. Of course, whether the President has the actual power in the sense of having the power to exercise his legal right, would require looking at other elements in the situation to see what resistance they offer to the President's actions. Because there are these other elements which, for an exhaustive analysis, must be introduced, the legal element fell short of a persuasive explanation of political activity. The point here, however, is that the legal element must not be overlooked. The extent to which it is an active determinant in any particular situation is a subject for empirical investigation at the time.

3. The Activity in Structure

When traditional political science turned its attention from the legal codes to the human beings acting within government, its data proved to be no less situational in character. The period from the eighties to the First World War can be described as the first stage of realism in research. It is essentially a period of transi-

---

[4] Unless otherwise indicated the idea of legitimacy will always be used in a psychological rather than a moral sense. Psychologically, an action is legitimate when it is popularly so accepted. An action would of course be moral only when it conforms to a given standard of right.

tion from the earlier legalism to the contemporary view of society as an interacting process among social groups.

For the purposes at which it aimed, the use of legal data could not be challenged. It sought to reveal the source and formal structure of the legally competent organs of government. The only genuine criticism of this approach to political issues was the tendency of its adherents to mistake a part for the whole. Swept away by the search for legal sovereignty they were predisposed to assume that this was the whole of political science, that the whole of the situation out of which policy arose could be described in terms of legal authority. The grip of legal analysis relaxed only gradually; it was pried away from political research by the appearance of a view of politics as a process. This new view led students to look behind the formal code.

In political research it is customary today to speak of political life as the political process; in a loose way the term is even used as a synonym for the ideas implicit in the political system. In its essence, the term political process refers to a method of interpreting phenomena as much as to the phenomena themselves. It suggests that all life is a pattern of interaction among social groups and individuals and that one aspect of this interaction relates to specifically political matters. Its orientation is towards the activity taking place in a political situation; this is its substantive implication. It also suggests that the various social units which act, each reacts on the other, ultimately shaping the policy that emerges for the whole society; this is its implication for method. Its crucial significance is, therefore, that it conceives of political life, not as the product of any one force, such as a class, a political structure, or some special social group, but as the product of multiple causes. In the search for these other factors influencing political life, students felt impelled to go beyond the legal structure to the activity which gave it life. Both the substantive and procedural implications emerge simultaneously.

In American political science this view of political life as a process of interacting parts grew only slowly out of deep intellectual roots in the nineteenth century. It is not my intention to probe into these[5] except to mention their obvious relation to the dynamic interpretations of social life so prevalent in the nineteenth century. The social dynamics of Comte, the dialectic of Hegel and Marx, the evolutionary movement of Darwin, the vitalism of Bergson, and the whole notion of stages of civilization endemic to this age are all associated with the intellectual matrix to which the view of social life as a process can be traced. These are the more general thoughtways that reflected the tendencies of the whole age. Our interest here, however, is limited to understanding the nature of the new kind of phenomena to which under the influence of the changing outlook, American political science turned. For this purpose it is more fruitful to look at the specific movement taking place in political science even though the full implications of this movement will thus be neglected.

The view of political life as a process did not take root immediately upon the demise of an exclusively legal approach to structure. The substance of its intent begins to appear, although not the term itself, by the eighties. Not until the end of the First World War, however, does the term in its present meaning definitely come into prominent use in American political science. The period from the eighties to the First World War is, therefore, one of maturation for this conception of political research.[6]

In this transitional stage, students of political life began to denounce the legal approach to institutions as sterile and superficial. They argued that if one wished to discover who had the power to make social policy, it was not only insufficient but misleading and erroneous to look to the legal provisions of the Constitution or the laws made under it. Instead, it became necessary to look at the "actual working" of these institutions and to relate

[5] See M. Lerner, "Social Process," *Encyclopaedia of the Social Sciences,* Vol. XIV, pp. 148-57.

[6] As late as 1927 the juristic outlook towards politics was still sufficiently strong to draw the attack of W. B. Munro in *The Invisible Government* (New York: Macmillan, 1928), pp. 3-4 and 32. See also G. H. Sabine, "Political Science and the Juristic Point of View," 22 *American Political Science Review* (1928), 553-75.

the various arrangements that were devised in practice to the actual locus of power. It was a period, in other words, when the emphasis in research began to shift from the discussion of legal competence to that of power or actual influence over policy. For this reason it is meaningful to call this the phase of realism in research.

Realism coincides with a similar development in Europe which had taken root perhaps a little earlier[7] but which in fact was a product and symptom of the same social forces at work in the Western world. Severe economic fluctuations towards the end of the nineteenth century and increasing imperial rivalries brought the golden days of the Victorian equilibrium to an untimely close. The dislocations of rapidly mounting urban industrialism and its accompanying agricultural readjustments gave birth to critical social problems, particularly in the United States. New social groups began to make their presence felt especially by trespassing on the ground of the older social forces. These domestic and international disturbances threw into bold relief the inadequacies of trying to understand political life as a rational adjustment to codes. During an epoch of relatively peaceful, linear social evolution, when the going values were accepted without serious challenge and the power of traditional social groupings seemed comparatively secure, political research could be indifferent to the actual patterns of activity in the struggles over social policy. But upon the disturbance of this relative stability, adaptation to the changing environment demanded inquiry into the actual working of institutions.

Perusal of the work of some of the more influential realists will put us in a position to appreciate their contribution to the development of the notion of political process and the kind of data that it implies. Woodrow Wilson, in his *Congressional Government,* was the first political scientist in the United States to make a significant effort to break the old legal pattern. But since

[7] See, for example, the work of H. J. S. Maine, W. H. Lecky, J. F. Stephen, K. Marx, G. Mosca, and V. Pareto, to mention only a few.

his discontent with contemporary research drew much of its strength from Walter Bagehot in England, a glance at the latter's work will illumine the nature and the limits of Wilson's breach with the past. Wilson regularly refers to Bagehot's *English Constitution*[8] but even if he had failed to mention it at all, not only the content of *Congressional Government,* but its very style might have suggested the author's affinity to the English writer.

While Bagehot does not stand alone, he is nevertheless one of the specific channels through which the growing changes in social science, the new realism of the nineteenth century, began to penetrate into American political research.[9] In the opening paragraphs of his *English Constitution,* Bagehot indicates his dissatisfaction with what he called the paper description or the literary theory of the English constitution, which saw power shared in a balance by King, Lords, and Commons. Bagehot rejected this paper description and sought rather to get at the "living reality" of the constitution. He finds it in the fact that the English political structure consists of two basic parts: the dignified or theatrical and the efficient parts. The dignified part he identifies with the monarchy and aristocracy. These elements which to Bagehot's time had been considered an intrinsic part of political power, Bagehot now considers to be of importance in the political structure only as a means of maintaining the loyalty of the multitude. They are vital in holding obedience to authority. The second fundamental part consists of those who wield this authority, the efficient elements in the political system. These he identifies with the Cabinet sitting in the House of Commons and deriving its moral and material strength from the middle class. Here lies the real authority and power in the political system.

[8] (World's Classics ed., New York: Oxford University Press, 1928).
[9] For a summary of the place of Bagehot in the history of American political research, see W. F. Willoughby's introduction to G. A. Weber, *Organized Efforts for the Improvement of Administration in the United State* (New York: D. Appleton, 1919), pp. 4-7; see also my own article "Walter Bagehot and Liberal Realism," 43 *American Political Science Review* (1949), 17-37.

In the introduction to one edition[10] of the *English Constitution,* the Earl of Balfour argues that since the Crown and the aristocracy contributed to the unity of the community, Bagehot had really erred in classifying it only as a dignified element in the constitution. In fact it is as efficient as any other operating part of the political mechanism. Acceptance of this interpretation would, however, conceal the essential revolution that Bagehot had introduced into traditional English thinking on the constitution. He was interested in discovering the real seat of legislative authority and the source of political power in the community. In this sense he was arguing that the Crown and the aristocratic class within the bosom of which it existed, no longer played an effective role in making decisions on social policy but rather contributed to maintaining the cohesion of the political system so that others could make decisions. For Bagehot, penetration to the reality led beyond the formal appearances to the social groups who held political power, in this case the middle class, or, in more general terms, to the locus of power in the political structure.

Today Bagehot is read largely for his views on the comparative merits of the British and American political structures as well as for his classic statement of the British constitution. Today, however, we tend to neglect the fact that he directed attention to a new level of data which had to be taken into consideration in all subsequent descriptions of political systems. Even those who contested his conclusions about the rigidities and the incapacities of the Presidential structure were nevertheless compelled, even to prove him wrong, to join him in rejecting the legal description of structure. This is true for example of Lowell.[11] Those who agreed with Bagehot in his views on the separation of powers, on the other hand, such as Woodrow Wilson, could do no less than to adopt his practice of seeking out the so-called realities.

Wilson never quite achieves the insight into political in-

[10] World's Classics.
[11] A. L. Lowell, *Essays on Government,* esp. Essay I on "Cabinet Responsibility and the Constitution."

stitutions shown by Bagehot. In his *Congressional Government* Wilson restricts himself largely to describing the locus of formal authority rather than of power. He leaves the impression that the basic influences on social policy emerge out of the committees of Congress, and he peers only momentarily beyond the committees to the other social factors that help to influence the decisions of the committees. Bagehot had anticipated the need to attend to the kind of phenomena that relate power to authority, an insight that for the United States was left to James Bryce, Henry Jones Ford, and others.

In emulating Bagehot, Wilson too inveighs against the literary theory, of the American Constitution in this case, which pictures the political structure as a finely adjusted set of checks and balances prescribed in *The Federalist*. He writes that

> one of the most striking facts, as it seems to me, in the history of our politics is, that that [constitutional] system has never received complete and competent critical treatment at the hands of any, even the most acute, of our constitutional writers. They view it, as it were, from behind. Their thoughts are dominated, it would seem, by those incomparable papers of the "Federalist," which, though they were written to influence only the voters of 1788, still, with a strange, persistent longevity of power, shape the constitutional criticism of the present day, obscuring much of that development of constitutional practice which has since taken place. The Constitution in operation is manifestly a very different thing from the Constitution of the books.[12]

In effect, Wilson urges that although authority may be formally divided among the various branches of the political struc-

[12] *Congressional Government*, pp. 9-10.

ture, in practice the power to make public decisions is distributed among the various committees of Congress. Whatever the *Federalist* papers may say about the political structure and however much the legal-political texts may continue to affirm this description, in practice neither the courts nor the President can interfere with the power of the committees. Exceptional circumstances may at times permit the courts or the President's will to prevail but the daily, continuous power lies with Congress. By the edition in 1900 of *Congressional Government,* when the Presidency had again begun to grow in stature, Wilson was ready to recognize its increasing political power. Although his interpretation was shifting, the kind of phenomena he felt it was necessary to look at, that which he considered the realities of power, remained the same.

As I have suggested, although Wilson had here contributed to a new conception of the political structure, he had still stopped short of the lessons urged by Bagehot. He had in fact only passed from an examination of the legal code prescribing the kind of political relations in which men ought to stand to a recognition that the location of power in the structure did not carry out the intention of the founders. Bagehot, on the other hand, had suggested that while one must look to the locus of power in the governmental part of the political structure, research must penetrate even beyond this level of phenomena to the social forces in the community which were the real movers of the governmental structure. In England he identified this as the small middle class. Wilson was not blind to the fact that the men in Congress did not cut their policy out of whole cloth but were themselves to some extent the creatures of other influences. He comments on the need to look at the social origins of legislators, at the activity of the lobbyist and at the responsiveness of the various political organs, such as the courts, to party passion and public opinion. But this awareness that policy may be formulated in the light of the power of groups external to the actual governmental structure is incidental to the main tone of his analysis. It was left to others to trace out more closely this connection with social forces.

In the historical period of which I am speaking, James Bryce was one of the most influential of these writers. Although his *American Commonwealth* stands with one foot securely lodged in traditional legal description—the bulk of his research deals with the legal prescriptions concerning political relations—it was modern and challenging for the time primarily because of its chapters devoted to the influence of party and public opinion on the makers of policy at Washington or at the state capitols. The novelty of his theme was unmistakable at the very outset of his work.

> There are three main things that one wishes to know about a national commonwealth, viz. its framework and constitutional machinery, the methods by which it is worked, the forces which move it and direct its course. It is natural to begin with the first of these. Accordingly, I begin with the government; and as the powers of government are two-fold, being vested partly in the National or Federal authorities and partly in the States, I begin with the National government, whose structure presents less difficulty to European minds, because it resembles the National government in each of their own countries. Part I therefore contains an account of the several Federal authorities, the President, Congress, the Courts of Law. It describes the relations of the National or central power to the several States. It discusses the nature of the Constitution as a fundamental supreme law, and shows how this stable and rigid instrument has been in a few points expressly, in many others tacitly and half-unconsciously modified.
>
> Part II deals similarly with the State Gov-

ernments, examining the constitutions that have established them, the authorities which administer them, the practical working of their legislative bodies. . . .

(Part III) The whole machinery, both of national and of State governments, is worked by the political parties. Parties have been organized far more elaborately in the United States than anywhere else in the world, and have passed more completely under the control of a professional class. . . . Part III contains a sketch of this party system and of the men who "run" it, topics which deserve and would repay a fuller examination than they have yet received even in America, or than my limits permit me to bestow.

(Part IV) The parties, however, are not the ultimate force in the conduct of affairs. Behind and above them stands the people. Public opinion, that is the mind and conscience of the whole nation, is the opinion of persons who are included in the parties, for the parties taken together are the nation; and the parties, each claiming to be its true exponent, seek to use it for their purposes.[13]

This excerpt reveals how closely he works within the pattern to which Bagehot had contributed and thereby probes further than Wilson into the elements shaping social policy. Bryce is not content to stop with a description of the way in which the governmental structure prescribed by a constitution works in practice. For him, this is merely the first step towards discovering the factors that influence activity within the formal governmental structure. He gives one of the most vivid descriptions available of the actual structure of political parties, for insight rivaled to this day

[13] J. Bryce, *The American Commonwealth,* Vol. I, pp. 5-6.

only by Ostrogorski and Michels. He visualized the party as a group of men dominated by the Inner Circle of full-time professionals, the party managers and ward politicians, and supported by an Outer Circle of part-time political workers. Together these are the wirepullers, a term popularized in England by Maine and Stephen, which expressively tells the part they were thought to play in molding policy. But driven by a relentless passion to pursue to their tap roots the elements out of which the political situation grows, Bryce was dissatisfied even with this novel insight into the party structure. He turned briefly from the structured relations of the party bureaucracy to the social circumstances that determine the nature of the men who participate in the party leadership—their educational background, class origins, and individual motivation.[14] He thereby displayed an inclination to reconstruct the whole situation instrumental in shaping social policy. His emphasis remains, however, with the party structure rather than with the social circumstances outside of it.

In summary then, as illustrated in this early work of Wilson and Bryce, political realism scarcely succeeds in escaping the clutches of legal utilitarianism. In viewing political research as largely a way of discovering where power over policy lies, it did not really go further than to substitute for a legal interest in the locus of competence within the governmental structure, a concern for the locus of actual power within the same structure. For the times, this was to be sure a tremendous stride beyond legal phenomena; but in retrospect, especially in the perspective of the whole progress of empirical political science, it recedes to a modest position. It becomes in fact only a short, although vital, step away from legal phenomena. For the legalist, the relevant element of the situation out of which policy arises was the formal structure of government. For the realist, the situation is still confined largely to governmental or such near-governmental structures as the political party. While legal description was rejected as a true picture of

[14] See op. cit., Vol. II, part IV.

structure, the realists were, nevertheless, still captives of the juristic framework of thought to the extent that they failed to pass beyond the study of the activity within the legal structure. Their awareness of the role of party did not in itself carry them far past governmental structure. They had simply added political parties to their inventory of governmentally relevant institutions. Just as legal research had viewed the supreme authority in a legal vacuum, so realistic research tended to see the actors in the governmental and party structures as autonomous, self-activating, and self-deciding groups rather than as a part in a complex interaction of political elements. There is no doubt that the realists showed signs of knowing better and, as I have suggested, strong hints of this knowledge appear in their work, but they were still too close to jurisprudence to be able to free themselves entirely.

Yet the germ of subsequent political research was there. Policy was no longer the product of men acting in relations prescribed by law. The situation out of which policy arose had been broadened from the legal to the actual patterns of political relations. It is true, the realists confined their attention largely to the same kind of structures as the legalists, and they did not see that the participants in these structures were linked to a broader political matrix. Nevertheless, to the extent that they went beyond the legal code, they were adding a new kind of phenomenon to the storehouse of political research. They were continuing to write about governmental institutions, but in such a way that they were really identifying a new class of phenomena that had to be taken into consideration when searching for the determinants of policy. Yet, at the same time, these new data were of the same genus as the earlier and continuing legal facts in that they contributed a new element to a description of the situation shaping policy. In effect, the realists had declared that in making social policy, the policy-makers must take into consideration, not only the legal disposition of authority within the governmental structure, but also the actual distribution of power in this structure and the related political parties.

Chapter 7

The Total Structure of the Situation

> But why do not the real leaders overturn the
> nominal and substitute themselves for their
> dummies? This ignores the whole basis of
> power which lies in a social situation,
> conditioning the actions of the leaders, and
> making it difficult or impossible for them
> to operate against the very basis of their own
> authority. They are not merely leaders
> per se, but they function in a total situation
> of which they are parts.
>
> Charles E. Merriam

EARLIER I noted that from the perspective of contemporary political science, the institutional elements conceived as interacting to influence authoritative policy could be reduced to two main types. I have discussed the first, governmental institutions. We are now ready to pass on to the second, nongovernmental groups.

1. The Group Element

In the twentieth century, a new concept crept gradually into political research, the idea that political activity is part of a process. With the spread of this new way of looking at political life, summed up in the term political process, we have the unwitting acceptance of the notion that social policy could best be viewed as part of a total situation. The conviction emerges that to understand how policy is formed and applied it is crucial to see political actors as part of a total situation which constrains, shapes, and directs their activity. Let us see just what is involved in the idea of a political process and how this idea strengthened and broadened the concern of political research for situational data.

Several unstated premises are involved in the idea of a political process.[1] The term signifies, first, that policy arises out of a situation consisting of the interaction of various social elements; second, that policy is not a final product but an aspect of an ongoing interaction among the various elements of the social situation; and third, that of the vast variety of activity involved in political situations, that of the persons within the governmental and party structure is only a manifest and small part, when compared with the importance of non-governmental social groups. For this reason, the term describes an extension of the work of the realists. It picks up their hints that a thorough understanding of the context of policy-making and execution would have to go beyond activity at the level of governmental institutions, hints that they themselves had never been able to put to intensive use.

In its origins and even today, the political process has been viewed principally as the interaction among governmental institutions and social groups. The process approach has implied

---

[1] Some of these premises are visible, for example, in O. Garceau, "Research in the Political Process," 45 *American Political Science Review* (1951), 69-85.

that to understand fully the matrix within which the policy is in constant process of formulation and application, one must reveal the role of groups, especially, although not exclusively, of pressure or interest groups. This helps to account for the deluge of interest-group studies in the last twenty-five years. Even governmental institutions are now customarily treated in this context as a species of interest groups acting back on policy in terms of its own interest in the situation.[2]

Since the First World War intensive examination of group activity has led to the analysis of policy as the continuing product of a situation defined largely in terms of participating groups. This is the meaning suggested, for example, when we read about the process in political parties. Research into the party process seeks to understand party ideology and actions as the product of group pressures surrounding them. These pressures may take the form of a bureaucracy with an interest divergent from the membership or of various class, functional, regional, and other groupings. Similarly, the study of the legislative process has come to mean more than the description of the procedures of the legislature and its component committees. It now means a study of the way in which policy is influenced by the existence of interest groups, lobbies, relevant non-organized publics, regional and class interests, and the like.

Political process has, therefore, been the special term used to denote the importance of the interaction of groups for social policy. Its use leaves the impression that the political process is above all a group process and that here political science has finally got down to rock bottom in describing the various elements of a typical political situation. In short, since early in the twentieth century the impression has been left that this view of the political process is final and if not exhaustive, at least definitive for all primary elements.

The origin of the concept of political process permits

[2] See for example, V. O. Key, "Administration as Politics," op. cit., chapter 7.

us to appreciate this almost inextricable relation with the group emphasis. It emerged towards the end of the nineteenth century in the United States, although it has a history in Europe, in the sociological and political literature in particular, that I shall not attempt to trace here. By the end of the nineteenth century sociologists, who in that day were often concerned with political problems, had adopted the concept as a valuable tool for describing the special subject matter of sociology.

The American sociologist, Albion Small, clearly sets this forth in his *General Sociology* (1905). There he seeks to show the limitations of the deductive and speculative sociology of theorists such as Comte or Spencer and to this end calls for a return to social realities. Deceptively, the fundamental reality in society for Small is the individual. The individual is a bundle of interests, desires, or wants, conditioned by geographic, racial, economic, aesthetic, and other considerations. But because of the nature of social life, the individual who seeks to satisfy these wants is compelled to unite in groups which represent these interests. Accordingly for Small the true datum of social science is group life and the forms of its interaction. Following Ratzenhofer, Small calls this interaction the *social* process. It is *"a continual formation of groups around interests and a continuous exertion of reciprocal influence by means of group-action."* [3]

In this way social process conveyed two major ideas which are not necessarily associated but which became closely linked together for some time in political research. In the first place, it conveyed the notion that social life is not a product or precipitate which can be examined at any moment in time in order to understand its nature. It is rather a constant flux of activity or social interaction. Comprehension of society would depend on knowing the nature of interaction rather than on formally depicting any set of relations as static at a specific point in time. But Small, following his European prototypes, developed the theme that for purposes of research the basic character of the

[3] A. W. Small, *General Sociology*, p. 209. Italics in original.

process lay in the fact that groups rather than individuals were the significant elements in it. Therefore, in the second place, the notion suggested by the term "process" was that group life provided the vehicle for social interaction.

Both these implications gradually penetrated research in political science. The political process analogously is a continuing flux of activity among social elements that seek to influence policy. The process conception views social elements as in constant tension or power struggle over policy, and the task of the political scientist is to extricate the various elements for independent study in order to determine the exact role of each. But for most political scientists, the political process is not only a complex network of human interaction; it is also specifically the interaction of groups. Political life is primarily to be viewed as group life. "The expansion and contraction of group patterns, the redistribution of individuals throughout the complex matrix —this is the social [and analogously, the political] process." [4] Or, as another author has put it: "This type of analysis has certain obvious attractions. . . . It directs attention to the frequently neglected richness of group and sub-group energy which goes into the making of public policy. It visualizes the development of public policy as a dynamic product of interacting forces." [5] We can see evidence of this conception of the process in the spate of studies during the late twenties and the thirties dealing with the interest group, class, ethnic, regional, and nationality basis of political activity.

[4] H. L. Childs, "Pressure Groups and Propaganda," in E. B. Logan (ed.) *The American Political Scene* (New York: Harper, 1936), pp. 205-42, on p. 205; see similarly H. L. Childs, *Labor and Capital in National Politics* (Columbus, Ohio: Ohio State University Press, 1930), p. 242.

[5] M. Fainsod, "Some Reflections on the Nature of the Regulatory Process" in *Public Policy* (Cambridge: Harvard University Press, 1940), pp. 297-323, on p. 298.

2. The Group and the Situation

For our present purpose, however, the importance of the process concept is not that it incorporated the notion of constant group interaction, but that in so doing it was adding to the elements of the situation. By the very way in which the group conception of the process is formulated, it suggests that the influence exercised by the groups in the process stems from the kind of situation they create rather than from the kind of people involved in these situations. In this sense, the discovery and application of the concept of process in the twentieth century, with its novel emphasis on group phenomena, was extending and intensifying earlier research by adding to it new kinds of phenomena such as social groups. These were now, for the first time, considered part of the total political situation. Although uncovering new phenomena, the concept of political process still referred to the same kind of data, namely, the impact of the situation, with an enriched idea of the elements in this situation.

The sociological origins of this concept give us the clue to the fact that it was directed to this unique and vital kind of data for understanding social policy. No work in political science better clarifies the nature of this conception of political data than Arthur Bentley's *The Process of Government*. The fact that Bentley wrote his book in 1908 does not impair the truth of this statement; it reflects rather his tremendous insight in being able to present in anticipation the kind of data to which political scientists would commit themselves, in large part, for the next fifty years. It is true that until recently Bentley's work has had no discernible influence on the growth of American political science; reference to it does not begin until the twenties with the rise of interest-group studies. It is only today, indeed, that a more general and belated revival of *The Process of Government* has become apparent.[6] But in spite of the fact that it preceded

---

[6] See most recently the heavy dependence on Bentley of D. Truman, *The Governmental Process* (New York: Knopf, 1951), esp. p. ix.

the main development in political research during the last half-century, that it is dated by an uncompromising hostility to introspective psychology and by an affirmation of an involved and antiquated psychological behaviorism, and despite the further fact that few students of politics have read the work until recently, it is still one of the best expressions of the kind of data to which political scientists have traditionally confined themselves.

Bentley stands as the watershed between the simple realism of Wilson and the more complex realism of the group approach to political process. He divides political reality in its direct empirical, rather than philosophical, sense into three levels: the formal legal structure, the action of men organized into the structure of government, and a deeper level of activity to which he claimed, with a great measure of truth, most political scientists had hitherto been blind.[7] Government, he says, is a product of the interaction of these lower-lying forces. These are the forces that really shape the activity of men. But action is a relationship between men who act and react on each other, and accordingly action can be viewed not as the product of individual behavior but solely as the product of the group. With Small, therefore, whose thinking much of Bentley's work reflects, Bentley concludes that the political process consists of the activity of groups. The process of government—and the term government in the title of his work means politics in general [8]—consists of the struggle among groups for the control of the activity of political organizations such as governmental organs.

Bentley comes closer than any earlier writer and most subsequent ones to discerning the true nature of the apparently changing data with which traditional political science has been concerned. The mere fact that Bentley understood political activity to consist of group interaction does not exhaust his interpretation of political life. He goes on to suggest what might be called a hydraulic theory of power; namely, that the pressure

[7] A. F. Bentley, op. cit., chapter 7.
[8] Ibid., pp. 260-3.

among interests over the content of social policy can be described as a "push and resistance between groups" [9] for control of governmental apparatus. Pressure here seems to be transmitted from one group to the other in much the same way as hydraulic pressure exerts its force on objects.

In a long introductory section to his work, Bentley deliberately rejects what he considers to be the customary psychological approach in terms of feelings, attitudes, and ideas of participants in political events. The actions of the groups must be interpreted, he holds, as responses to the pressures of other groups. Implicit here is the notion that one group responds to the pressure of the other because, in anticipation, it can visualize the response that a particular activity will stimulate and then, in terms of its own estimate of the effect of this response on its own interests, it acts accordingly.[10] The hydraulic theory of power suggested in Bentley is implicitly asserting that each group responds to the actual and anticipated activity from outside itself and is limited in its actions by the presence, actual or imputed, of these activities. "All phenomena of government," he writes, "are phenomena of groups pressing one another, forming one another, and pushing out new groups and group representatives (the organs or agencies of government) to mediate the adjustments. It is only as we isolate these group activities, determine their representative values, and get the whole process stated in terms of them, that we approach to a satisfactory knowledge of government." [11]

This is a specific and concrete way of saying that the power structure of the situation, the activity, as Bentley puts it, determines the policy adopted and the way it is put into effect. He himself feels constrained to adopt the very term "situation" and to show its relevance. "No matter how highly generalized or how specific the ideas and feelings are which we are consider-

[9] Ibid., p. 258.
[10] Cf. C. J. Friedrich's "rule of anticipated reactions" in *Constitutional Government and Democracy*, pp. 589 ff.
[11] A. F. Bentley, op. cit., p. 269.

ing, they never lose their reference to a 'social something.' . . . Neither anger, nor liberty, nor any feeling or idea in between can be got hold of anywhere except as phases of social situations. They stand out as phases, moreover, only with reference to certain positions in the social situation or complex of situations in the widest sense, within which they themselves exist." [12] In his enthusiasm for the identification of the structure within which activity takes place, Bentley would recognize, other than activity, no such variable as the personalities or the feelings of the participants.[13]

The tendencies of contemporary studies of interest groups admirably demonstrate the extent to which political science has largely been preoccupied with this situational kind of subject matter. Why have political scientists undertaken to study groups? The obvious answer is that the activities of groups, their numerical strength, the intensity of feeling behind them, and their techniques in persuading the electorate and politicians to support them all have a bearing on the kind of decisions and actions which such political mechanisms as an agency or Congress or the Presidency will make and take with regard to the pressure group's interest. When traditional political research is called upon to describe the way in which the activity of these interests influences the activity of formal policy-makers and administrators, the resulting policy is viewed as a product not only of the motivations or personalities of the actors, but also of the activity-response that the makers of policy anticipate will be evoked by their decision. Underlying traditional research is the assumption that, for example, when a governmental agency acts on policy, it will speculate on a number of decisions and will hope to choose that alternative which, in anticipation, would seem to evoke from groups in its environment the least number of responses considered by the agency to be hostile to its objectives. The structure of the situation for the agency will therefore include

[12] Ibid., pp. 169-70.
[13] Ibid., all of Part I and p. 198.

the constellation of pressures arrayed for and against it and an estimate of their relative strengths and of the consequences that might flow from any of the possible alternative decisions and actions. It is to this kind of data that traditional research looks.

The activities of interest groups are, of course, not the only factors relevant to a decision or to part of the structure of a political situation. A complete understanding of the determinants of the action of an agency, for example, in terms of the concept of political process, would take into consideration the way in which all interacting groups, including the agency as a group with an interest of its own, and as we shall see later in this chapter, other kinds of social aggregates, acted and reacted on one another.[14] This process of group interaction can be described, however, as the product of how groups respond to the structure of the situation. In effect, research students have been saying: Let us keep the motivations of the actors constant and thereby delete them from the situation. Whatever the feelings of the individuals within the group may be, if we are looking at the process from the point of view of any one group, then its decisions and actions (policy) will be modified by the power of varying constellations of groups arrayed around it.

3. Types of Social Aggregates in the Situation: Social Groups

Up to this point I have been trying to show that latter-day research into the role of various social groups in the political process has led to the identification of situational data. Further evidence to point up this argument can be adduced if we in-

---

[14] Bentley has sometimes been accused of depicting governmental institutions as devoid of independent interests of their own and therefore as pure creatures of the will of pressure groups. Such an interpretation forces Bentley farther than he actually goes. He was sharply aware of what we today call the politics of administration. See ibid., pp. 443-4.

quire into the kind of social aggregates which contemporary political science has discerned as elements in the structure of the situation.

In political science research workers tend to lump all social aggregates together as though for purposes of research no one aggregate was different from another. In fact, aggregates of human beings come together in a variety of different relationships which can be conveniently classified. For example, an individual who belongs to the aggregate we call a crowd interacts with other members of the crowd in one way. If he and other individuals were all members of an audience at a formally called political meeting he would interact in another. A crowd and an audience, in turn, both display kinds of interaction among their members quite different from those prevailing in a numerous geographically-dispersed public. To offer generalizations about the behavior of different social aggregates it would be necessary to recognize a variety of differing types. For our purpose, however, it is enough to say that traditional political science has quite unwittingly been seeking to isolate the effect of such aggregates on authoritative policy. Every aggregate, in so far as it is relevant to the formulation and execution of policy, becomes a new element in the structure of the situation in traditional research.

We can see how unerringly this research has sought for situational data, whatever the kind of human collectivity it undertook to analyze. Historically, those interested in the relation of the group to the political process have never clearly distinguished among such varieties of social aggregates as interest groups, economic and social classes, ethnic, religious, regional, age, sex, skill groupings, and the like. They have all been thrown together into a heterogeneous mixture of social aggregates. The major distinction made, as I have already indicated, has been between governmental institutions on the one hand and all other kinds of aggregates on the other. This distinction rested on the ground that the aggregates of human beings in institutions we call governmental are said to have a sanctioning power significantly different from any other in the community.

For purposes of understanding how power is amassed and used by social groups, however, there is another way of classifying some of the important social aggregates found in recurring political situations. As traditional political science has maintained, an element of the structure of a situation consists of groups. In the large body of research concerning interest groups —and governmental groups are viewed as a species of interest groups—what is obviously meant by a group is an organized collection of individuals.[15] The significant fact about governmental and interest groups for present purposes is not the distinction in their legal competence. It is rather their similarity as groups in which the participants interact with each in an enduring way for the purpose of achieving stated or implied common purposes. Such groups have come to be called formal organizations.[16] The fact of deliberate organization for common goals distinguishes both governmental groups and interest groups from other kinds of institutional patterns of activity. Congress or the Supreme Court is no less a formal organization than a trade union or a farmers' organization, however different the needs served by these various institutions may be. Accordingly, there is essentially no difference in the form in which either interest groups or governmental institutions are related to policy. Since both kinds of activity take the form of formal organizations, the task has been to discover their place in the power situation.

[15] See, for example, the research of H. L. Childs, P. Herring, V. O. Key, or E. E. Schattschneider.

[16] See H. Simon, D. Smithburg, and V. Thompson, op. cit., p. 85; P. Selznick, "Foundations of the Theory of Organization," 13 *American Sociological Review* (1948), 25-35. Cf. P. Herring, *Group Representation Before Congress* (Baltimore: Johns Hopkins Press, 1929), p. 6, where a group is defined as "a number of individuals bound together in a common cause or united by similar interests into an articulate unit"; and cf. H. L. Childs, *Labor and Capital in National Politics*, p. 7, who writes: "In any case the perception of such common attributes gives rise to a conscious attempt to marshal them and to regiment into groups the individuals concerned."

An example referring to formal *governmental* organizations alone, demonstrates that, with regard to this type of activity-pattern, political scientists have traditionally been searching for its consequences on the situation. Indeed, a large part of political science is concerned with the study of the situational impact of formal governmental organizations. The American Constitution sets up a body of organizations that we call the national government, and one of its critical characteristics is the separation of powers. Students of political behavior (psychology) have complained of the lifeless way in which this institutional arrangement has been analyzed—and with considerable justice, since traditional research, even in the realistic phase, seldom penetrates to the actual patterns of activity of which this complex relation is composed. But in spite of this obvious handicap, what is usually neglected by those who challenge the value of traditional political research is that the latter has been coming at the problem from the point of view of the consequences of the situation for social policy. In effect, although not in these words, it has been suggesting that in a community in which the patterns of activity summarized in the phrase "separation of powers" is prescribed by law and in which legality is a norm for action, any social group participating in this pattern will have to take into consideration, when it acts, the response that its action will evoke in others who can invoke the law. The separation of powers creates a situation in which any one of a number of social groups, Congress, the executive, or the courts, can each either on its own independent initiative or under the influence of other social groups in the community, act so as to circumscribe and in some cases to veto the policies of the other. This power arises not from the kind of personalities acting in Congress, the executive branch, or the courts, but from the relationship in which each organization stands to the other.

Political science has in a rough and imprecise way been describing the statuses and roles of participants in this complex relationship called the separation of powers. It has been showing that each group of participants acting in this complex network of relations must take into account the power of others. Whatever the personality of the members of Congress, for example, their decisions must take into account the possible reaction of a President carried into office by widespread popular support. The legal definition of the situation in the Constitution, as modified by practice, is an important element of the situation only because social groups in society have given the Presidency their support. This circumstance, once recognized by Congress, helps to define for Congressmen the power of the Presidency and in that sense, the power elements in the situation within which Congress must make its own decisions. Congress makes up its mind with constant reference to the power that both the President and the courts have and will wield if they obtain sufficient social support. Congress must constantly evaluate its own power as a function of the power of the other major policy-influencing groups.

Perhaps the best illustration of the way in which traditional political science is concerned specifically with the situational circumstances surrounding policy is the perennial dispute, sparked by Bagehot, with regard to the merits of the Presidential as compared with the Parliamentary system of government. One school of disputants argues that the situation created by the separation of powers tends to paralyze action, regardless of the people involved; a second school maintains that the situation provides for a more flexible representative system. According to the latter interpretation, a variety of means are thereby made available for social groups to bring their influence to bear. If they cannot persuade the Presidency of the merits of their claim, then social groups can appeal to Congress or the courts. The separation of powers, therefore, is said to be a structural device for the peculiar conditions of a large country in which diversified interests might easily be stifled by what some would argue are the more limited channels of access to legal authority in the Parliamentary system.[17] Although interpretation of

[17] For a succinct expression of this view see P. Herring, *Presidential Leadership* (New York: Farrar and Rinehart, 1940).

the way in which it operates varies, the separation of powers is here conceived as a situation in which each organized group acts in the light of its expectations about the activity of other group-participants in the same situation.

A further illustration can be taken. The political situation may be the point of intersection of the activities of several formal non-governmental organizations. The leadership in a large interest group is constantly confronted with the need to make a decision which, ultimately through the political process, affects authoritative policy. In making such decisions, the leadership must take into account the threat to itself of the existence of various external and internal groups such as parties, other interest groups, and semi-organized competing leadership groups within its own organization. These groups are all part of institutionalized patterns of activity which have consequences for the survival and destinies of the particular segment of the organization, the group's leadership, whose activity is of immediate concern. They are all power elements in the situation, although they are not all the elements. These are the elements within which the group leadership must decide and act and which must be taken into consideration in these decisions and actions. No less than the obvious limitations of the physical environment, the formally institutionalized human environment serves as a constraint on decision and action, independent of human motivations. To lose sight of this is to ignore an important determinant of action.

4. Types of Social Aggregates in the Situation: Social Groupings

Two points are obvious, however. First, the study of the political process is not conducted by traditional political science purely in terms of formal organization, whether of the governmental type or otherwise. "The population is not neatly apportioned into [group] pigeonholes according to primary interest. Great numbers of people do not belong to associations." [18] And second, even if political activity were confined to organized groups, it would be superficial to try to explain their changing character, numbers, and strength solely in terms of themselves. This brings us to a second kind of so-called groups which are traditionally included within the political process. We shall call them social groupings. They are strictly speaking not groups since they are patterns of activity or relations of individuals to one another that are not formally organized, that require no close interaction among the members, and that are not deliberately directed to the pursuit of specified purposes. They are collections of individuals who are classed together as a result of the fact that they have specified characteristics in common. Because of this we come to expect similar kinds of activity-responses from them in typical circumstances. Individuals fall into such groupings as a result of the possession of certain common social characteristics rather than because of a common effort for the achievement of collective purposes.

These characteristics are varied and numerous but quite familiar. Society defines the positions and expected behavior of individuals in the light of their belonging to the same age, sex, skill, economic, social, religious, sibling, and other groupings. Individuals of the same sex do not have to be pursuing any objectives in common, and yet every society sets up certain expectations with regard to the role or activity associated with such individuals in varying circumstances. Groupings of individuals according to these criteria are obviously of a different level of importance from the classification of individuals in accordance with the formal organizations to which they belong. The expected behavior of individuals in formal organizations is in part determined by the combination of social groupings from which they come as well as the interests they share in common as members of the organization.

[18] V. O. Key, *Politics Parties and Pressure Groups*, p. 208.

The existence of social groupings is an element of the political situation which must be distinguished from social groups. Analysis would show that social groupings are analytically prior to social groups in the sense that the activity and even the interpretation of goals of a formal organization reflect the fundamental social groupings from which its members come. The actions of an interest group or of a governmental organization, for example, are very closely related to the social composition of its members, that is, to the social groupings such as economic or social class, region, and so on from which they are drawn. Furthermore, and this is the point of primary importance here in terms of situational data, the groupings are directly as much a part of a situation as the groups. Every authoritative decision must take into consideration the response of the various social groupings throughout the society; or to put the matter directly, social groupings as well as groups are part of the structure of the situation.

An illustration or two will throw some light on this point. Let us consider the economic institutions about which much has been written in political science under the topic of the relation between the political and the economic institutions. Economic institutions is a very loose undifferentiated phrase. It refers to the two kinds of phenomena about which we have been speaking. It refers to a broad area of institutional activity consisting, on the one hand, of organized groups such as corporations, various kinds of business enterprises from the small shopkeeper to the large corporation, trade unions, trade and consumer organizations, and the like; and, on the other hand, economic institutions include a vast body of activity about which society has developed certain expectations and to which certain statuses have been ascribed. We have the buyer-seller relation, the employer-employee relation, the owner-nonowner relation, and so on almost indefinitely. We can classify individuals into groupings each characterized by one or more of these and many other economic relations.

In arguing that economic institutions are a vital element in the political process, traditional political science has been trying to say more than that organized economic groups have brought pressure to bear within the process. It is true, the literature on interest groups often leaves the impression that these groups are the sole channel of influence between economic patterns of life and social policy. To this extent the literature tends to be superficial. Others have been suggesting, however, that the economic groupings are an effective part of the structure of the general political situation. They have stressed particularly the impact of the grouping classified according to the criterion of property ownership.

In arguing for an economic interpretation of the Constitution Charles Beard,[19] for example, was not necessarily maintaining a psychological thesis, namely, that men are motivated by a desire for profits. He was, in fact, urging that those who were making constitutional decisions, whatever their motives, were confronted with patterns of economic activity, analyzable into social groupings, that in themselves were a force compelling decisions in a direction that would not violate certain economic expectations of men. He was asserting that the expectations relating to property give birth to economic classes and that these are influential groupings in society. Decisions and actions regarding the political structure which ignored their power would have little chance of surviving. Beard was here trying to isolate one variable, the expectations in relation to property ownership, to show how, as part of the situation in which constitutional decisions were being made, it helped to shape these decisions. His zeal sometimes carried him to the point of maintaining that this economic part of the situation's structure was the only important variable worth considering, whereas in his more temperate

[19] See *An Economic Interpretation of the Constitution* (New York: Macmillan, 1913) and *The Economic Basis of Politics* (New York: Knopf, 1922).

moments he meant only that it was a most persuasive factor at the time.[20]

Similarly, Marx's attempt to isolate the influence of social classes on policy is a search for the role of class groupings in the situation. Marx never insisted, as we have often been misled into believing, that the officials of government are calculating hypocrites carrying out conspiratorial designs against the working class in favor of the capitalists. It is the popularizers who have offered this interpretation as a useful stereotype in the actual struggle over power. For Marx, the reason why the officials in governmental institutions use their power in favor of the possessing class is not that they are personally venal and morally corrupt. On the contrary, his argument is that in the relationship of forces in a society, groupings formed around expectations with regard to the mode of production and property relations confront the policy-makers with a power situation in which they must meet the needs of the dominant class or lose their positions of authority.

In a cogent emendation of Bentley's premises, Merle Fainsod corrected Bentley's defect of insisting on a purely group interpretation of the elements in a political situation and ignoring the broader institutional setting within which groups as well as government must act. Later interest-group studies showed the same tendency as Bentley's to ignore the broader institutional matrix within which the groups themselves functioned. These institutional patterns circumscribe not only the decisions of government, of course, but equally the decisions of other formal organizations, such as the interest groups themselves, as I earlier indicated. As Fainsod points out in a study of the regulatory process, the "nature of that process is most satisfactorily revealed when the analysis proceeds on three interrelated levels," two of which are of concern here: "(1) the conditioning factors which

[20] See the latest edition of *The Economic Basis of Politics* (New York: Knopf, 1945) where Beard amends his earlier views.

made up the institutional context of regulation, (2) the parties in interest who are concerned with the character of regulation. . . ." [21] The "institutional context" is suggested as an element of the situation within which a regulatory agency makes policy in addition to the element of the "parties in interest," a legal phrase for interest groups. The "institutional context" described as the technology, economic organization, ideology, law, and the like, helps to determine the direction which regulation takes and the limits within which it must confine itself, Fainsod points out. One of the reasons for this, I am suggesting, is the fact that the institutional setting as part of any complex of political relations creates power centers that cannot be ignored.

The division of the so-called group elements into organized groups and groupings does not exhaust the variety of identifiable social aggregates. As I have already indicated, an exhaustive analysis would compel us to differentiate among crowds, publics, audiences, and similar phenomena. My immediate objective, however, relieves us of the need to pursue the classification of social aggregates any further.[22] My purpose here is to indicate the kind of data to which political science has historically been committed.

The important classification into groups and groupings demonstrates what would simply be confirmed by exploration of the place in research held by other classes of social aggregates. It would confirm that the study of institutional patterns of activity, as crystallized in organized groups or diffused in social groupings, gives us the clue to the situational emphasis of this research. This helps to explain why we sometimes hear traditional research called institutional as contrasted with recent psychological investigation. Psychologically oriented research workers often deplore the traditional treatment of institutions. I am urging

---

[21] M. Fainsod, op. cit., p. 299.

[22] For a good generalized treatment of the subject matter which has suggested some terminology here, see J. W. Bennett and M. M. Tumin, op. cit.

that this concern for institutions really displays a traditional lack of interest in the personality of participants in political life and a major concern in political science for the impact of the structure of a situation. To say, therefore, that process analysis is institutional is simply another way of saying that political science has been concerned with the extent to which policy is dictated by the nature of the relations in a pattern of activity rather than by the motives and feelings the participants bring to the situation.

Beginning with the legalists and continuing to contemporary times, when policy is viewed as the changing product of a process, it is clear that the burden of research in traditional political science has been to add to the variety of phenomenal elements considered part of the structure of the situation. At the same time, however, it has included an examination of the impact of this structure of the political situation on social policy. I need only add here that this commitment to situational data has been so strong that almost inescapably it has led to a revolt against itself in favor of an important aspect thereby neglected, the psychological.

5. *Structure of the Situation*

Before turning to this reaction, let us try to clarify somewhat further the meaning of situational data. What is implied by the concept of situation? A complete answer to this question will not be attempted here as it would require an independent work of considerable length. The concept is endemic to contemporary social science,[23] especially sociology and social psychology, although there too it is often used casually even when it is crucial to an analysis. Nor has its widespread use in the social

---

[23] See a review of its use by P. Meadows, "The Dialectic of the Situation: Some Remarks on Situational Psychology," 5 *Philosophy and Phenomenological Research* (1944-5), 354-64.

sciences been accompanied by an equally extensive agreement on the meaning to be given to the term. Since all social activity takes place within structure, it would indeed be strange if all social scientists were not compelled in one way or another to fall back on the conception of the situation, or a substitute synonym, to help understand a problem at hand. The type of data underlying traditional research in political science, therefore, does not in itself distinguish political research from that in the other social sciences. On the contrary, the very fact that political science has been committed to situational data, and the accompanying awareness of this, serves to bring political science into close integration with the other social sciences. The apparent backwardness of which political science has been so often accused is due, in this respect, less to its observation of entirely different classes of data than to its failure to make unimpeachably clear the kind of data with which it has been concerned.

Although political science is thus concerned with situational data, it directs attention, of course, to the *political* situation. Therefore, it is not enough to ask what the situation is; we must also be prepared to show what makes it political. In the light of our earlier discussion of the nature of the relations we call political, this is possible. We have a political situation whenever activity arises over the authoritative allocation of values, however indirectly this activity may be related to policy. Two citizens disputing over the foreign policy of the United States create a political situation. This is one step in the direction of influencing the whole political process and one part of the whole political system. It is a form of political activity as contrasted with the limiting case of utter apathy.

The question that requires further analysis, therefore, is the meaning of the concept situation. American process theorists, like Small and Bentley, had identified the heart of the research problem in the social sciences although they promptly ignored it. It is the individual who acts and interacts with others. Without action there are neither social problems requiring solution nor the need for social sciences to investigate the uniformities involved. People do not interact politically in a vacuum, however. Interaction always occurs in relation to other people, to a physical environment, and to a non-human biological environment. The total situation consists of those circumstances which shape activity. The point is so obvious that it is often neglected. It is only another way of saying that, when people act, there are various elements in their social, physical, and biological environment limiting and determining their activities.

Once we consciously use this elemental idea as the center of research, however, we are immediately confronted with the need to specify just how we are to classify the total situation so that we can be certain that, in any concrete research project, we do not through error, habit, or neglect, omit any important determinant of political activity. If the task of political theory is to provide a guide for selecting the significant variables, then obviously one of the major problems in the formulation of conceptual theory will be an adequate identification of the major aspects or elements in the political situation.

Although political research has never posed the question in quite this way, and therefore its response does not emerge distinctly, it is clear from our recent discussion that traditionally political science has been classifying the elements of the situation in terms of legal or constitutional, as contrasted with extra-legal political, phenomena. We see law on the one side and activity on the other. Now undoubtedly this is a valuable kind of classification for some purposes. It directs attention to the fact that the ordering of men's relations provided for in formal codes is not without some influence on policy. He who has the law on his side thereby acquires one kind of influence. But having said this, the traditional approach to the political situation stops. The classification has little further utility, and we are left only with an enumeration of the kinds of extra-legal activity, such as that of interest groups, the informal actions of people in governmental organizations, and the like. In a sense, political science is still operating within the frame of mind set for it by the juristic outlook of the nineteenth century. It adopts a classification of phenomena based on the principle of their formal legal structure.

I am here urging that when, from the point of view of systematic theory, we approach the problem of the kinds of data relevant to a complete piece of research, it is necessary to use a different axis of classification. Classification, according to these new criteria, would enable us to identify a major kind of data to which political science has really been directing its attention over the years—the situational. Let us therefore look at the possible form of such a classification.

Examination of traditional research has led to the conclusion that we must identify at least two generically different kinds of data in every political situation: first, what for want of a more expressive term, I have called the situational; and, second, the psychological. The situational refers to those determinants which shape activity in spite of the kind of personalities and motivations in the participants. There are at least three separate categories of situational data to be identified: (1) the physical environment; (2) the non-human organic environment; and (3) the social environment or patterns of human activity flowing from social interaction.[24]

It goes without saying that our physical environment influences our activity, regardless of the kind of people we are. Our non-organic resources, topography, and spatial location, such as

---

[24] I have learned much in this regard from a study, while it was still in manuscript stage, by T. Parsons and E. Shils, "Values, Motives and Systems of Action" appearing in the volume edited by them entitled *Towards a General Theory of Action* (Cambridge: Harvard University Press, 1951), pp. 47-278. For the source of much thinking today about the social situation see the work of Max Weber, esp. *The Theory of Social and Economic Organization* (New York: Oxford University Press, 1947), ed. by T. Parsons.

being near or distant from the seat of government, influence the kind of political lives we lead. Geopolitics and the study of regionalism attempt to explore the effect of physical environment on social policy. The geographical dispersion of nations has helped to create certain permanent needs throughout the long span of history, however much the personality structures of the political leaders and the whole population may have changed.[25]

Similarly, the flora, fauna, and micro-organisms of a situation play a significant part in shaping all social activity, including the political. For example, their influence upon population movements is well known. The American Indian in his pursuit of the buffalo, the location of fur-bearing animals in relation to early American development, and the existence of the bread-basket of Europe outside Italy, Germany, and Great Britain are sufficient to confirm at first glance the clear relation between social and political life on the one side, and the non-human organic environment on the other.

Finally, the fact of social life, that people act and react on one another, leads to the establishment of stable, regularized modes of activity in our political life that we call institutional patterns. The very fact of their existence, as this and the earlier chapter have sought to show, helps to determine the way in which social policy is made and executed.

These three aspects of a situation are some of the more important elements which represent varieties of situational data. They have been so termed because they are the conditions which do not depend upon the feelings, attitudes, or motivations of an acting individual, but rather upon the form that the activity or presence of other persons or things, physical and non-human organic, take. At times writers have called them the objective conditions limiting and shaping action. This description is satis-

---

[25] See H. J. Morgenthau, *Politics Among Nations* and J. Mattern, *Geopolitik: Doctrine of National Self-Sufficiency* (Baltimore: The Johns Hopkins University Press, 1942).

factory as long as it does not lead us to believe that the subjective factor of personality is any less objective as a datum than any other aspect of a situation. When situational data are described as the objective conditions, however, what is normally implied is that they help to determine activity with an influence entirely separate from that of the kind of people who are acting.

We can appreciate the independent influence of situational data on activity if we look at the role that a fourth and final element, the personality, plays in a situation. I am not denying here the obviously indubitable, that how a person reacts to a given set of so-called objective circumstances is conditioned in part by the kind of person he is. A party leader who is stable and free of severe internal tensions will clearly be able to evaluate his surrounding circumstances, such as the strength and tactics of his opponents, more reliably than a leader who is riddled with frustrations and a deep sense of persecution. Identical situations will elicit quite divergent responses from each of these leaders. Each will define his situation differently in terms of the predispositions of his personality.

But what we tend to ignore today, while we are riding the crest of psychological research—and the history of American political science brings this out—is the fact that although personality variations are an undeniable dimension of a situation, another aspect consists of the patterns of activity in the situation surrounding the participants. Assuming that each of the party leaders just mentioned is mentally stable enough to grapple with reality, however the two types might otherwise vary, when confronted with the existence of powerful social groups making claims on their parties, the leaders would have to consider the presence of these groups and their strengths. There would be a tendency on the part of the decisions and actions of differing party leaders to converge, in spite of the differences in their motivations, because of the presence of powerful groups in their environment. To take a decision or step which ignored their presence would be impossible without inviting the nullification or later radical modification of the decision or action itself.

Basically this is the theme of a recent revealing work on the Tennessee Valley Authority.[26] In it the author shows how the social environment in the Valley led the Authority to adopt a necessary policy of conciliation to prevailing white-dominated, wealth-oriented agricultural practices. However much personalities in responsible places have differed, their decisions in this case were influenced by the situational elements in the Valley to such a degree that the varying personalities left only an imperceptible mark on the fundamental policy of the Authority towards agriculture. Even the liberal-minded top-level executives were powerless to overcome the influence of the situation. Their personal predispositions were of no avail. Presumably, if the strength of traditional agricultural groups had been less pronounced, the personal predilections of the administrators in the Authority, if they had led to a different policy, might have prevailed. The point is that the situational data are vital in any piece of research. The extent of their influence as contrasted with psychological data is always a matter for concrete investigation; but that they normally play some part, however slight, is difficult to contest.

It will be clear that I have not examined all three kinds of situational data with which traditional research has been dealing. I have chosen to treat only one of the three or more possible varieties of these data, the social. The reason for this is simple. My purpose has not been to show exactly how varieties of data ought to be used in developing a systematic theory but rather to emphasize the need to explore the possible classes of data. By trying to show how the corpus of political research, that dealing with political institutions as they interact with one another, has been concerned with the situational as contrasted with the psychological dimension of political life, the hope is that the reader could easily visualize analogically the importance of other situ-

---

[26] P. Selznick, *TVA and the Grass Roots* (Berkeley and Los Angeles: University of California Press, 1949).

ational determinants such as the physical and non-human organic. Intensive treatment of other situational components, while vital for other goals, would for our purposes needlessly duplicate what has already been said in relation to political institutions. In briefly sketching the recent history of American political science, I have been seeking to show the variety of sub-elements, legal and extra-legal, which we can subsume under the broad category of the institutional environment.

On the basis of this description of the structure of a situation the point of this and the preceding chapters can be restated with greater clarity. This point is that the structure of the situation helps to mold the political process and that traditional political science has been particularly suitable for illuminating these situational determinants. The starting place is an individual acting to influence policy. With him as the point of reference, we can see that the structure of the enveloping environment will serve to resist his endeavors, whether singular or in groups, where they threaten established expectations. He must either permit the latter to deflect his activity to some degree or he must seek to change these expectations.

The identification of situational data and of their importance for political science opens up a large area of research which has as yet been untouched. There are few reliable generalizations geared to the problem of how actors, in groups or as individuals, respond to various kinds of typical situations. Furthermore, there is little knowledge about the variety of classes of situations which may exist and their component elements. Although some theoretical frameworks have been proffered in other social sciences for the analysis of situations, such as the means-end schema,[27] these have yet to be tested for their applicability to the political system. My primary purpose here, of course, is neither to evaluate those that do exist nor volunteer

[27] T. Parsons, *The Structure for Social Action* and also *Essays in Sociological Theory Pure and Applied*.

one of my own; it is simply to raise the problem as one to which theoretically oriented political scientists might well address themselves. Otherwise it will be found difficult to utilize effectively an important variety of data in the formulation of a general political theory.[28]

[28] In addition to the work of T. Parsons already mentioned, it is fruitful to look at W. I. Thomas, "The Behavior Pattern and the Situation," 22 *Publications of the American Sociological Society* (1927), 1-13; L. S. Cottrell, Jr., "Some Neglected Problems in Social Psychology," 15 *American Sociological Review* (1950), 705-12; and of course the extensive writings of Max Weber. G. E. G. Catlin is one of the few political scientists to raise situational analysis to the level of consciousness. See his *A Study of the Principles of Politics,* chapter 2.

Chapter 8

Behavioral Data

> *The choice of these terms [actor, act] as a
> starting point results from the conception of
> political science as a branch of the study
> of human behavior. Central throughout are
> persons and their acts . . . what people say
> and do.*
>
> Harold D. Lasswell and Abraham Kaplan

As I have already indicated, the structure of the situation represents only one of two possible kinds of determinants helpful for understanding the way in which power is used to influence policy. The personality is a second dimension of any activity which, concurrently with the situational, contributes to the outcome. To explain the determinants of any particular political act, we need to know not only the various circumstances or objective conditions surrounding it, but also the kind of personality, the improperly called "subjective" conditions, that individuals bring to the activity. No two individuals will define a situation and react to it in exactly the same way. The same facts may be so interpreted by two different persons as to lead to totally divergent decisions and actions. A source of the divergence lies in the individual's personality.

In traditional research, political science has shown a marked indifference to the relevance of the motivations and feelings of participants in political activity. Within the last three decades this has given birth to sharp dissatisfaction, so pervasive that it has led to the adoption of a new concept, that of political behavior, to express the measure of the discontent and the need for a new outlook towards research. This concept mirrors a deep sentiment in favor of closer, if not almost exclusive, attention to the motivations and feelings of the human actor. Whereas situational research had its roots in sociology, concern for behavior seeks its categories in psychology. Against the background of traditional situational research, it is the task of this chapter to explore the kind of data students of political life seek to unearth in the use of such psychological concepts as attitudes, feelings, motivations, and personality. We shall conclude that if traditional research has lost sight of the acting human beings, to the same degree but at the opposite pole, those who have turned to psychology threaten to ignore the relevance, and sometimes even the existence, of situational data.

1. The Study of Political Behavior

To precisely what kind of research does the concept of political behavior refer? It is clear that this term indicates that the research worker wishes to look at participants in the political system as individuals who have the emotions, prejudices, and predispositions of human beings as we know them in our daily lives.

This use of psychological terms with regard to political problems is by no means a modern innovation. It can be traced back to the very origins of serious political thought. Every novitiate in the history of political values learns that each system of political speculation rests on a unique set of notions about human nature. In this sense political science has always been psychologically oriented. One has only to call to mind the work of Plato, Hobbes, or Bentham to realize the prominent role that psychological assumptions have played in speculations about the functioning of the political system.

Only within very recent times, however, with the publication of Graham Wallas's *Human Nature in Politics*,[1] if a rough date is to be set, has a body of thinking arisen in the United States which uses psychological categories, not to lay the foundations for later speculation or research, but as an intrinsic part of that very research. It no longer suffices to make an assumption either about the intellectual and rational character or the irrationality of human nature and then to act as though this premise were the definitive statement about the role of human motives and emotions in political life. With the developments of the last twenty years, the application of psychological categories extends to all political life. Since we may no longer assume that human nature is given, the task is to determine the relation of human feelings, attitudes, and motivations to each set of political circumstances.

Behavioral research—remembering that we are using this adjective without thereby imputing outmoded behaviorist views to contemporary political psychology—has therefore sought to elevate the actual human being to the center of attention. Its premise is that the traditionalists have been reifying institutions, virtually looking at them as entities apart from their component individuals. At best, in studies of political parties and legislatures, as an illustration, the individual recedes into a shadowy background. He becomes an impassive creature whose presence is never doubted but who seems to act in the organizations without the normal attributes of a human being.

In the studies of Congress, for example, there has traditionally been little attention, except in passing, to the way in

[1] First edition in 1908.

which the attitudes and personalities of the participants influence Congressional activity, or to the impact of the institutional patterns of activity on the feelings and attitudes of the individual. Traditional situational analysis has dealt largely with the way in which one pattern of activities conditions another, without probing behind the activities to the feeling human being to discover how this is so. As a result, the individual has become a wooden automaton who does not seem to vary in his predispositions or feelings under any political situations. This neglect of the most obvious element, the human being, has led to the wholesale rejection of the study of institutional "shells." In its place there has arisen a search for the way in which the feelings and motivations of the individual act and react in any set of political circumstances. It is now customary in political science to call this the study of political behavior or the use of psychological categories in relation to political phenomena.

Before turning to explore the meaning of this concept, political behavior, we must see what its relation is to the concept of the political process. The use of these two phrases has been ambiguous. Political behavior is the newest concept to appear in the firmament of political terms. Although it can be found sprinkled through the literature ever since the First World War,[2] appearing at about the same time as the concept of political process itself, it has been adopted for general use only within the last ten or fifteen years. Of late it has so gained in favor that it even threatens, if not to displace the concept of process, at least to reduce it to a secondary, less consequential position in research. Today we hear as much, if not more, about investigations of political behavior as of research into the political process.

It is evident that its popularity is in no small measure

[2] See for example its use by C. E. Merriam, "University Research and Equipment," in *Report of the Committee on Political Research*, p. 308. Today it sometimes appears as though the use in political research of knowledge from psychology were something new; a reading of the literature of the 1920's indicates that this is the period when the first wave of enthusiasm had its origin.

due to the psychological connotations of the term. With the social sciences all newly saturated in psychological terminology, it would indeed have been unnatural for those political scientists who are sensitized to new developments to fail to adapt this kind of analysis to their own research. Whether the concept of political behavior appropriately applies to the research which it is used to describe or whether it is improperly employed in a loose use of a fashionable term is a matter for our immediate consideration.

In spite of the prevalence of both the concepts of political process and political behavior in the writings of political scientists, and in the face of the central role they play in designating the character of research, there are few specific studies of either term.[3] A survey of their use and necessary meaning, however, leaves little doubt that they are neither exclusive, irreconcilable, nor identical approaches to political data.

The incautious use of the terms has led to the appearance of two conflicting tendencies. On the one hand, political process and political behavior seem to be used almost as synonyms. In one and the same work it is not unusual for the concepts to be used indiscriminately to refer to the general body of political data as though they were alternate ways of referring to the same subject matter. We hear about research into the political process or in relation to political behavior without discovering any intention thereby to identify different things.[4] It will shortly become apparent however that whereas the political process refers to the concrete system of intertwined activity

[3] See the very conscious use of the idea of political behavior in D. Truman, "The Implications of Political Behavior Research" in 5 *Items* (1951), 37-9; and E. Frenkel-Brunswik, "Interaction of Psychological and Sociological Factors in Political Behavior," 46 *American Political Science Review* (1952), 44-65.

[4] Illustrations of this appear in such works as the following: E. S. Griffith (ed.), *Research in Political Science* (Chapel Hill: University of North Carolina Press, 1948); E. E. Schattschneider, *Politics, Pressure and the Tariff* (New York: Prentice-Hall, 1935); O. Garceau, *The Public Library in the Political Process* (New York: Columbia University Press, 1949).

which shapes authoritative policy, political behavior properly indicates an intention to look at a particular aspect of data, the psychological, to help provide an understanding of political activity. Research workers often use the term political behavior, therefore, to indicate that they are studying the political process by looking at the relation to it of the motivations, personalities, or feelings of the participants as individual human beings. The term is not used to signify that they are studying something different from the process.

On the other hand, with almost equal frequency the concepts are encountered in conflict with each other. In the literature there often persists an overtone that those interested in political behavior are really devoting themselves to the study of something different from those concerned with the political process.[5] This feeling cannot be lightly set aside with the statement that it is unfounded or misleading. Its source needs to be explained and in doing so we shall be able to discern just what it is to which the concept of behavior really stands in contrast.

The grounds for this feeling that the concepts refer to entirely different subject matters can be appreciated if we recall that until the recent appearance in political science of knowledge consciously borrowed from psychology, the political process was discussed almost exclusively in situational terms, denuded of reference to the feeling human being. As a result, in the absence of deliberate analysis of the meaning of the political process as a concept and of an identification of the kind of data at the heart of political research, it has seemed only natural for political scientists to assume that by the political process they have been referring to something inherently non-psychological. As the utility of psychology has become increasingly apparent, it is understandable that the study of political behavior should be opposed to the study of the political process.

If we accept the fact, however, that the earlier approach to political problems was unique not only because it had in-

[5] See footnotes on page 204.

volved the study of political life as a process but because it had
led research workers to direct their attention to the situational
aspect of the process, the following conclusion forces itself upon
us. If the phrase political behavior does designate a new kind of
data, it stands in contrast to the situational aspect of political
activity rather than to process analysis. Political behavior refers
to a new kind of data different from situational data, to which
political research had been almost exclusively devoted in the
past. But like situational data, the study of political behavior is
nothing more than a way of exploring the functioning of the
political process. It is therefore ambiguous and an index of
theoretical indifference either to juxtapose or identify the concepts of process and behavior.

2. Concealment of Situational Data

Today the relevance and critical significance of the individual's personality and feelings for political activity is of course
beyond dispute, so that there need be no effort here to prove the
accepted.[6] What, however, does require special attention is a
seldom-observed consequence of the use of psychological categories. At times, commitment to them tends to become so intensive that it threatens to conceal the fact that there is a genuine
difference between situational and psychological data, a difference that no sense of the urgency to explain action in terms of
human feelings and personalities can possibly destroy.

The role of motives and feelings are often so over-
weighted that political research overlooks two considerations:
first, the nature of the psychological effects *on* the situation,
and second, the psychological effects *of* the situation. The first
refers to the fact that there exists an isolable influence of per-

[6] One need only to look at the work of H. D. Lasswell and H. Simon,
and most recently of D. Truman in *The Governmental Process* for evidence
of this.

sonality and attitudes on political activity; it does not thereby signify, however, the impossibility of a concurrent influence from the direction of the situation. The second refers to the fact that quite often even though we may describe activity in terms of the feelings and motivations of individuals, this in itself is no sufficient proof that we are dealing with a psychological rather than a situational determinant of political activity.

Let us look first at the predisposition to attribute to human motivations the primary force shaping the political system. The main burden of the discussion in this and the two preceding chapters has been not the contradictory, but rather a less inclusive interpretation of the scope of the situational determinant. I have suggested that since we always act in social situations, we are invariably confronted with patterns of activity in our environment that deflect our decisions and consequent actions. In maintaining this position, however, I have not been implying that the structure of the environment alone determines actions. This is only one factor. Another, equally significant, is the kind of human being involved—what his personality is like, how he is predisposed to interpret situations, how he responds to demands made upon him, what his attitudes are towards the various political prejudices of the groups in his social environment, his loyalties, and so forth in an endless catalogue of the motivations, feelings, and attitudes of the individual.

A rounded analysis of a political event therefore requires some attention to the situational as well as to the psychological data involved. Although this fact seems at this point to be obvious, the truth is that numerous efforts at investigating the psychological aspects of activity still tend to ignore the situational determinant. A good portion of psychological research leaves the unmistakable impression that motivations are the primary, if not the exclusive, factor in shaping political institutions. In this kind of commitment to psychological research, if situational data are not consciously rejected as valuable material for understanding the political system, at least these data are neglected so consistently that their utility might just as well be deliberately denied.

We must confess that in political science there are few authors indeed who have felt sufficiently equipped to explore political relations in the light of the feelings and motivations of the participants.[7] Most comment on the psychology of politics has come from persons who function within the framework of the discipline of psychology itself. From among these, examples of psychological determinism can be amply cited. A case in point is a recent work by Abram Kardiner, *The Individual and His Society*.[8] On numerous grounds it is an exceptional work, but this does not concern us here. Although the author views institutions in broad cultural classifications and therefore he does not directly deal with political institutions, by implication his analysis applies to these as well. This work illustrates in almost classic terms how inordinate commitment to psychology can lead to the concealment of the situational aspect.

Essentially, the author seeks to show that the personalities generated by the fundamental institutions of a culture, acting on primitive, biological drives, are primarily responsible for the existence and characteristics of the secondary institutions. He does not argue that all institutional patterns are shaped by the need to gratify biological drives; indeed, he carefully distinguishes his own from this position.[9] His point is that the "primary" institutions alone mediate between the inherent drives and their gratification in a culture; each culture produces as a result certain basic personality types. The "secondary" institutions, on the other hand, among which would be included the political, are the mechanisms through which the basic person-

[7] For the paucity of studies in political science using psychological material see C. E. Hawley and L. A. Dexter, "Recent Political Science Research in American Universities," 46 *American Political Science Review* (1952), 470-85.

[8] (New York: Columbia University Press, 1939).

[9] Ibid., p. 16.

ality structures seek to satisfy the needs and tensions generated by the process of socialization through the primary institutions. The character of the secondary institutions is therefore determined largely by the impact of the personality on them.

As Kardiner writes, "the primary institutions are those which create the basic and inescapable problems of adaptation. The secondary institutions are creations of the result of the primary institutions on basic personality structure";[10] and secondary institutions "are derived from the constellations created in the ego structure by the basic effective realities."[11] The essential characteristic of secondary institutional patterns of activity is, therefore, that they reflect rather than help to mold and modify the basic personalities in any culture. The flow of influence is from typical individual constellations of motivations towards the institution.

With rather similar premises in mind, others have sought to prove that the breakdown of the community is primarily a matter of the loss of faith by which men live, or that war can be accounted for as a device for the dissipation of mass tensions or release of innate destructive impulses, or that it is a protective device for the defense of what one loves, or that the authoritarian personality is the source of the authoritarian society. In most cases, if the situation is not entirely ignored, the nod made to it in passing scarcely compensates for its neglect or substitutes for its analysis.[12]

What has so obviously been neglected here is the fact that personality is not a constant throughout life; the assumption that the early experiences in a life history permanently mold the personality and its motivations does not withstand the test of first inspection. The individual possesses the capacity of testing reality and readjusting to it, which means that his personality undergoes constant modifications in the light of his experience. Essentially this interpretation underlies the whole assumption of

[10] Ibid., p. 345.
[11] Ibid., p. 132.
[12] See ibid., chapters 1 and 2.

personality reconstruction through psychotherapy. Such restructuring of personality is part of the continuous process of living. The personality is not a constant which plods through life's experiences dutifully leaving its imprint on institutional patterns. Since reality adjustment does take place, the so-called secondary institutions themselves, while often less influential than the primary, do nevertheless play some role in the process. This is just another way of saying that the stable structured relations of men, what we have identified as part of the situational dimension, bear some relation to our actions. The extent of action and reaction between institutions and personalities is of course always a matter for empirical determination.

Today there are few students of human behavior who would sanction, on theoretical grounds at any rate, any attempt to insist exclusively on motivational causality. If this were the only source of neglect of situational data, it would suffice to refresh our minds from time to time with regard to the limited claims that can be made on behalf of personality as a determinant and insist upon the recognition of this modest position in actual research.

In fact, however, the statement that personality and situation are concurrent and mutually dependent variables does not exhaust the discussion of their relationship. Often in political science we meet the idea that the ultimate and only meaningful explanation of political life can be obtained through a description of activity in terms of the feelings and motivations of the participants. Psychology, in other words, is presumed to provide the fundamental categories for understanding the political system. Since in this way political behavior is conceived as simply an aspect of human behavior in general, psychology becomes if not the only, at least the most appropriate, lens through which to view political life.

The point here is that within this view there lurks the premise that the use of psychological terms is of itself unquestionable evidence that we are thereby examining a psychological determinant of political activity. To the extent that this notion prevails, it helps to conceal the role of situational data. The presence of psychological terms is in itself no proof that a research worker is in fact isolating a psychological determinant. Very often what he is really doing is trying to understand the psychological mechanisms and responses set in operation by the impact of the situation. In the last analysis, the so-called psychological approach in a great deal of research is a description of the psychological effect of the situation, rather than the effect of psychology, that is, of motivations, on the situation. This is the second consideration which, as I indicated earlier, is often overlooked by those devoted to political psychology. We need carefully to distinguish the effect of psychology *on* the situation from the psychological effect *of* the situation.

As this suggests, we can approach a situation from two points of view. First, we can examine the impact of motivations and personality on the situation. In his *Psychopathology and Politics,*[13] for example, Lasswell sought to distinguish the way in which one's private affects were displaced on public issues. Although the author has here been sometimes accused of arguing for the exclusive neurotic basis of all political participation, a moderate interpretation of this early work in the application of psychoanalytic theory to politics would suggest that he did not intend to exclude the influence of other than psychological factors on the behavior of the individual. He was simply trying to show how the neurotic aspects of the personality left their mark on political life. Since such a piece of research seeks to trace the flow of influence from the individual and his motivations to the situation, it can be said to be using pure psychological categories.

However, research that seeks to trace the flow of influence back again from the situation to the individual, even though it describes that influence in terms of the feeling-response of the individual, is in effect isolating the impact of the situation. For

[13] (Chicago: University of Chicago Press, 1930).

example, the desires for power and prestige, which are often called attitudes or motivations typical of Western culture, may be sentiments evoked by the situation rather than pre-existing sentiments which individuals carry to the political situation. If we wish to continue to participate in an institution, we may have to accept the institution's definition of the conditions for participation. Whatever particular predispositions we may have developed as a result of our exposure to a particular culture, the desire to continue to participate in a specific institutional pattern that puts a premium on power and prestige may well influence the actions of the individual. In some cases the institutional pattern will dominate over the individual's pre-existing personality, and he will be constrained to adopt attitudes in harmony with the needs of survival in the institution. The desire for power or prestige in this case would be a motive generated by the institution rather than one brought by the individual to the institution. The desire for power and prestige appears to be a psychological, but in fact may be a situational, category. The institution in this case molds the personality.

This is a point long known but not generally assimilated in every-day analysis. W. I. Thomas adopted it as a central theme in the twenties[14] and more recently in similar vein Talcott Parsons has written:

> Once a situation is institutionally defined and the definition upheld by an adequately integrated system of sanctions, action in conformity with the relevant expectations tends, as pointed out, to mobilize a wide variety of motivational elements in its service. Thus, to take one of the most famous examples, the "profit motive" which has played such a prominent part in economic discussion, is not a category of psychology at all. The correct view is rather that a system of "free enterprise" in a money and market

[14] See the earlier reference to his work and also *The Unadjusted Girl* (Boston: Little, Brown, 1923), pp. 43 ff.

economy so defines the situation for those conducting or aspiring to the conduct of business enterprise, that they must seek profit as a condition of
survival and as a measure of success of their activities. Hence, whatever interests the individual may
have in achievement, self-respect, the admiration of
others, etc., to say nothing of what money will buy,
are channeled into profit-making activity. In a differently defined situation, the same fundamental
motives would lead to a totally different kind of
activity.[15]

The failure to identify situational data as an isolable influence on activity has left considerable uncertainty as to the
intentions of the student of political life. We do not know when
he is searching for genuinely psychological variables, that is, for
the extent to which behavior stems from the motivations of the
individual as they are brought to bear on the situation and when
he is talking of the situational dimension, that is, of the extent
to which the situation calls up certain predispositions and attitudes from the individual personality or requires readjustment
of attitudes.

A good indication of this is the pioneer work of Simon,
Smithburg, and Thompson on *Public Administration*. Among
its numerous merits, this book cuts new patterns of thought in
the study of administrative services, particularly in its efforts to
remedy the manifest reluctance of traditional administrative research to utilize psychological analysis to the full. The authors
begin with the premise that "to avoid sterile formalism and
dogmatism [a textbook in public administration] must be
grounded thoroughly on the psychology of human relations in
organizations. . . . In particular, we believe that a clear understanding of the problems of top-level organization and of the
relation of administration to politics can be reached *only* through

[15] *Essays in Sociological Theory Pure and Applied*, pp. 37-8.

an analysis of the basic psychological processes involved in administration." [16] This opinion appears as a constant refrain throughout the book.

By psychology, however, the authors mean two things: first, that the ideas, prejudices, and personalities of a group of people will influence the organization of which they are part; and second, that the organization itself will have a determinable effect on their behavior. As they put it, at the same point in which they speak of their predilection for a psychological approach, "an administrative organization is a group of people— of flesh-and-blood human beings—who behave in certain ways, partly because of the ideas, prejudices, personalities, and abilities they bring to the organization, and partly because of the influence upon them of the other members of the administrative group and the society about it." [17] It is quite obvious that, in spite of their interpretation of their data as psychological, they are concerned only in part with the influence of the personality on the institutional patterns. For the most part, on the contrary, they search for the impact of the situation on human feelings and motivations. It would be manifestly impossible to discuss the functioning of an administrative group without taking into account the way in which the group organizes its members for the making of decisions, the taking of action, and the maintenance of cohesion.

Except in a very loose way, it is deceptive to call research into the impact of the structured group on the behavior of its individual members investigation exclusively into psychological processes. Here what is being isolated is the way in which the situation, formed by a group of people who come together collectively to fulfill certain purposes, creates conditions which help to determine the activity of each individual. On the one hand, the participating individuals act as they do because of

[16] H. Simon, D. Smithburg and V. Thompson, op. cit., p. vi. Italics mine.
[17] Ibid.

motivations and attitudes stemming from extra-organizational factors. This is the influence of the personality. On the other hand, however, how they would act, if there were no other influences playing upon them, is circumscribed by the fact that the administrative situation in which they find themselves compels them to act in a slightly different way, if the group is to maintain itself.

The authors are quite conscious of these diverse kinds of influence but are content to call them both an examination of the psychological processes. Thus in an early chapter of the text,[18] in which they sketch the major framework of their approach, they list the influences from outside the organization which determine the kind of person who comes into the group. Such influences are the mores of the community, personality differences, prior training which sets up professional and other kinds of attitudes, and so forth. Items such as these are the influences shaping the personalities of administrators from outside the administrative group. For our purposes we can view these as the psychological determinants in the administrative situation.

The authors also point, however, to numerous influences from within the organization: the value premises which are laid down as the basis for decisions, the legitimacy of accepting certain instructions or persuasions from others in the organization, the expectations of how organizational roles are to be performed, the formal structure itself, and the informal cliques that grow up. All these, which we can identify as situational factors, they recognize as the more important of the influences. And indeed the situational quality of these factors quite unwittingly impresses itself on the authors, for they are constrained to remark, at one point, that the "individuals placed in organizational situations [sic] . . . do behave differently than they would if they were outside organization, or if they were in different organizational situations [sic]."[19] They immediately

---

[18] Ibid., chapter 3.
[19] Ibid., p. 79.

point out that the whole of their book will "be concerned chiefly with these organizational influences upon behavior—with the fact that the organization in which he finds himself is an important determinant of what the individual does and decides." [20]

It is just because the authors do in fact deal largely with situational data, rather than with psychological, that their work in the end explores the same kind of administrative problems with which administrative research has traditionally been engaged. Traditional research has always been confined essentially to situational data, trying to plot the effect of administrative organizations and related groups upon the so-called administration of policy. The authors of the present work do, of course, go beyond traditional research in that they reformulate many problems for a better understanding of them, and what is even more important, they seek to specify more accurately the effect on the individual. The latter had been lost from sight in earlier work. But it would be misleading to conclude that the character of their data was generically different.

This may at first seem rather puzzling, for a premise of our discussion of situational data was that for the moment the feelings and attitudes of the participants could be ignored. And yet here I have begun to discuss the way in which a situation molds attitudes and motivations. The contradiction, however, is apparent rather than real. We can still talk of the influence of the situation without looking at the feelings with which the individual responds. We need simply talk of the activity that ensues. As we saw earlier in reference to Bentley, this was the crucial insight of his work.

We can, for example, understand easily enough the reasons why the open ballot would lead to considerable restraint in voting without turning to the psychological mechanisms that are called into play in the restriction of this activity. Not that this would give us a complete explanation, but it would describe one aspect of what takes place. The relations of men are such that

[20] Ibid.

the open ballot would expose us to a variety of sanctions from those who have some control over our lives. We would anticipate certain kinds of activity-responses from others which would help to decide how we would cast our open ballot. Anyone who has participated in a group divided into numerous passionate factions knows the struggle that revolves around the issue as to whether the vote shall be closed or open. We can say that the situation relevant to our voting would in our contemporary culture help to restrain our freedom. We could, however, gain further insight into just how the situation accomplishes this by tracing the effect of the open ballot on our attitudes towards voting. We would then have to seek out the psychological consequences of the situation, tracing out why, in the light of the feelings and attitudes of the participants, they acted as they did in the circumstances. While the examination of situational data does not require the use of psychological data, we obtain greater explanatory depth through their introduction.

What we must stress again, however, is that although institutions may themselves mold to their own requirements the personalities of their participants, this does not thereby deny the importance of the contribution of personality to the nature of an institutionalized pattern of activity. The political institution can shape the matured individual only within limits; he is not infinitely malleable. This essentially is the underlying truth of Kardiner's work, which we discussed earlier. It is patent that both the individual and the situation act and react on each other. It is only for analytical purposes that we can isolate the situational from the personality determinant. Quite properly, psychological research into the relation between political institutions and personality would tend to leave the impression that the role of the personality in ordering human relations is a determinant of high significance. But if it stops there it would fail to recognize that the institutional aspect of the situation itself is another and equally important variable deserving the same deliberate and careful attention as the other.

.   .   .

In conclusion, therefore, I am suggesting that political science has been slow in identifying and distinguishing two major classes of data, the situational and the psychological, and in allocating to each its appropriate place and meaning in research. In so far as students of the political system have felt the need to adopt the idea of political behavior as a description of their newest data, they have thereby been groping towards a way of clearly distinguishing recent research from that traditional to their discipline. But since behavior has been used to refer both to the impact of personality on the situation as well as to the converse, it has been a term only of general ambiguous reference rather than of clear analytical value. A barrier in the way of systematic theory, therefore, is the lack of knowledge in political science about the nature of each class of data and the consequences of each for research into the political system. The existence of such knowledge would put political research in a favorable position for determining the place that each must play in a general conceptual framework.

Chapter 9

The Moral Foundations of
Theoretical Research

*It seems impossible to determine the facts in the
case; what we always have is a selection
of more or less pertinent facts, and if we have
a selection, then some fallible human being
must select them, and in spite of the best
endeavors, he is likely to get his desires
mixed up with his realities.*

Charles A. Beard

OUT of the many areas critical for an understanding of
the problems encountered in formulating systematic theory, I
have selected for comment only a few. These have appeared to
me as prior on any scale of urgency, taking into consideration, in
political science, the relatively early stage of thinking about systematic theory. These problems, basic to any study of systematic
theory, have turned on the general characteristics of theoretical
analysis itself, the relation of theory to the present state of affairs
in political research, the need to clarify basic orienting concepts, and, in the last few chapters, the place of recurring kinds

of data in an understanding of political activity. At least one further point remains for discussion: the connection between a research worker's moral frame of reference and the kind of general theory he formulates. This relationship is of special importance for political research if only because few other matters have given rise to as much dispute and ambiguity as the part played by value judgments.

In this and the succeeding chapter, I shall urge, first, that moral views influence theoretical thinking to such a degree that a conceptual framework would be incomplete without a clear knowledge and understanding of its moral premises; second, that mere description or formal knowledge of these ethical premises does not meet this requirement for moral clarity; and third, in conclusion, that the need for closer attention to systematic theory automatically imposes on political science the obligation to re-examine and ultimately to revise the way in which moral theory has been studied over the last half-century. In its most general terms, I shall argue that while moral views may be logically separable from factually oriented knowledge, in actual research our moral frame of reference plays an influential and inextricable part in conditioning our observations and conclusions.

1. The Properties of a Value Judgment

Up to this point, I have not said much about the ethical premises of theoretical work. What little has been offered in passing, as in Chapter 2, did not go further than to indicate that there was a fundamental logical distinction between causal and value (moral) theory. But I did not pause to explore this difference. Indeed, my laconic reference to it might have aroused the suspicion that I considered these two kinds of theoretical thinking to be so entirely independent that they could be mingled only at the risk of inconsistency and confusion. Leaving this impression undisturbed until this stage of the discussion has been largely a matter of convenience. It seemed wise to be un-impeachably clear at the outset about the unique problems in developing an analytic framework as compared either with the collection of facts or with the discussion of the desirability of a political system. But now that the argument has been made that there is a genuine problem with regard to a conceptual framework, divisible into manageable elements, we are ready to inspect more closely the relation between causal and value theory.

To avoid any possible doubt that may arise later, how-ever, I must dwell for a moment on my working assumption about the properties of a value judgment, an assumption which has informed and will continue to prevail in the present work. This assumption, generally adopted today in the social sciences, holds that values can ultimately be reduced to emotional responses conditioned by the individual's total life-experiences. In this inter-pretation, although in practice no one proposition need express either a pure fact or a pure value, facts and values are logically heterogeneous. The factual aspect of a proposition refers to a part of reality; hence it can be tested by reference to the facts. In this way we check its truth. The moral aspect of a proposition, however, expresses only the emotional response of an individual to a state of real or presumed facts. It indicates whether and the extent to which an individual desires a particular state of affairs to exist. Although we can say that the aspect of a proposition referring to a fact can be true or false, it is meaningless to characterize the value aspect of a proposition in this way.

The adoption of this view of values does not exclude the possibility of examining values as observable facts associated with human activity. That a person holds values and that these have consequences for action are social facts in the same sense as any other part of his activity or convictions. We can say that it is true or false that a person expresses certain preferences, that they are internally compatible, or that they have specified im-plications for action. Such observations are different, however, from arguing that the sentiments expressed are themselves warrantable by evidence.

A simple example will illustrate this well-known interpretation. Let us assume that we agree that democracy is a political system in which power is so distributed that control over the authoritative allocation of values lies in the hands of the mass of the people. To say that "the United States is a democracy," can obviously be proved or disproved, given accessibility to appropriate data. We can speak of the truth or falsity of such a proposition. But to say, "I prefer a democracy," introduces a proposition with a logically different aspect. It expresses my sentiment in favor of this kind of political system. We can say that it is true or false that I hold this kind of sentiment, or that it is incompatible with an equal preference for an authoritarian political system, or that, to be consistent, I ought not to give my political support to a movement that would destroy democracy. To assert that this value judgment is true makes sense in another way as well; namely, that it is true that I made the statement or that it expresses the sentiment that I feel and is not an attempt at deception about my emotions. But it has little meaning to say that my preference for democracy is true while someone else's dislike of it is false.

In thus adopting as my own the going interpretation of values in the social sciences, I do not intend to minimize the utility of raising the disputed issue of the nature of values. It would be quite rewarding, for other purposes, to inquire whether values are objective, substantive principles, or periphrastic modes for expressing what are essentially indicative moods, as, for example, pragmatism implies. For the present discussion, however, a final decision in this matter would not turn out to be vital. In assuming that values are expressions of our preferences and essentially dissimilar to factual aspects of propositions, I am in fact adopting a conception of values which will prove least convenient for the defense of the kind of study of values I find necessary today in order to develop rounded systematic theory.

I am, however, deliberately operating on this assumption because, if the need for value theory can be justified in these terms, it must by this very fact be reasonable and convincing even to those who would begin with contrary premises about its nature.

2. The Possibility of Value-Free Political Research

With these introductory remarks concerning my assumptions, let us now examine my original contention that the development of a satisfactory general theory depends upon a full exploration of the moral premises with which we undertake such research. Briefly stated, the reason for this lies in the impossibility for political research ever to free itself from involvement with values. Verbally, research may carefully avoid any mention of values but this in itself need be no evidence of their absence. And their presence is far from innocuous; they have a deep influence on the adequacy of research, pressing upon systematic theory through the moral premises of the research worker. If we look at the reasons for this we shall be able to appreciate why the goal of value-free research is a myth, unattainable in spite of the best of intentions.

Like all social knowledge, political science has its origins and continuing support in the obvious fact that human beings find it useful. If men did not feel that political science does or might ultimately satisfy some human purposes, it could scarcely have existed for over two thousand years. And as we saw in Chapter 4, the utility of political research stems from the fact that it helps men to decide upon the kind of political system they would prefer and to understand how to go about changing social policy to obtain it. The inspiration behind political science is clearly ethical. Men want to understand the political system so that they can use this knowledge for their own purposes.

If such knowledge exists to meet human needs, however, the definition of these needs is always provided by individual research workers in the particular culture, and it is this definition which leaves its deepest mark on factually oriented research. I would argue that no factual proposition uttered by a human being can be devoid of all relevance to moral preconceptions. For even though I am assuming that factual and moral propositions are logically heterogeneous, this does not mean that in practice it is possible to discover a proposition which expresses only a sentiment or states only a factual relationship. When we talk about justice as a moral problem, we invariably refer to some factual condition which we consider just or otherwise. And when we describe a factual situation, our propositions invariably flow from some moral purpose that has led us to investigate these facts.

It is only recently that this conception of the relation between facts and values has begun to be accepted generally. Among political scientists, as among most other social scientists, no more than a decade ago it was possible to find a considerable number who subscribed to the conviction that complete freedom from value premises was possible.[1] Here they joined what we can now designate as the classical view of positivism, typical of the closing decades of the nineteenth century, which construed objectivity and, therefore, reliable knowledge, to depend upon the moral neutrality of research.

In recent decades, social science has been undergoing a slow transformation of its views, especially under the belated influence of Ernst Troeltsch and Karl Mannheim and, generally, through the efforts of the whole field of the sociology of knowl-

---

[1] See G. E. G. Catlin, *The Science and Method of Politics,* esp. part 3; C. E. Merriam, *Political Power;* H. D. Lasswell, *Politics, Who Gets What, When, How;* W. F. Whyte, "Challenge to Political Scientists," 37 *American Political Science Review* (1943), 602-97; "Politics and Ethics, A Symposium," 40 ibid. (1946), 283-312; W. B. Munro, *The Government of the United States* (5th ed., New York: Macmillan, 1946) esp. p. 6; V. O. Key, op. cit.; A. L. Lowell, *Essays on Government,* esp. p. 8. Compare with F. Kaufmann, "The Issue of Ethical Neutrality," 16 *Social Research* (1949), 344-52.

edge.[2] Through work in the latter, it has now become as evident as the converse was to early positivism, that whatever effort is exerted, in undertaking research we cannot shed our values in the way we remove our coats. Values are an integral part of personality and as long as we are human, we can assume that these mental sets and preferences will be with us. The ideal of a value-free social science has revealed itself as a chimera. Even where a research worker should claim utter impartiality, there can be no doubt that he has simply driven his moral views so far underground that even he himself may no longer be aware of them.[3]

The mere statement, however, that values underlie all research, does not in itself lead to the inevitable conclusion that these values must, by virtue of their presence, influence this research. Conceivably they could be there, but remain quite innocuous and even irrelevant. Evidence indicates, however, that in practice the impact upon research of one's moral outlook is both wide and varied. Mannheim was one of the earliest to document in detail this relationship from the point of view of political philosophy.[4] Values, we now know, not only provide the matrix which shapes the selection of an empirical problem for investigation, but they mold the formulation of the problem, the selection of data, and even their interpretation. If truth were obtainable only upon the exile of our moral premises, it would become forever unattainable because of the inescapable presence of values.

This influence does not mean, however, that the validity of empirical research depends upon the kind of values with which one approaches his data; validity still is determined by

[2] For scrutiny of the literature in the whole field of sociology of knowledge see R. K. Merton, "The Sociology of Knowledge" in G. Gurvitch and W. E. Moore (eds.), *Twentieth Century Sociology* (New York: Philosophical Library, 1945), chapter 13.

[3] For an illustration see my article on "Harold Lasswell: Policy Scientist for a Democratic Society," 12 *Journal of Politics* (1950), 450-77.

[4] K. Mannheim, *Ideology and Utopia*.

the correspondence of a statement to reality.[5] Whether or not a statement is true depends upon whether, when verified through the known procedures of good reasoning and observation, we find that it accords with experience. Our ability to perceive certain relations among facts, however, may depend upon insight gained from immersion in one or another moral outlook. To put the same thought in a different way, certain moral premises may blind us or dull our senses to the presence of a relationship. Thus, while the truth or falsity of a proposition is not finally determined by the presence or absence of particular moral premises, the fact that we have been able to perceive a relationship or even the truth or falsity of a proposition may well depend upon these premises.

This relevance, as Max Weber phrased it, of empirical research to values, has asserted itself clearly in American political science. Most research in the last seventy-five years shows its affinity to a belief in democracy as the best kind of political system.[6] In its most general sense, democracy has been interpreted as a set of institutional patterns that guarantees the rights of minorities, provides respect for legal procedure, and somehow casts the bulk of power into the hands of the numerical mass of the population. With some exceptions, the problems selected for research display this commitment to current democratic views of what is right. Political science seeks to understand the mechanism whereby the formal organs of government, such as Congress or the Presidency, are subjected ultimately to the control of a vaguely conceived majority; the way in which the whole process of adjustment among competing groups functions, evidence of an obvious interest in the achievement of free consensus as a goal; how the power centers of leadership in parties,

[5] See K. R. Popper, *The Open Society and Its Enemies* (rev. ed., Princeton: Princeton University Press, 1950), chapter 23 and G. H. Sabine, "Logic and Social Studies," 48 *Philosophical Review* (1939), 155-76, esp. p. 176.

[6] See, for example, B. E. Lippincott, "The Bias of American Political Science," 2 *Journal of Politics* (1940), 125-39.

interest groups, and governmental organizations are controlled and limited; the way in which people participate in political life, especially with regard to the sources of political apathy, an obvious derivative of an interest in popular rule; and how political authority in all phases of the political system is brought to a sense of responsibility, morally and factually. We could construct an indefinite catalogue of the principal foci of research in American political science as evidence of the way in which its adherence to democratic standards, however variously we may define them, has shaped and guided the selection of problems for research.

There is, of course, little about this adaptation of research to our moral premises that is inherently malignant to satisfactory work. Without some criteria for choosing areas for research, we would have no knowledge of where to begin in the search for generalizations significant for human living. If, in an effort to avoid taking a moral position, we shunned conscious criteria of our own, but simply followed traditional lines of research, then we would not be genuinely cleansed of all moral standards. We would just be adopting the values implicit in traditional research. Until recently, however, social scientists have been prone to question both the wisdom and validity of research undertaken with obvious moral inspiration.

What is true of research in general is no less true of systematic theory. Without attempting to argue here what I have sought to demonstrate elsewhere,[7] it can be said that the kind of variables which a theorist considers cogent for his theory, the type of data he selects to test it, even the kinds of relations he sees among his variables, normally show a significant relation to his moral premises. In systematic theory, as in purely factual research, we may banish all verbal reference to values, but this does not in itself prove that our ultimate preferences may not have exercised an unobtrusive influence on our observations and reasoning.

[7] See my article, op. cit.

3. The Meaning of Moral Clarity

A consequence with far-reaching implications for the study of political theory flows from this inextricable relation of facts and values. Within the last decade or more, social science has come generally to acknowledge that what cannot be exiled from research ought to be brought into the open. There it can be scrutinized to estimate its possible results. Accordingly, it is said that our task as rational social scientists who seek to improve the reliability of our knowledge is to make our values explicit, to assert, avow, affirm, indicate, or clarify them in some way as a kind of moral prelude to our main empirical theme. Having made a formal statement in this way with regard to our moral views, it is held, we can then push on with the task of discovering verifiable propositions, factual or theoretical. In effect, this is an exhortation to present a summary of our moral postulates so that we ourselves and our audience may be aware of their potential influence on our thinking. As one author phrases the matter, "there is no logical reason why a social philosopher should not postulate any value he chooses, provided only that he avows what he is doing. . . ." [8]

This obligation on the social scientist to clarify his moral convictions, if he is to increase the reliability of his knowledge, presents a serious problem. Its merit is that it shows an awareness of the close relation between analysis and observation, on the one side, and moral outlook on the other. But its credit in this respect is almost erased by the purely formal character of the obligation it imposes on the social scientist. The purpose presumably is to communicate an accurate picture of the political scientist's ethical convictions. It is highly doubtful, however, that the demand for a purely formal exhumation and presentation of moral premises would enable the research worker to present an accurate picture of his moral views. Self-clarification requires

---

[8] G. H. Sabine, "What Is a Political Theory," 1 *Journal of Politics* (1939), 1-16, on p. 13.

more than a simple self-questioning with regard to one's preferences.

As anyone who has attempted seriously to elaborate his moral views will readily perceive, the attainment of moral clarity, sufficient to allow a person to affirm a particular position, can be achieved only at the end of a long process of moral inquiry. Such a process is not easily understood or learned, no more easily in fact than the canons and procedures of scientific method; and it requires the same creative insight that the discovery of causal relations demands of the most fruitful empirical research. In a word, moral self-clarification requires training and experience in the concepts and procedures of moral inquiry, the kind of analysis we usually associate in political science with the study of strict political (value) theory. When the demand is made that the research worker make his values explicit, it is usually assumed that to do this, he need simply ask himself what his moral preferences are, and a quick answer will be forthcoming. It presupposes that the student of politics is clearly aware of his ultimate preferences and their modifications or elaborations when applied to political life.

Let us ask for a moment just how such moral awareness in relation to politics is achieved. It is well known that very few people really understand what they value, or if they do, in what order or hierarchy they would prefer things. Furthermore, immediately upon reflection, it is equally clear that we never quite know how much of each desired goal we would be willing to yield in order to achieve some part of another goal. In short, we are not unambiguously aware of our ultimate preferences, of their general ranking or hierarchical arrangement, and finally, of their specific ranking in a concrete political situation.

There are at least two ways in which clarity about these moral questions can be achieved. One is through the actual experience of a situation which calls forth an expression of all our basic preferences in circumstances in which not all can be equally achieved. When we have to act, we have no alternative but to make moral choices. Such an experience would immediately solve the problem of what we wanted and how much we would yield of any one preference to achieve another. It would establish in a practical way, discernible through our actions, the nature and ordering of our values.

It is obvious, however, that values which impinge on our political research are infrequently called into action as a system. We seldom find it necessary or possible to act out the total configuration of our preferences and their political consequences. Only if we were presented with the possibility of reconstructing a political system *de novo* in our own image, would we then be called upon to act out our total scheme of preferences. But not even a Danton or Robespierre at the height of his power was able to obtain practical expression for his ideas about the best kind of political system. If the achievement of moral clarity were possible only through the actual application of our moral premises to political life, we would never be able to make known our actual values. We would be able to present only a formal statement based on momentary reflection upon what appeared to be our moral postulates.

But this practical barrier preventing us from passing beyond merely formal clarification can be overcome. There is a second way in which it is possible to trace the consequences of our moral views as a means of clarifying them. This is through the traditional method of political theory whereby we reflect upon, analyze, and project our moral views into practical political life. Failing an action situation which compels choices among all possible alternatives, clarity becomes possible, not through the formal presentation of a few premises in a page or two, but through the laborious task of constructively forming an image of the kind of political system that flows from our moral premises.

Rational research requires a complete definition of the way in which we conceive our goals. These goals cannot be fully clarified unless we explore our basic moral views. The latter, in turn, lack full meaning and expression until their knowable consequences are fully worked out. The consequences, however, are social in character and, therefore, a rational understanding of the moral frame of reference for an activity such as research compels us to enter into a full inquiry with respect to the application of our goals. We are compelled to project our moral views into an image of the kind of society and political system we would accept as desirable and in this way to formulate a view of what we conceive to be the good political life. Only through an enterprise such as this could we then say that we had clarified our values or made them explicit. Moral clarification requires more than the formal postulation of a few interrelated values. It requires the positive task of constructing an image of the political system flowing from these moral premises. This task we can call the constructive approach towards moral clarification as contrasted with the largely formal approach implicit in the exhortation to avow, affirm, state, or make explicit our values. A constructive approach requires the synthesis of values with facts to bring out the full meaning of the values.

The constructive approach is well illustrated by the political theory of any of the great social philosophers of the past. An analysis of the components of any political theory shows how a theorist communicates his values, not through the assertion of a few dogmatic premises, but through the elaborate construction of the consequences of his moral views for the political structure and processes. The values are never fully appreciated until the essential knowable consequences have been elaborated. Bentham, for example, carefully presents his fundamental moral outlook through a description of what he means by the ethical principle of utility or moral hedonism. The full meaning and implications of his description, however, do not become apparent even from *An Introduction to the Principles of Morals and Legislation*. Full understanding requires investigation into his conception of the practical consequences of his views for jurisprudence and for the general political structure, as elaborated in other works. Moral judgments are too complicated for any individual to summarize them in a few pages or to clarify their full meaning without testing them through their hypothetical application to the political facts.

We can conclude, then, that the development of systematic theory will normally be related to the moral views of the theorist. Knowledge of these views may be helpful in understanding the particular kind of theoretical system proposed and its strengths and weaknesses as a tool to analyze the political system. But the theorist cannot check the impact of his moral views on his theory unless he is thoroughly aware of the nature of these views. It is deceptive, however, to accept formal assertion of belief in certain moral postulates as a meaningful description of the ethical premises behind theoretical research. For the student of general theory, full moral self-clarification requires that he devote serious attention to a constructive approach to his values.

Chapter **10**

The Decline of Modern Political Theory

But there have not been wanting brave souls who have taken the historical faith quite seriously and have actually attempted to make the historical point of view replace or supersede all independent method or standpoint of valuation.

Morris R. Cohen

In the last chapter, the point was made that rational inquiry into systematic theory requires intimate knowledge of the moral frame of reference within which the research takes place and that such knowledge is attainable only through a constructive approach to moral problems. In this chapter we shall continue this discussion by asking just how well prepared political scientists are to explore their moral premises in this way. In answer, I shall suggest that the study of political values in American political science during the last fifty years or more has failed to provide the student of political life with the skills and knowledge necessary to explore fully his own moral preconceptions.

The study of value theory has traditionally fallen to political theory, although, as we shall see in the final chapter, this need not be the only task of political theory. Implicitly political theory has dealt with causal as well as value theory. Nevertheless, in the division of labor among political scientists, it is customary to attribute to political theory an exclusive interest in philosophical, normally meaning moral, problems. However much this may unnecessarily narrow the scope of theoretical thinking in political science, the fact is that research into political theory is now equated with the study of value theory. Our question, therefore, concerning the adequacy of value theory for helping political scientists to reveal their moral convictions must be directed to political theory.

1. Decline into Historicism

With certain exceptions that definitely lie outside the main pattern, political theory has been devoted to a form of historical research that has robbed it, as it has descended to us in the European tradition, of its earlier constructive role. In the past, theory was a vehicle whereby articulate and intelligent individuals conveyed their thoughts on the actual direction of affairs and offered for serious consideration some ideas about the desirable course of events. In this way they revealed to us the full meaning of their moral frame of reference. Today, however, the kind of historical interpretation with which we are familiar in the study of political theory has driven from the latter its only unique function, that of constructively approaching a valuational frame of reference.

An examination of some classic American works in the study of theory over the last half-century, such as those by Dunning, McIlwain, and Sabine, will uncover a vital source of the contemporary decline in constructive moral inquiry in the United States and, therefore, of its inadequacy as a tool for helping political scientists lay bare their moral premises. In the past, theory was approached as an intellectual activity whereby the student could learn how he was to go about exploring the knowable consequences and, through them, the ultimate premises of his own moral outlook. He studied the history of theory in much the same way that Rousseau, for example, might have inquired into the work of Aristotle: as a means to inform himself of the way in which others viewed standards of right so that he might himself be better able to solve the same problems to his own satisfaction.

Scrutiny of the works by the American political theorists just mentioned reveals that their authors have been motivated less by an interest in communicating such knowledge than in retailing information about the meaning, internal consistency, and historical development of past political values. There are, of course, others who are genuine exceptions to this trend, but they are a mere handful among the vast majority that confines itself to this kind of historical interpretation.

As it has been practiced by the majority, the historical approach has managed to crush the life out of value theory. Not that the historical treatment of political ideas need in itself produce this result; rather, it is the kind of history, which can be described as historicism, that, having seized the minds of theorists in the last half-century, must bear the blame.

It is with considerable hesitation and reluctance that I describe this approach as historicist. Like so many other concepts current in philosophy, it has assumed a variety of meanings and its use here, unfortunately, must add another. On the one hand, historicism has normally been used to suggest the hypothesis that all ideas are historically conditioned and, therefore, that all ideas, both moral and causal, are purely relative. There can be no universal truths except perhaps the one truth that all ideas are a product of a historical period and cannot transcend it.[1] On the other hand, some have called this view historism or sociologism—

[1] Consult especially the work of Wilhelm Dilthey and Karl Mannheim.

the sociology of knowledge carried to an extreme—and have reserved the term historicism for a different purpose.[2] In this case, historicism is defined as the belief that history is governed by inexorable laws of change and that human actions are guided by permanent ultimate purposes.

As I have indicated, historicism in the present discussion does not go so far as the meaning attributed to it in either of these two contexts. Historical interpretation in political theory today does not necessarily lead to the belief that universal generalizations are impossible or that history is governed by inevitable laws of evolution. Instead, the contemporary historical approach is historicist solely because it believes that very little more can be said about values except that they are a product of certain historical conditions and that they have played a given role in the historical process. Political theory today is interested primarily in the history of ideas. This preoccupation with problems of history, rather than with problems of reflection about the desirability of alternative goals, is what gives contemporary research in political theory its special significance.

The historical approach to values, which I am calling historicism, has led theorists to concentrate, first, on the relation of values to the milieu in which they appear; second, on a description of the historical process through which such ideas have emerged; and third, as part of these two objectives, on the meaning and consistency of the ideas expressed. In political theory, students have been devoting themselves to what is essentially an empirical and a logical, rather than to a value, problem, at least in terms of the prevailing disjunction between facts and values. They have been learning what others have said and meant; they have not been approaching this material with the purpose of learning how to express and clarify their own values. They have in effect assimilated political theory into empirical and causal

[2] K. R. Popper, op. cit., esp. chapter 23; see also a series of articles by the same author in 11 and 12 *Economica*, New Series, (1944 and 1945), which appraises historicist methodology.

social science and have thereby abandoned its genuinely moral aspect.

True moral reflection would not, of course, neglect the history of value theory. Such history would be invaluable as a source for appreciating the nature of other kinds of moral standards. Since the meanings of words depend upon the culture and its historical moment, full understanding of a moral idea, as of any other, requires an investigation into its meaning in the light of the cultural conditions under which it arose and was in use. The sociology of knowledge, which seeks to reveal the ties between knowledge and the historical circumstances, would provide vital material for a moral inquiry into earlier political theory. But even though moral research would include history, it would use the latter for purposes entirely different from those of historicism. History would be a means for informing the inquirer of alternative moral outlooks with the hope that this would aid him in the construction of his own political synthesis or image of a good political life.

Although there is solid unity in the disregard for constructive moral inquiry, differences do exist in the general approach which each theorist has adopted towards the role of ideas in the historical process. There are at least three main points of view. Some attention to these will serve to bring out the intrinsic nature of the prevailing historicist approaches and, thereby, the main reasons for their effective disablement of theory. It will show how theory has come to lose its utility for training students of political life in the knowledge and skills necessary for understanding those moral premises within the matrix of which they conduct political research.

2. The Historicism of Dunning

In a very broad sense, W. A. Dunning in his three volumes entitled *A History of Political Theories*,[3] published in the

[3] (New York: Macmillan, 1902, 1905, and 1920).

first two decades of this century, set the tone for research in political theory. His training as a historian furnishes the key to his work; he approaches political theory with a primary interest in problems of historical change and seeks to reveal the role of political ideas in this process. History, he assumed, is a product of the interplay between social practices or institutions and political ideas. An adequate understanding of historical change will require investigation into the way in which each of these aspects of the historical process influences the other. As a result, political theory, for Dunning, becomes a historical account of the conditions and consequences of political ideas. He seeks to uncover the cultural and political conditions which generate and shape the prevailing political conceptions of an age and to isolate the influence of these ideas, in turn, on the social conditions.

This interpretation of the function of theory recurs as the major unifying theme throughout his writing. "The only path of approach to an accurate apprehension of political philosophy," he writes in the opening pages of his first volume, "is through political history." [4] "The criterion of selection," he writes in the same vein, "will be a pretty definite and clearly discernible relationship between any given author's work and the current of institutional development." [5]

Dunning is clearly historicist, therefore, in his conception of political theory, but he goes even further in helping to divert attention from moral reflection. Relentlessly he rejects the value of dealing with moral problems even in a purely historical context. For him, political theory is essentially historical research into views that derive from observation of political facts and practices, especially as they are related to the legal form of political life. Later, with the growth of political realism,[6] his disciples broadened this interest in legal ideas to the history of all em-

[4] W. A. Dunning, *A History of Political Theories,* Vol I, pp. 1-2.
[5] Ibid., pp. xviii-ix.
[6] See above, chapters 6 and 7.

pirically based theories of political activity.[7] But, as for Dunning, there was no doubt that so far "as discrimination and selection are inevitable, the present history will prefer those lines of development in which political ideas appear as legal rather than as ethical." [8]

He does tolerantly accept the possibility, it is true, of writing about political theory from a variety of points of view, each of which may have its own justification and among which ethical analysis might hold an important place. He was undoubtedly thinking of the moral emphasis of Paul Janet's *Histoire de la science politique dans ses rapports avec la morale,* one of the prominent texts in use at the time, which Dunning's work was to displace in a few years. Dunning's catholicity, however, was only nominal. In his own work he rejects the utility of historically scrutinizing the varieties of moral views about political life, except perhaps as an accidental by-product of the analysis of empirical ideas. Moral views, for him, were "dogmas, with endless varieties of shading and detail." [9] Implicitly he views moral premises as the product of mere caprice or whim, dogmas without warrant and therefore scarcely worth analyzing or interpreting. To the extent that they must be included in a history, they can be treated only with regard to their place as a variable in the historical process.

In Dunning's hands, therefore, the study of political

[7] C. E. Merriam, *American Political Ideas* (New York: Macmillan, 1920), writes in his Preface: "The purpose of the writer is to trace the broad currents of American political thought in their relation to the social, economic and political tendencies of the time. Sometimes these ideas have been best expressed in political institutions; sometimes in laws, judicial decisions, administration, or customs; again, in the utterances of statesmen and publicists or leaders of various causes; sometimes by the formal statements of the systematic philosophers. . . . This study is the outgrowth of investigations begun in the Seminar on American political philosophy given by Professor Dunning, in Columbia University, 1896-97, and the writer wishes to acknowledge his deep sense of obligation for the inspiration then given, and for subsequent encouragement in the prosecution of this work."

[8] W. A. Dunning, op. cit., Vol. I, p. xxi; see also pp. 302-3.

[9] Ibid., Vol. III, p. 422.

theory is virtually converted into the history of factual ideas and theories. There can be no objection, of course, to including the history of causal theory in the tasks of political theory as a field of specialization within political science. In fact, in the concluding chapter I shall urge the need for the inclusion of causal theory in the general study of political theory. From the point of view of the present discussion, however, Dunning's was a sin of omission. He would exclude from political theory the treatment of moral ideas even as a variable in the historical process. Confronted with the task of writing three volumes about political ideas, in practice he did find it impossible to banish all reference to moral views; they are too intertwined with factual statements in any political theory. Nevertheless, he sought consciously and successfully to locate moral ideas in the penumbra of his work.

It is symptomatic of the general attitude towards moral questions in the early part of this century that Dunning's interpretation of political theory should have been acceptable. It is equally reflective of the premises of contemporary political science that with important, although not fundamental, modifications (especially with regard to the place of moral ideas), his approach continues to color research in theory today.

Although he directed theory towards a historical examination of the interaction between ideas and the social environment, it was impossible for him to neglect entirely other aspects. He did pay considerable attention to the meaning and logical consistency of ideas; without logical analysis of a theory the relation to the times could scarcely be explored. Further, in spite of the fact that his critics universally noted that "the most striking characteristic of the *opus magnum* was its dispassionate and objective quality, its detached point of view," [10] his readers could not fail to discover that Dunning favored representative democracy, even though moral views found only a grudging place in his thinking.

[10] C. E. Merriam in "News and Notes," 16 *American Political Science Review* (1922), 689-94, on p. 694.

And where a theorist offered an idea that could be checked against known facts, Dunning did not hesitate to express his opinion about its validity. But in spite of these excursions into logic, moral interpretation, and empirical verification, his motivating concern in writing his three volumes was for the interaction of factual ideas with institutions in the historical process.

It would be saying too much to isolate Dunning as the source of contemporary historicism in American political theory. Rather, he reflected social conditions which formed the hospitable soil in which such a conception of theory could flourish. But if personal responsibility can be fixed in a complex historical process, Dunning must accept a large share of the blame for establishing a pattern from which research today still shows few signs of departing. Subsequent works differ in emphasis, and later histories of theory often show greater depth of scholarship and perception, but they do not fundamentally broaden the limits imposed on the study of political theory by its early historical orientation at the hands of Dunning.

3. The Historicism of McIlwain

The Growth of Political Thought in the West by C. H. McIlwain,[11] one of the most inspiring teachers of theory in this century, illustrates a second variation on the historical theme. Whereas Dunning had turned to history because he saw political ideas as a possible influence on the course of events, McIlwain adopts historical research because for him a political idea is an effect rather than an influential interacting part of social activity. Being virtual ciphers in the changing patterns of actual life, ideas can have meaning only as part of a history of theories in which ideas may condition subsequent ideas, but in which they leave no impact upon action. McIlwain comes to history, it will ap-

[11] (New York: Macmillan, 1932).

pear, primarily because there is in his understanding of the nature of theory as a set of ideas no other meaningful way in which it can be discussed.

As the title of his volume indicates, the purpose underlying his study is historical; it seeks to show the way in which Western political thought has emerged from antiquity to the end of the medieval period.[12] Ideas, he assumes, have a history, and it is necessary to inquire into this history. The question here, however, is just why he feels he should make a historical study.

McIlwain's conclusions about the place of ideas in social life help to explain why his attachment to history in the realm of political theory was not simply a matter of caprice. To put in its bald form a view that he puts consciously, but more subtly, a political theory for him is normally a rationalization, not a determinant or influential condition of action. Ideas for him are epiphenomena, the mere froth on the ocean, as it were, that has little effect on the movement of the waves. They justify behavior but are scarcely instrumental in influencing political activity. Verbally at any rate—for his actual practice and even a few of his comments would indicate a contrary view—he does not conceive that ideas have even the power of a myth in persuading men to act.

This view is, as I have suggested, the product of a conscious judgment, not the derivative of a hidden assumption. In the very concluding chapter of his work, McIlwain carefully draws attention to his reflections on the subject. "But as we have seen," he writes, "it is almost a law of the development of political thought that political conceptions are the by-product of actual political relations, and oftentimes in history these relations have changed materially long before this change attracted the notice even of those most affected by it, or became a part of their unconscious habits of thought, much less of their political speculation, when they had any." [13]

[12] Ibid., p. v.
[13] Ibid., p. 391.

Although he speaks here with conviction, McIlwain is not completely at one with himself. Sometimes, in passing, he is reluctant to do more than pose as an empirical question, to be answered for each time and place, the extent to which ideas and practices interact.[14] At other times he states without reservation that "the constitutional doctrines concerning the basis of the Emperor's authority, and the ideas political and religious that gathered about his person or his office, had effects upon both the theory *and the practice* of monarchy in the later western world. . . ." [15] However much the actual writing of his history may have compelled a less extreme view about the effectiveness of ideas, his own conception of their role served at least to provide for him a justification for his way of dealing with theory.

Although McIlwain explicitly rejects the conclusion that ideas can influence action, in doing so he does not mean to imply that they are totally devoid of effect. They may be influential, but their influence lies exclusively in the realm of ideas. When men search for a justification or rationalization of a particular act or set of institutions, McIlwain does not hold that they cut their ideas out of whole cloth. They adopt, modify or elaborate the arguments of their predecessors, in this way contributing to the development of these ideas. The fact, however, that ideas have a history does not convert this history into a causal element in the whole historical process. For McIlwain, it merely shows that political ideas in Western civilization have some kind of continuity and this provides a good reason for tracing their development. Without the possibility of ideas leaving some kind of impact on succeeding ideas, there would have been little occasion for a book dealing with "the *development* of our ideas about the state and about government." [16]

With these clear assumptions about the role of political theory, as sets of ideas, we can understand why McIlwain should

---

[14] See, for example, ibid., p. 201.
[15] Ibid., p. 132. Italics mine.
[16] Ibid., p. v., italics in original; see also p. 131.

not feel compelled to question the historical pattern of research already popularized in the United States by Dunning. If political ideas follow upon practices, then an examination of moral criteria prevalent in other ages, as an aid in formulating our own, would seem to have little utility in and of itself. This does not mean that McIlwain must summarily reject any criterion other than the historical for judging political thought; for that matter, as we saw, neither did Dunning. But the point at issue here is not what other variety of tests or modes of examination an author could conceive as legitimate, but what prompted him to adopt his own as the most meaningful context for the study of theory. McIlwain's explanation is unambiguous. Since research reveals the inconsequential nature of political theories, he who wishes may explore them as a means to help him to understand his own moral standards; but for McIlwain, research into the continuity of ideas yields the richest rewards for scholarship.

This interpretation of ideas as a reflection of activity leads to certain consequences for the study of the history of theory. It transfers the emphasis of history from a causal study of the contribution ideas make to the actual process of social change, as it had been conceived by Dunning, into an exploration of the historical conditions surrounding the emergence of an idea. These are the bounds that McIlwain sets for himself. As he phrases his task, when discussing the reasons for the decline of the Western Roman Empire, "the chronicler of the growth of political thought is concerned *only* with the changes in men's conception of the state produced by the new political conditions that accompanied and followed this decline." [17] In effect, political theory is here construed as a branch of the sociology of knowledge, which deals primarily with the circumstances shaping knowledge as it has varied over time. The task of the political theorist is to show the way in which a social milieu molds and shapes political thought. It is concerned with the exclusively empirical task of uncovering the determinants of ideology.

[17] Ibid., p. 167. Italics mine.

In spite of this reduction of political theory to the study of an aspect of history, there was imbedded in McIlwain's approach to the history of theory a respect for moral views that saved them from the utter eclipse they had suffered in Dunning's work. For McIlwain, a theory includes more than propositions anchored in observation. He prefers rather an inclusive history of theory, one that does not neglect any aspect of a political idea that seeks to justify political practices and institutions. And the moral justification appears to him primary. In fact, his very formulation of the kind of ideas which constitute the subject matter of a history of theory suggests his initial concern for men's views on the good political life, rather than their conclusions about the way in which men do act. " 'Man is born free and everywhere he is in chains. . . . What can make it legitimate?' It is the central question of all political thought." [18] With this moral question from Rousseau as the opening comment of his work, he sets as his task the history of men's reflections about the moral basis of political obligation.

McIlwain thus selects moral ideas for special attention not only because they are in fact the preoccupation of theorists, but also because in his own interpretation they have special significance in men's lives. He leaves the definite impression that moral views are worth discussing and affirming. For example, in the light of his own values, there is little doubt that the moral premises associated with contemporary democracy, especially when viewed as a constitutional order, are of paramount significance and that a person would be eminently rewarded in discussing them. In a sense, the inspiration behind his whole volume is an attempt to depict the early origins of these moral convictions.[19]

Since McIlwain attributes such special significance to moral judgments, it might appear inconsistent to characterize his historical work as historicist. If he felt that a person ought to as-

[18] Ibid., p. 1.
[19] Ibid., pp. 1-3.

sert his allegiance to a particular set of moral ideals, then this might appear to be the basis for a direct inquiry into the way in which we go about formulating such ideals. McIlwain, however, does seem to be strongly influenced by an interpretation of the nature of moral judgments that bars him from approaching theory in anything but a historical context.

Let us look for a moment at his conception of the nature of values to trace its influence on his thinking. This conception is nowhere unambiguously set forth. Inference from his scattered comments does lead to the conclusion, however, that he considers values to be a product of the individual's response to his environment. Moral standards, he holds, are essentially unprovable. Political theory, he argues, cannot be discussed without penetrating to the philosophical premises underlying a theory, that is, to the attempts to "solve the mysteries of existence and knowledge." [20] But he holds that in the past some of these "profoundest assertions remained unproved because in their nature unprovable." [21] Presumably, the most perplexing of these mysteries concerns the purposes of men. If it is true that these purposes are indeed unprovable, then our values cannot be a matter of cognition. They can be only expressions of a point of view or personal opinion. To this extent his interpretation of the nature of values does not vary substantially from that common to modern social science—values are an emotional response to experience. While differences in refinements may exist, the essential point is that McIlwain aligns himslf with those who see moral experience as subjective in origin and nature.

This subjective view is conclusively upheld when McIlwain finally asserts that when a person's duty is at stake, "the individual opinion or conscience is the ultimate test in all cases." [22] If we could know what our moral obligations were in the same way that we know about the existence of a fact, mani-

[20] Ibid., p. 97.
[21] Ibid.
[22] Ibid., p. 369.

fest evidence, not individual conscience, would be our guide. Conscience sets our moral purposes when, because of the nature of moral judgments, the latter are considered to be the product not of rational inquiry but of responses to social circumstances.

This relativistic interpretation of the nature of values raises a dilemma which we shall meet again in Sabine's work and which I shall treat more fully at a later point. If moral judgments are subjective and relative, then how are we to justify ourselves in adopting one set of preferences as superior to all others? Although McIlwain makes no attempt to answer this question, it is clear that he does believe decidedly in the need to affirm one's moral premises. And yet, in spite of this belief, he does not avoid one of the consequences that is often said to flow from moral relativism; namely, that if all moral beliefs are a product of the life-experience of each individual, then no one belief can lay claim to any higher worth than any other. There is, therefore, so the argument runs, little use in discussing values; let each man simply set forth his own with the knowledge that the values of any other person are just as good as his.

Historicism is a natural outgrowth of this kind of reasoning. If we begin with a belief in the equal value of all moral judgments, then there is little use in inquiring into such judgments; whatever our moral convictions, they are no better than the standards held by any one else. Accordingly, if we must deal with moral problems, the only approach that has any meaning is the historical one. It instructs us in the analysis both of the meaning of terms and of their relation to the historical process. In the matter of moral issues comprehension in historical terms alone makes sense.

Obviously McIlwain, from the standpoint of his conscious convictions, would not agree with this sequence of reasoning. His belief in the superior moral worth of his own outlook does subtly assert itself. But the fact that he does not go beyond a historical analysis is equal evidence that he has not avoided entirely the consequences of this kind of reasoning. In fact, his historicism, in practice, indicates the firm grip that this interpretation of the consequences of moral relativism has upon his study of political theory. There is a possible interpretation of relativism, to be examined later, that can help us to restore the study of moral theory to its natural place in political science. The fact that McIlwain confines himself to historicism, however, indicates that he has not availed himself of this alternative conception of the meaning of moral relativism.

When we join his view of the nature of values to his conviction that ideas can have little consequence for practical human affairs, we can understand why his work in the realm of ancient and medieval political theory should have been so hospitable, in its basic assumptions, to historicist research. In spite of his undoubted conviction that it is worth while to affirm moral views, his conception of the role of ideas in general bars him from advocating anything other than a historicist treatment. We must infer that moral views, being a species of ideas and, indeed, being in his own interpretation the central part of a theory, are really not influential in the course of history. Logically, he cannot escape from the inference that, like all ideas, moral views are products, not interacting causes in historical change. As such we can say no more about moral theories than we can about ideas in general. We can speak of their meaning and of the circumstances molding them, but beyond this, little can be said. We are therefore forced to conclude that McIlwain never makes clear why it really is worth while to assert one's moral views vigorously; presumably they do not guide action. We can understand, however, why he should be led to history as the most meaningful mode for interpreting moral ideas.

4. The Historicism of Sabine

A third type of approach to the history of political theory is represented by G. H. Sabine's *A History of Political Theory*.[23] Without doubt this brilliant volume has exercised deeper influence over the study of political theory in the United States during recent years than any other single work. With Dunning and McIlwain, Sabine does not pause to question whether a historical study of theory is an appropriate approach to the subject matter. It is true, he does show exceptional insight into his own method. He is able to explain, however, only what his historical research involves, not why it is justified. We are left with the impression both from his work and from his own description of his method, that a historical study of theory provides its own self-evident justification. The very nature of Sabine's understanding of moral judgments seems to point to no other kind of useful approach.

In his attitude towards the history of theory, Sabine falls into a category separate from that of Dunning or of McIlwain. He combines elements from the approaches of both. With the former he agrees that the examination of political thought merits attention because it is an aspect of the political process that interacts with and influences social action. With the latter he maintains the necessity of describing and analyzing the moral judgments in each theory. Through this blend he lays the basis for a serious inquiry into the values of various thinkers. For Sabine, moral judgments need not be viewed as mere rationalizations of activity; rather they may be influential factors in history. As a subject matter they are not inferior to factual proposition, as by implication Dunning insisted. Thus, while in his basic interpretation of the relation of ideas to action, Sabine does not go beyond Dunning, his conception of the nature of the history of political theory does differ in the emphasis he gives to the role of ethical judgments.

[23] (1st ed., New York: Henry Holt, 1937).

Every political theory, Sabine points out, can be examined from two points of view: as social philosophy and as ideology.[24] In the latter aspect theories stand as psychological phenomena and, as such, their truth or falsity is not in question. Regardless of their validity or verifiability, theories are beliefs, "events in people's minds and factors in their conduct." [25] They are, therefore, influential events in history. As Sabine writes, "political theory is itself a product of, or factor in, politics." [26] For this reason, the task of the historian is to determine the extent to which the theories have helped to shape the course of history.

But a theory can be scrutinized for its meaning rather than for its impact on human actions. When it is viewed in this light, Sabine suggests that it contains two kinds of propositions: factual and moral. Although we can inquire into the logical consistency of both kinds, Sabine adopts the conception of values traditional to social science and argues that it is possible to warrant by evidence only those statements that refer to factual conditions. Moral statements cannot be described as either true or false. They just are. Values, he states, in complete awareness of his own position, are "always the reaction of human preferences to some state of social and physical fact." [27] Values are not *deducible from* facts; moral laws cannot be rationally discovered either in the actual course of events or in the nature of man.[28] Nor are they *reducible to* facts; they are expressions of emotions.

Nevertheless, Sabine holds that since a political theory invariably includes some statements of preference, and indeed since the exposition of preferences is the occasion for the development of a theory, value judgments lie at the heart of a theory and are the very reason for its existence. The moral element

[24] Ibid. (2nd ed., 1950), p. 704; also G. H. Sabine, "What Is a Political Theory."
[25] "What Is a Political Theory," p. 10.
[26] G. H. Sabine, "Logic and Social Studies," p. 170.
[27] *A History of Political Theory* (1st ed.), p. viii.
[28] Ibid., esp. in chapters 29 and 32.

seems to him so to color a political theory that he considers the latter primarily a moral enterprise. This is why, in spite of the obvious factual propositions within a theory, Sabine did not feel it anomalous to conclude, in the light of his premises about the nature of a value judgment, that "taken as a whole a political theory can hardly be said to be true." [29]

From Sabine's careful exposition of the nature of a theory, the tasks of a history of political theory become quite clear. In such a study we ought to isolate the influence of a theory on the actions of men; this is its psychological aspect. We can analyze the factual statements implicit in any theory and set them against the facts as we know them today. In this respect, political theory is concerned with empirical truth. This is clear from Sabine's own history of theory in which he feels free to pass judgment on the validity of various causal theories and factual assertions. The history of theory, in this respect, is a stimulus for reflection on the truth of empirically oriented propositions.

Sabine is less sanguine, however, about the utility of the study of theory for moral reflection. We can and ought to examine the logic of the statements embodying value judgments and comment on their compatibility; we can and ought to reveal the full meaning of statements of preference. And yet, while the study of theory may help us to make up our minds on the validity of causal theories, apparently it is no important part of its task to help us to formulate our views on moral matters. In this respect the study of theory is reduced to historical narration.

If Sabine's interpretation of the meaning of value judgments had led him to believe that any one man's moral preferences was equivalent in worth to another's, then his reduction of moral research to pure history would have been understandable. It is true, he calls himself a social relativist.[30] But he does not feel

[29] Ibid., p. vii.
[30] Ibid., p. viii.

it is inconsistent with this position to affirm vigorously the superior value of one moral position.[31] He feels free to offer a forcible defense of his own values. It is undeniable that he believes firmly in the reality and meaningfulness of ethical predicates.

In spite of this deep conviction about the merit of personal self-expression in the realm of values, historicist preconceptions nevertheless do govern the execution of his history of theory. In his work, moral inquiry does not use the history of political theory for purposes other than of historical understanding. This historicism becomes quite apparent when we ask the question: What can a student of theory learn about the tasks of research into value theory from Sabine's *History?* He can learn how to describe a variety of value systems that have emerged in the past and how to inquire into their meaning and possible consequences. He can learn about the need to demonstrate their historical continuity, and perhaps he can indicate the path of growth of certain ideas of importance, such as liberalism or democracy. He can discover categories for describing the social and psychological conditions which influenced the growth and form of ideas and contributed to their diffusion and perpetuation or decline. In fact, the student would be taught that a complete study of political theory must inquire into all these problems. But a question would remain: To what end?

There can be no doubt about the purpose behind the clarification of a theorist's empirical propositions. Here, as we saw, the student is permitted and encouraged, by Sabine's example, to pass judgment, where it is relevant, on the empirical validity of a part of a theory. But when we approach values, there is little to guide the student of history with regard to what he is to learn from his research that passes beyond a mere report of a theorist's moral speculation. The student may always indicate the presence of logical incompatibilities; the assumption is that inconsistency violates good reasoning even where it involves values. It is even possible to argue from what Sabine says that the historian of values may evaluate a moral system in terms of its acceptability to himself, as long as this judgment is undertaken consciously and clearly. With Max Weber, Sabine recognizes that although knowledge in any science "is independent of moral values . . . such values are [nevertheless] involved in its origin and in its use." [32] However, beyond the description of the social conditions molding values, the analysis of their meaning and a comparison with his own or other values, the student is never encouraged to interpret the study of value theory as the examination of a process of valuation that may instruct him in the nature and problems of this process. The analysis of a theory appears to be a prerequisite primarily to an understanding of the theory's place in history, not to its use in helping one formulate his own moral outlook. Any help it may give appears to be largely accidental and incidental.

I have inquired into the approach of these three truly distinguished historians of political theory because there can be little doubt that in the United States today they are representative of research in this field. Political theorists are primarily historicist in their orientation. They do not use the history of values as a device to stimulate thought on a possible constructive redefinition of political goals. Their fundamental outlook prevents this.

In political theory today, if these authors are representative, there lurks a conception of values that prevails in social science, a misconception as I shall maintain. According to this view, all a social scientist can legitimately and significantly say about moral propositions is that they have a certain meaning and logical coherence and that they are a part of a historical situation to which they may contribute something and from which they take their character. It is true, of course, that McIlwain, and especially Sabine, believe that their interpretation of the nature of moral judgments, which is relativistic, does not stand as a bar to a strong

[32] "Beyond Ideology," p. 2.

attachment to and affirmation of these judgments, or indeed to their elevation as a superior moral frame of reference for all men. It is nonetheless apparent that, in the exclusive place they give to the historical study of values, they do not feel that moral judgments are really worth talking about directly, *qua* moral judgments.

The fact is that political theorists have so construed the consequences flowing from their conception of values that they are forestalled from attempting a radical reconstruction of their moral heritage. They are driven to assume that, aside from historical description, their major task in moral matters is to clarify, like extreme semanticists, and not to reconstruct, like imaginative moral architects. As I mentioned at the outset of this discussion of historicism, these two tasks are not, of course, unrelated; formal clarity and historical perspective are obviously prerequisites for any intelligible formulation of views about the good political life. But they are not ends in themselves.

As a result of this preoccupation with historicism in moral matters, the study of political theory, as for the most part we know it today, is manifestly unsuited for training political scientists in the skills and knowledge of genuine moral clarification. Without such clarification, a research worker is unable to estimate the full extent to which his moral frame of reference might limit and distort his efforts towards the construction of systematic theory. To permit exhaustive inquiry into moral premises, political science is compelled to revise its approach to value theory and to set as one of its central objectives the study of moral problems as such, and not their history largely for the sake of narration.

5. The Source of Decline

To this point, the objective of the discussion about the moral premises of research has been, first, to show that knowledge of these premises is vital to any empirically oriented research, especially with respect to the construction of systematic theory; and second, to indicate that today political theory, which in political science assumes responsibility for research in moral matters, has in fact failed to help research workers in achieving a full understanding of their moral frame of reference. Effective moral clarification requires a constructive rather than a historicist approach to values.

We must now look for a moment at some of the reasons for the decline of theory and research into historicism. These need to be stated, for they indicate the path that research in value theory might well follow if it is to prove useful in helping research workers to understand their moral frames of reference. Since the reasons go beyond the circumstances particular to the United States, they must be viewed in the context of value theory in the Western world. My theme will be that moral historicism, of the kind described here, has emerged from three sources: the proneness of political scientists, for broader social reasons, to conform to the moral presuppositions of their own age; the general misconstruction of the consequences of a relativistic interpretation of values; and finally, the very historical epoch, stretching back a century, out of which we are just now passing.

Most students of political theory today accept, as given, the moral premises of Western civilization. The assumption is that they must be considered eternally right. For this reason, when we insist upon a research worker revealing his values, we need only ask him to clarify, avow, or affirm them. The task is simple because there does not appear to be any real conflict over what is desirable in the long run. Presumably research workers agree on ultimates even if they may disagree violently about means. Whether this is genuinely true could not be determined, of course, without closer examination; but the feeling that it is true has important consequences for the role of research into value theory. It inhibits students of moral theory from making a radical exploration into their values. Such an inquiry would demand the assumption that something new can be said about what is desirable and that the prevailing moral theories are not necessarily the last word. It may be that they are, but only by beginning with the contrary assumption could a theorist hope to prove to himself that no other alternative is more acceptable.

This tendency toward moral conformity is both a symptom of and a cause contributing to the lack of a constructive approach; therefore it prevents the very kind of inquiry necessary for a thorough understanding of the values underlying research. By indicating that a student can discover his values merely by postulating or clarifying them through avowal or affirmation, political science thereby places its imprimatur on the going values. To avow or affirm implies that a research worker knows what he wants to express or that what he wants can be easily uncovered. We do not ask mathematicians to *avow* a solution to a problem; we merely require them to avow their axioms, a less difficult task. Where there is a problem, we ask them to *think out* or worry about a solution.

Value clarification is normally placed at the same level as a declaration of axioms. The assumption is that it is a relatively simple task to uncover and make known one's preferences; hence a research worker does not need to worry through this problem. And a significant reason for this assumption is found in the prevalence of a feeling that values are well-known. But when we ask just what values are well-known we see that normally they must be the commonly accepted ones. Because we are very familiar with them, we feel we know their meaning well and no longer need bother to explore them in depth. The exhortation, therefore, that a research worker need only avow his preferences, in effect makes the assumption that he need not go beyond the accepted values of the day.

Since political science is thus operating on the assumption that it needs only to avow what it knows, the problem that remains to challenge it is not inquiry into the merit, that is, acceptability, of these moral goals, but at most an examination of their origins, development, and social impact. There seem to be few operations political theory can perform on moral views except to explore their apparent meaning and to trace their history. The irony of this procedure, however, lies in the fact that through it political research is rapidly caught up in a vicious circle. Once it traces the history of moral ideals, the fact that they have a long and respected ancestry associates them with all the glamor and sanctity of tradition. And although in general history we have long ago given up the idea that the world inevitably progresses from worse to better, in the realm of moral history we still feel that our moral premises have been enriched over the ages. What we believe today appears to have moral worth exceeding that of most earlier ages. History, therefore, reinforces the tendency in political research to conform to current moral ideals, and conformity, in turn, leads political science to history as the only approach useful in moral research.

We have numerous examples today of this appeal to history that well illustrate how this predilection in political research for adopting the going values ultimately converts moral clarification into a study of historical roots. This approach to history differs in its purposes from the three modes of historicism which we have discussed earlier, although even in the work of those political theorists, the present kind of outlook towards history is present in varying degrees.

The history stemming from conformity begins with the deliberate choice of contemporary values and then seeks to understand their meaning more fully by examining their growth through a special tradition, such as the Machiavellian in some few cases, or the liberal and democratic in most. It uses history to illuminate the meaning and to establish the worth of contemporary moral postulates, whereas other historians of political ideas emphasize the objective description of growth. In effect, the first kind of approach to political theory assumes, in Burke's traditionalistic vein, that the political values which have evolved through trial and error of a civilization over the centuries have thereby acquired a sanctity and truth which no re-analysis can fundamentally impair or radically modify.

A recent work by A. D. Lindsay, *The Modern Democratic State*,[33] well represents this approach. Although this example is not drawn from an American work, nevertheless for two reasons it is permissible and desirable to turn to it as representative. First, it is well-known and used in the study of political theory in the United States; and second, it provides a mature and self-conscious use of the method and for this reason lends itself to a less complicated and briefer analysis.

In the very first chapter of *The Modern Democratic State*, Lindsay clearly demonstrates that he uses history to place the stamp of approval on his interpretations of conventional values in a democratic society. In this chapter he maintains that at his best the theorist must confine himself to an attempt to understand the "operative ideals" [34] which have proved effective in determining men's political relations. From this starting point, the subject matter of theory consists of the beliefs and purposes which actually operate at any time to help determine men's relations to the law, to authority, and to the kind of political organizations they establish.[35] Since these ideals, he holds, differ with each time and place, the task of a student of theory is to decide upon the culture he wishes to study, to identify the operative ideals, to make these "explicit" [36] so that men will "understand what their purposes and will regarding the state actually are"; [37] finally, the student must discuss "how this type of state [and ideals] came into being." [38]

Lindsay is, therefore, exceptionally clear about his intentions and about the place of political theory as an area of research. He does not intend to inquire into a theory of a good

[33] (New York: Oxford University Press, 1943).
[34] Ibid., pp. 37-8.
[35] Ibid., p. 47.
[36] Ibid., p. 47.
[37] Ibid.
[38] Ibid., p. 51.

political system that may serve succeeding generations as well as our own; as the title of his work indicates, he intends to restrict himself to *modern* democratic ideas. After clarifying them and as part of the process of making them explicit, he will trace their historical development. "This volume," he writes, "is not about a general ideal called democracy but an historical type called the modern democratic state. . . ." [39] He therefore devotes himself to the explanation of what he conceives to be the true meaning of contemporary ideals, in terms of which men seem to act, as they have been handed down and modified through the centuries.

In the execution of this work he is forced, of course, to interpret contemporary democratic ideas, since there is no clear unanimity about their content and meaning. Furthermore, in no more than half of his book does he really adhere to his initial commitment; instead, he attempts in limited measure to redefine democratic premises. But in terms of his avowed approach, which describes accurately an important rationale of contemporary historical research into theory, the reformulation must be considered secondary and incidental to his main purpose: the attempt to present a historical understanding of what we seem to cherish today.

This essentially uncritical commitment to prevailing values as necessarily the most acceptable to the present and immediately succeeding generations, while a distinct source of current historicist tendencies, has strengthened the hold of tradition. It aborts any attempt on the part of students of theory to think in terms of new formulations of their moral goals. No one could argue that historical research is solely to blame for the lack of what, to parody Robert Lynd, might be called outrageous moral hypotheses.[40] But since research into moral theory presumably could give intellectual leadership here, the failure of

[39] Ibid., p. 1.
[40] R. S. Lynd, *Knowledge for What?* (Princeton: Princeton University Press, 1939).

political theory to do so must leave theory with a share of the blame for an almost casual resignation to our moral traditions.

Conformity in moral theory has been the more easily accepted because of a widespread misconstruction of the consequences that flow from the usual relativistic view of values adopted by social scientists. This relativism constitutes a second factor contributing to the current preoccupation of theory with history.

In the long span of time, ranging from its birth in ancient Greece to the middle of the nineteenth century, ending perhaps with Hegel and Marx, political theory was more than a mere offshoot of political history. As we have had occasion to observe repeatedly, in that long epoch, political inquiry, which in retrospect we misname political theory,[41] began and adhered to an elemental question for which people, as laymen, have always sought an answer; namely, what criteria ought one to use in evaluating the variety of social programs offered by groups competing for political power? As we saw in Chapters 4 and 5, the resulting concern of political science with social policy led to innumerable questions. But in the whole field of political science, contemporary political theory has undertaken, as part of its task, to engage in research into standards within the framework of which practical policy might be established.

As long as men thought it possible to arrive at some moral standards in terms of which a future political system could be conceived, there was sufficient incentive for a constructive examination of past moral ideas. But once the conclusion was drawn in the nineteenth century that all values are the expression of individual or group preferences and that these preferences, in turn, reflect the life-experience of the individual or group, then the impetus for the constructive study of values disappeared. If values are only the expressions of sentiments, then there seemed to be no ground upon which a person or an age could argue for the superiority of his or its moral views. Varying preferences were construed to be neither better nor worse than others, simply equal in moral worth. Social scientist A could say to his colleague B that his, A's, preferences were just as good as those of B; if B was a relativist, it appeared that he had no grounds for denying this. However strongly he might believe in his own moral position, there was no rational evidence that he could present to demonstrate that A's views were inferior. At most he could say only that his moral views differed. If no one preference could be proved to be better than another, then it seemed, if not a waste of time, at least a purely aesthetic and, therefore, politically meaningless task for scholars to devote themselves to the constructive elaboration of value systems.

This interpretation and conclusion, as I shall try to show in a moment, was quite incorrect and misleading. The adoption of a correct conception of moral relativism need not in itself have led to the decline of the critical appraisal of values. Yet, however illogical this conclusion was, since its truth was accepted, its effect was to turn political theorists to a study of the source, origin, and historical importance of moral ideas as the most meaningful way of dealing with them. The hitherto constructive functions of theory promptly evaporated.

This belief in the ultimate equal worth of all moral views is the product, however, not of logic, but of preference itself. To say that a moral position is relativistic need not mean more than that it stems from the life-experiences of an individual and that by factual evidence no one value can be proved to be superior to another. To borrow Mannheim's term, it means that a preference is relational; [42] it relates to the social conditions in which it appears. The vital fact about this meaning of relativism is that the description of the conditions surrounding the emergence of moral preference does not by itself necessarily imply any opinion about the merit or demerit of these preferences. It does not demonstrate values to be either equal or unequal in worth. It merely indicates that they are equal in their origins, in the

[42] K. Mannheim, *Ideology and Utopia,* p. 70.

sense that they are each a product of historical circumstances. If we wished, we could of course compare them with regard to other qualities such as their moral worth. This would however be a separate and independent task. To do so we would need first to establish an acceptable moral standard in terms of which varying preferences could be compared. But barring agreement on such a standard, two differing value judgments can be said to be neither better nor worse when each stands by the side of the other. They just differ and are incommensurable until some third standard of comparison is adopted.

Let us assume, for example, that we know clearly what we mean when we talk about the desirability of freedom and of security. We can talk about the relativism of these moral preferences. When we say they are relative, we need only mean that we happen to accept them as desirable and that this acceptance can be explained in terms of our response to the historical circumstances in which we live. If we were to argue, however, that in terms of their varying life-experiences, one person considers freedom preferable and another person, security, and, therefore, that each statement of preference is equal in worth to the other, such an argument would carry us beyond the bounds of good reasoning. The mere fact that each expression of a preference is equally relative to circumstances does not in itself mean that we must necessarily conclude that they are equally valuable. Whether freedom is considered superior, inferior, or equal in moral worth to security depends obviously upon some prior moral standard or preference in terms of which these two preferences are themselves evaluated. The relativism of freedom and security implies no statement about the merits of these two goals. The position which holds that because preferences are relative, they are by virtue of that fact of equal value is itself an evaluation and I shall call it equalistic relativism. Equalistic relativism is a moral position; it argues that because no value judgment can be proved superior, all values must be treated as equally good. Moral relativism, or properly, relationism, is a statement of fact; it simply declares that all value judgments are responses to historical conditions.

Yet, however untenable the conclusion of equalistic relativism, it has been implicit in most social science; as I have already suggested, this invalid interpretation succeeded in converting the study of moral ideas into the history of these ideas. Without identifying equalistic relativism by name, we have already witnessed its impact on political theory, as for example, in the work of McIlwain and Sabine. There its influence was indirect but nonetheless present. Although, as we saw, Sabine and McIlwain verbally would reject the idea of equalistic relativism, in the execution of their work they are unable to escape its consequences, so prevalent is this outlook in our age. A moral problem for them is therefore primarily one of historical description, not of constructive inquiry.

The preoccupation of theory with the history of values can be traced, finally, to a third source, the very historical conditions out of which it has emerged. The ultimate reason for the deliquescence of the hitherto constructive functions of theory can be attributed to the historical circumstances of the last hundred years. With the recent change in these conditions, any historical justification for the refusal publicly to re-evaluate moral frameworks must now be considered destroyed.

In the latter half of the nineteenth and in the early twentieth centuries, there was undoubtedly sufficient agreement in western Europe for the indifference to value reformulation to have little important meaning in every-day political affairs. There were no deep cleavages in ethical opinion that could so sharply divide antagonistic groups as to require a choice among fundamentally irreconcilable and competing values. Since there was this greater unity in moral outlook than we know today, it did not seem inconsistent or neglectful for contemporary and later value theorists to devote their energies largely to the history of moral ideas. Since men did not feel that these ideas could be fundamentally disputed, there was little left to do but to explore their history.

With the growth of fascism, however, at the end of the First World War and the subsequent spread of totalitarianism in the West, the fact that Nietzsche had foreseen decades earlier, and which is now popularized through social anthropology, namely, that men can act on the basis of widely divergent ethical standards, has become all to apparent. And this realization that the Western moral heritage, however we may describe it, is not universally or eternally acceptable must gradually lead to a reconsideration of the need, not only to analyze and describe historically but also to question prevailing political values and their institutional implications. The fact is that, unlike the nineteenth century, we do feel the need for some conscious guidance for our conduct in practical matters. In our period of conflicting value patterns, reinforced by almost irreconcilable power relations, the mere adoption of the values of our ancestors begins to pall unless they are seriously subjected, before acceptance, to critical analysis and imaginative reconstruction. In its approach to moral problems, however, theory still operates on the assumptions of the nineteenth century; hence it is reluctant to abandon its historical orientation.

These are a few of the more important reasons for the decline in the study of theory today as compared with its earlier days. While helping to explain the source of captivation with historicist research today, at the same time these reasons do suggest part of the remedy if research workers are to receive the training necessary for genuine moral self-clarification. There can be little doubt that research workers need to be sharply aware of the historical position in which they now find themselves. Mere avowal or affirmation of preferences was satisfactory for an earlier period when ultimate moral assumptions appeared to be clear and settled. Conformity to prevailing values involved fewer dangers than it does today. Research workers could even afford the luxury of misconstruing the nature of moral relativism to mean moral indifference. Social purposes had not been substantially and profoundly challenged. Now, however, if purposes are to receive full clarification, historical perspective itself opens our mind to the need for a deeper kind of moral inquiry, one that is freed from commitment to prevailing values just because of their prevalence or to relativism as a moral position rather than as a descriptive concept.

The discussion in this and the prior chapter has therefore sought to show that research into empirical theory must be inadequate unless it is undertaken with a full awareness on the part of the research worker of his own moral premises. These premises are not easy to identify. Special competence is required for this purpose. We might have assumed that training for this competence was available in political (value) theory, but examination of the contemporary historicist approach indicates the deficiency of theory in this respect. Political theory is no longer able to aid political scientists in going beyond a formal clarification of their values. The very needs of work in systematic theory, therefore, demand the rejuvenation of political theory. Without the knowledge of how to go about clarifying their moral premises through a constructive approach, political scientists can scarcely expect to be able to acquire the competence necessary to detect the influence of moral views on their research in systematic theory.

Chapter **11**

Critique of a General Political Theory

> In order to understand the organic laws of a
> political system, it is necessary to examine
> it as a whole, and seek to discover not only
> the true functions of each part, but also its
> influence upon every other part, and its
> relation to the equilibrium of the complete
> organism.
>
> A. Lawrence Lowell

OUR attention in the last two chapters to the relation of values to a theoretical framework brings to a close our discussion of specific areas of research to which an interest in the development of systematic theory might initially lead. Numerous other problems would, of course, require exploration. My objective in this work, however, is only to draw attention to the need for theoretical research and to broach some of the more important issues. In this chapter I shall foresake the pattern of inquiring into specific problems and turn to a general appraisal of one systematic theory which can be detected in recent empirical research. We shall discuss, not what I might consider to be a new

266

and useful theoretical framework—a problem beyond the limits of this work—but instead, the extent to which an existing one merits conscious adoption or continued use.

Although in the last half-century American political science has wandered among the facts of political life, it has not entirely lost sight of its horizons. Here and there in the literature over the years some interest has arisen in formulating a body of theory to guide empirical research. The mind is prone to search for uniformities as the most economical way to organize the body for action, and the collective mind of political scientists is no exception. If the pieces of interest in theory are accumulated and assembled, like the surprising coherence in the kaleidoscope, they fit together into a theoretical pattern. The pattern emerges, however, less by design than by accident. Its form is the theory of political equilibrium, the only discernible suggestion of a theoretical framework on the broad horizon of empirical research.

In calling the idea of a political equilibrium a theory, I am ascribing to it greater pretensions than it actually possesses. It is used more to describe the results of political activity than to represent a central concept in a mode of analysis. It is so pervasive, however, and, in spite of the modest claims made on its behalf, it has so many theoretical implications, that by treating it as the key concept of a broader theory rather than as an adjective applying to a condition of the political system or as an isolated analytical device, we can see its vital, even though latent, meaning for political research.

At the outset we must distinguish two different senses in which the idea of an equilibrium is used: first, as a mode of analysis, implicit in a substantive conclusion, for understanding the process within a political system; second, as a description of the kind of mutual restraint obtaining among various power groups usually associated with a constitutional political system. In the second sense, it is sometimes used objectively to describe a system composed of power elements that limit each other. But often it is used to depict a condition an author would like to see come into existence, and therefore it has a pronounced value orientation. We shall call the two major senses in which the term is used the general equilibrium and the constitutional equilibrium respectively. To be able to understand the role and utility of the concept as a possible framework for research, we must distinguish between these two meanings. Let us turn first to the idea of a general equilibrium since through it, if at all, a framework might conceivably emerge.

1. Meaning of General Equilibrium[1]

As we would suspect from our knowledge of research into the political process, the concept of equilibrium regularly occurs when the idea of process is uppermost in an empirical investigation. There is a reason for this close relationship. At the minimum, the concept of equilibrium in the present sense conveys two ideas: first, that all the elements or variables in a political system are functionally interdependent; and second, that they will tend to act and react on each other to a point where a state of stability, if even for a moment, obtains.

[1] For suggestive discussion of the use of this concept in the various social sciences see: G. J. Stigler, *The Theory of Price* (New York: Macmillan, 1946); P. Sorokin, *Contemporary Sociological Theories* (New York: Harper, 1928), chapter 1 and *Social and Cultural Dynamics* (Chicago: American Book Company, 1941) 4 vols., Vol. IV, chapter 14; J. L. Henderson, *Pareto's General Sociology* (Cambridge: Harvard University Press, 1935); J. A. Schumpeter, *Business Cycles* (New York: McGraw-Hill, 1939), esp. chapter 2; V. Pareto, *Mind and Society* (New York: Harcourt, Brace, 1935) 4 vols., Vol. IV, esp. chapter 4; G. Myrdal, *An American Dilemma* (New York: Harper, 1944), appendix 3. For discussion directed to political science see M. A. Ash, "An Analysis of Power, with Special Reference to International Politics," 3 *World Politics* (1951), 218-37; D. Black, "The Rationale of Group Decision-Making," 56 *Journal of Political Economy* (1948), 23-34, "The Decisions of a Committee Using a Special Majority," 16 *Econometrica* (1948), 245-61, and "The Unity of Political and Economic Science," 60 *Economic Journal* (1950), 506-14; H. Simon, *Administrative Behavior,* chapter 6; C. I. Barnard, *The Functions of the Executive* (Cambridge: Harvard University Press, 1940), *ad hoc.*

The first of these ideas is clearly fused with the meaning of political process. The very notion of process implies that there is a variety of elements interacting with one another to produce the changing states of the political system. Interest groups, parties, legislatures, relevant publics, international pressures, and the like are kinds of political activity which interact to shape the condition and policies of a political system. This is just a concrete way of saying that all parts of the political process depend upon all other parts, and collectively they all determine the state of the political system in the same way that celestial bodies help to determine one another's position and the general configuration of the universe.

The popularity of these ideas of process and mutual interdependence can be traced back in political thought to the growth of pluralism. They reflect a form of empirical pluralism which corresponds to the emergence of ethical pluralism in political philosophy. Modern ethical pluralism appeared at the turn of the present century with the increasing recognition of the multiplicity of social forces, especially groups, contributing to the condition of society, and specifically in politics, to the formulation and execution of authoritative policy. In contrast to ethical pluralism, which speculated on the variety of political systems that became possible once the moral value of group life was acknowledged, empirical pluralism is practically coterminous with the notion of process. It leads on the descriptive level to the recognition of the multiplicity of causes, especially of a group nature, that influence social policy. In contrast to a tendency in the nineteenth century to view social causation in terms of single factors, the process approach sought out the variety of mutually dependent factors underlying the distribution of power and its relation to the authoritative allocation of values. Almost ineluctably the need appeared for a concept to link this idea of interdependence to a mode of analysis that would permit students to relate simultaneously varying elements to the state of the political system at any given time. Thus, once the notion of process with its pluralist causal assumptions crept into practical research, it was easy for the idea of equilibrium, already familiar to economics and sociology, to filter in as well.

The idea of a general equilibrium has a logic of its own, however. Its adoption could not help committing political science to the corollary that the interdependence can best be understood as a system in which the interacting parts tend to come to rest. This is the second idea implicit in the notion of equilibrium. It suggests that because the parts of a system vary simultaneously, that is, determine each other and the whole complex of relations among themselves, there will be a tendency for these relationships to maintain themselves in the face of any force that seeks to upset them. There is always a tendency to maintain the given equilibrium. Without this additional idea of maintenance of the equilibrium there would have been little point in adopting the concept of equilibrium except as a more elaborate synonym for the idea of process.

This association of process analysis and equilibrium theory is apparent at an early date, as their appearance in Bentley's *Process of Government* testifies. Bentley leans as heavily on the idea of equilibrium as he does on process. For him the political process is synonymous with "the equilibration of interests, the balancing of groups." [2] Although he uses the term equilibrium only occasionally, he turns to numerous other terms to express the same idea. Society consists of a multiplicity of groups which are always jostling one another to establish a "balance" or "adjustment," his two favorite terms. The fact that he feels free to speak of the process as one of equilibration, an alternative expression to the balancing or adjusting of group interests, indicates that in his own mind these are all identical ideas. [3]

In turning to the idea of an equilibrium Bentley adopted a framework that quite unobtrusively has come to embrace most

[2] A. F. Bentley, op. cit., p. 274.
[3] Ibid. For frequent use of these terms see especially chapters 10, 14, and 20.

political research. He urged that students begin to consider the manifold political activities as constituting an interacting process. But he went beyond this simple idea of interaction. In describing it as an equilibrating process, unless the term was simply redundant, he was implying, first, that the process tends to maintain itself in a system; that is, there is a natural coherence or relatedness among the parts of the process. The activity hangs together because it all relates to "political phenomena," [4] a phrase of Bentley's. Second, he was suggesting that the law and governmental institutions, or the formal expression of policy and the high level agencies forming this policy, were all intertwined with underlying groups in a complex reactive system that constantly tended towards a moment of balance or equilibrium. For Bentley the task of political science, therefore, became one of discovering just how this equilibrating tendency came into existence, took its form, and changed over time. He sought the answers by turning to group activity.

It would have been instructive to witness the way in which Bentley himself would have applied his equilibrium framework to the details of political research. He relieved himself of this obligation, however, by specifying in a footnote (where he expresses his intention more clearly than in the main body of the text) that he was interested not in stating a substantive theory but in advancing a mode of analysis.[5] Through the use of it he hoped that others would be able to explain or understand how the balancing process functioned. This is why he failed to elaborate in anything but the most casual detail the implications of the mode of analysis suggested by the concept of equilibrium. What he took for granted as almost self-explanatory subsequent political science has accepted with equal nonchalance. One is tempted to say that because of the lack of a serious challenge of Bentley's conceptual premises in this regard,

[4] Ibid., p. 259.

[5] Ibid., p. 263, fn. 1, where he says that the object of his book is "to illustrate the possibilities of the application of a particular manner of statement [mode of analysis] or scientific method to the material."

political science lost the chance to open up the whole problem of the merit of an underlying scheme of analysis.

As I have said before, until quite recently Bentley has been almost entirely neglected. Nevertheless, his writing is of significance not only because it has come belatedly to exercise a growing influence upon the outlook of political scientists but also because in it Bentley was able to anticipate a main framework of research subsequent to his own day. He reacted earlier and more sensitively than others to those pluralist influences impinging on political research that led it in later years to absorb the idea of equilibrium as a nuclear analytic concept.

A reading of significant empirical literature in the United States since the First World War reveals the astonishing extent to which the equilibrium notion has been adopted. It appears so frequently that it is amazing that theoreticians in political science have neglected to distill the thoughts on the subject for special attention. A few quotations here will suffice to illustrate how frequently and naturally the notion is used in political research, with seldom a pause to inquire deeply into its implications and utility. Indeed, penetration into the concept normally seems unnecessary because it is so acceptable to both reader and author alike as an obvious image of the political process. The clarity of this analogy is of course totally deceptive, but we shall come to that in a moment.

One author writes of the "notion of politics as the relationships between governor and governed, or as the pattern of balance or equilibrium between groups of diverse interests struggling for ascendency. . . ." [6] Another, in summing up the influence of social groups on governmental institutions, concludes that "in any case, all groups, whether they realize their objectives or not, play a part in making the existing political equilibrium what it is." [7] Still another says that "the functional situation

[6] V. O. Key, op. cit., p. 5.
[7] H. L. Childs, "Pressure Groups and Propaganda," in E. B. Logan, op. cit., p. 208.

out of which the political arises is . . . the need for some form of equilibrium, adjustment, *modus vivendi* between the various groups and individuals of the community." [8] The concept has gained such wide acceptability that in a text noted for the advanced theoretical level of its approach the discussion of the separation of powers is imbedded in a broad equilibrium framework. "If we consider the history of the institutional development of divided powers," the author writes, "it is very clear that such division has facilitated the maintenance of an equilibrium between various rival groups and claims, not a stable equilibrium, but a moving one which continuously adjusts itself to the shifting balance of these groups as they evolve." [9]

The idea is used in describing not only the general configuration of the political system but also special aspects of the political process. As another author notes: "Observation discloses a succession of Congressional sessions and chief executives different in personal characteristics and in surrounding circumstances. The equipoise [read equilibrium] noted in any moment of time is the instant product of the interaction of the variable characteristics of the forces in conflict." [10] The prevailing tone of the whole book in which this statement appears also embodies the notion of equilibrium. It insists that public policy in a democracy is the product of an adjustment among conflicting interests. By leaving open more than one path of access to government, the separation of powers allows interests to choose the best medium to express themselves. It has proved to be a valuable

[8] C. E. Merriam, *Political Power*, p. 21.
[9] C. J. Friedrich, *Constitutional Government and Democracy* (1950 ed., New York: Ginn), p. 186. See also the deliberate use of the concept in the analysis of formal political organizations and other institutional patterns by H. Simon, D. Smithburg, and V. Thompson, op. cit., esp. chapter 18; D. Truman, op. cit., pp. 26-32. And see its use with regard to other data by M. Fainsod, op. cit., esp. pp. 297-9; R. C. Spencer, "Significance of a Functional Approach in the Introductory Course," 22 *American Political Science Review* (1928), 954-66, esp. pp. 962-4; A. L. Lowell, *Essays on Government*, pp. 3-4; R. Hildreth, *Theory of Politics* (New York: Harper, 1854).
[10] P. Herring, *Presidential Leadership*, p. 7.

mechanism for bringing about the necessary balance or equilibrium among antagonistic social groups.

I have cited here only a few illustrations of the use of this idea. To say the least, it would be revealing, if not startling, to review in some detail all outstanding political research in the last half-century or more; throughout the idea of equilibrium constantly emerges either in direct use of the term itself or as an inarticulate premise.

2. General Equilibrium as Descriptive Conclusion

We can now turn to an examination of the possibilities for developing the general equilibrium concept into a full-fledged conceptual framework for political research, as it is, for example, in economics. The opening step in such an analysis is to find out just what is meant in the literature when a writer talks about the competing groups in the political process reaching an adjustment, accommodation, balance, equilibrium, or the like. Although I shall examine them later, we can assume for the moment the synonymity of the terms.

Singling out the concept of equilibrium as representative, we find that the literature differs considerably in its use of the term. Two recurring descriptions of a general equilibrium do appear however. One defines it as an actual condition that occurs at some moment in time; the other describes it as an equilibrating or balancing tendency, a potentiality which never works itself out to the point of equilibrium. Let us look at each of these.

The first meaning is usually implied in the ordinary day-to-day use of the term outside technical works. It leaves the impression that activities which are functionally interrelated act and react until they ultimately reach a condition wherein no actor is willing to change his position in relation to the others. This need not be a condition of absolute rest or lack of motion;

interaction among the competing actors continues. This condition parallels the hypothetical situation in mechanics when a ball, although in motion, is said to be in equilibrium as long as it is moving at a constant rate on a straight line without stopping.

A clear-cut example of this meaning appears in George Catlin's *A Study of the Principles of Politics*. Unfortunately, to this day this work has had only a peripheral effect on the movement of American political science. It stands as a lonely structure which no one has sought to remodel or embellish. The structure, is, however, well worth examining closely since it accurately mirrors the conventions of its day; unerringly Catlin caught the unobtrusive spirit of American political science. The apparent opacity of his work is due to the fact that he tried to carry some latent tendencies in the discipline to the logical extreme. This is true, for example, in his identification of situational data, although the formulations in his whole work have left his remarks quite inaccessible except to the initiated or extremely patient reader; it is true also in his search for an intrinsically rather than superficially homogeneous subject matter for political research. Similarly, the fact that the concept of general equilibrium pervades his work shows how close he was to the basic currents of thought in empirical research.

Catlin deliberately uses the idea of equilibrium to mean a condition of rest. He finds that the essential homogeneity of political relations lies in the fact that each person in society, and each group, seeks to assert his or its will over others through control or power over them. But sociality or the need to live together with others is as fundamental as individual assertiveness. The result is that the political process consists of the means and paths whereby these conflicting wills are brought into some sort of consensus, harmony, balance, or equilibrium, terms which Catlin indiscriminately uses as synonyms. Each person or group seeks to assert its control over others; the primary object of all political relations is to procure "some personal adjustment of the will of another man to my will." [11] Ultimately a point is reached where it is to the "balance of advantage" [12] of each participant to call a halt. This is the point of equilibrium. At this point no one considers it to his advantage to change the existing relations or patterns of interaction.

It is apparent here that by the concept of equilibrium Catlin is suggesting an actual state of relations which exists at any moment in time. From whatever aspect we look at the political process, whether at a partial phenomenon or at the process as a whole, each picture is the product of an equilibrium. When human beings co-operate, for example, they do so because temporarily their wills run parallel and a "stabilized harmony of wills" [13] ensues. When one group dominates another, there too is an equilibrium, although in Catlin's opinion a less durable one. The equilibriums so established also give birth to political conventions, the law, and even the political structure. "The traditional structure, institutional and conventional, [is] built up by wills and [takes] shape as a network of related wills in equilibrium." [14] It is clear that Catlin considers the political relations existing at any moment in a political system to be the product of an equilibrium among a number of competing wills, individual or group.

Superficially, the use of equilibrium here to describe the state of the political system seems replete with insight. Men do struggle for power in our society and yet utter chaos is not the rule. Some sort of "equilibrium" must prevail, and presumably the task of political scientists ought to be to explain the process by which this is achieved and the particular pattern that it takes. In effect, what empirical research was unconsciously doing in bits and pieces, Catlin was seeking to do consistently and coherently at a high level of abstraction and generality. Closer in-

[11] G. E. G. Catlin, *A Study of the Principles of Politics,* p. 71.
[12] Ibid., p. 165.
[13] Ibid., p. 69.
[14] Ibid., p. 232.

spection of the concept, however, raises certain questions that undermine its apparent utility.

In the first place, Catlin uses the notion of equilibrium with a meaning that is not inherent in it, although because of the casual use of the equilibrium idea in political science it often appears with his meaning. His interpretation of every moment and aspect of the political process as the point of rest of mutually dependent variables leads one to ask when the political system is ever out of equilibrium. Since the term does not discriminate between moments of disequilibrium and those of equilibrium, it is too undifferentiated. Indeed, the work of others, such as Bentley, shows that it is possible to interpret the political process in the antithetical sense as a constant movement in disequilibrium. Catlin seems in fact to contradict himself. Certainly if he can say that any set of political relations are the product of an adjustment of wills at the time, then if these relations change, as they must, at some point the equilibrium must be disturbed; the old equilibrium is therefore destroyed to make way for the new one, however little the latter may differ from the former. Otherwise, change would be impossible. Catlin is not totally blind to this, and yet he ignores its implications for the use of the idea of an equilibrium. In this he is typical of others in political science who assume that the existing state of affairs is the result of a momentary equilibrium of the elements involved. If everything is equilibrium, then the term is indeed barren of meaning.

In the second place, is it possible to prove that an empirical system ever reaches a condition of equilibrium? Is equilibrium a condition of rest and how do we discover when change stops? To answer these questions we would have to be able to define quite sharply, more than we have done to this point, the meaning of the term. Catlin sensed the inadequacy of his own formulation but did little about it because of insurmountable obstacles in his way. We shall discuss these in a moment.

Catlin's sensitivity arose from the fact that he was more

conscious than many of his fellow political scientists that he was trying to emulate economics and physics, in which the idea of equilibrium is prolific with insights. What he sensed and yet what he and others failed to realize sufficiently is that in both these disciplines the term is used with a precise meaning. The point at which the relevant interdependent variables of these disciplines come to rest can be identified precisely at the level of theory. But these disciplines have never aspired to identify this point empirically. For the physicist, for example, a point is in equilibrium when the vector sum of all the forces acting on that point is zero; in the case of an extended object it occurs when the sum of all the torques and forces equals zero. Similarly for the economist, equilibrium occurs when a given price brings supply and demand into accord. It is possible to determine the quantity of goods or services being supplied together with the quantity that will be demanded at each price until a point is reached when the demand just equals the supply. This will be the equilibrium price. It is so called because at this point no one will seek to change his position either by supplying more goods or services or by demanding more. The interdependent variables of price, supply, and demand are at rest. Exchange continues to take place, of course, and in this sense there is no cessation of life or activity. But there is stability in the sense that outputs and prices do not change.

In contrast, however, to its use in political science, neither in mechanics nor in economics has the theory been designed to prove the existence of an equilibrium in reality. On the contrary, it has been recognized only as a "theoretical norm" [15] or point of reference against which any empirical set of relations can be contrasted or compared. In mechanics, an essential ingredient of the equilibrium position is that it can be reached only in a frictionless world. In the real world the position can only be approximated. Similarly in economics, only if certain conditions were stable would the economic system settle down into an

[15] J. A. Schumpeter, op. cit., chapter 2.

equilibrium position. All novelty in the basic circumstances surrounding economic choices, such as in the tastes, technology, and resources, would have to be eliminated. Barring the existence of these conditions, the empirical economic system never does settle down. It is in constant state of disequilibrium, moving to or away from an equilibrium, always in the *"neighborhoods of equilibrium"* [16] but never arriving. In describing political life as passing through moments of equilibrium, research in political science has therefore been seeking to convert a heuristic device into a substantive description of the empirical world.

Since traditionally the term has been used in an imprecise, almost intuitive way, political scientists could not help but fail to overlook its full significance for research. Therefore, instead of viewing the state of equilibrium as a theoretical model, helpful in simplifying reality for purposes of analysis, rather than as an exact picture of reality, they have committed the natural mistake of considering the equilibrium a possible condition of the empirical system.

Catlin is not the only one who has fallen victim to this fallacy. It is equally apparent in the work of others—for example, of Charles Merriam. Various problems arise in connection with Merriam's work in this respect, and these will be touched on later. Here I wish only to point out that although his astute political instincts lead him to sense the inadequacy of characterizing the political system as a state of equilibrium, he does not really escape giving such a description. To avoid leaving the impression that he believes the political system is in a constant state of equilibrium, he repeatedly describes it as a "moving equilibrium." [17] This is an apt and persuasive phrase to catch the sense of periodic disorganization and reintegration which we certainly experience in political life. In depicting the equilib-

[16] Ibid., p. 71. Italics in original.
[17] See C. E. Merriam, *The Role of Politics in Social Change* (New York: New York University Press, 1936), where he uses this phrase frequently. It appears regularly in many of his other works as well.

rium as one that moves, however, Merriam must mean that at certain stages in the process moments of equilibrium do occur. He leaves us with an image of the process as a series of discrete states of rest linked by periods of movement toward and away from equilibrium. Although no moment of rest is permanent, nevertheless real moments of equilibrium are part of the political pattern. To this extent, therefore, he joined Catlin and others in converting what economics and physics had found to be a useful tool of analysis into a misleading picture of reality.

In strict logic, of course, we are not permitted to object to this attempt to prove that the empirical political system does arrive at varying equilibriums. The onus would rest, however, with its users to prove that the political process, unlike economic or physical processes, actually does come to rest. At any rate, as a beginning it would be necessary to have a strict definition of the point of equilibrium so that we could clearly recognize the object of our search. We shall shortly return to this problem.

Some political scientists have instinctively realized the difficulties of using the term and have avoided entirely the notion of a point of equilibrium while continuing, however, to use the equilibrium concept. As we shall see, there is considerable justification for this approach. But it too encounters certain obstacles inherent in the logic of the equilibrium idea, obstacles that destroy most of its utility for empirical research in political science, at least at the present time. This brings us to the second of the two substantive meanings which the idea of a general equilibrium assumes in research. The first was that of a condition of rest. The second is the idea of a balancing or equilibrating process, in which an equilibrium never obtains although there is a tendency towards it. This is why it can be called an equilibrating tendency. By conceiving of the political system in this way, a few political scientists have thereby implicitly rejected the likelihood of the process settling down in equilibrium.

The work of Bentley is a classic example of this view although, like most other uncritical users of the concept, he sometimes inconsistently writes as though the system did reach an equilibrium.[18] Most of the time, however, he conceives of social groups as constantly in process of balance but never succeeding in establishing even a momentary, much less a prolonged, equilibrium or balance. He speaks of the equilibrating or adjusting that goes on among groups without contending that this is more than a tendency that never quite works itself out. There appears to be perpetual disequilibrium.

Similarly, and much more prominently, in contemporary literature on international relations, it has become the entrenched custom to talk not of the balance of power but of the balancing of nations, each against the other, with no state of rest or equilibrium being achieved. Students of international politics have long pointed out that the international process could never attain a state of balance because the most important conditions which would permit this are themselves constantly changing. An equilibrium could not be achieved even for the briefest moment because technology, populations, resources, and other such conditions upon which national power depends are themselves in constant flux. The most that can be said about the international process is that a balancing takes place. The tendency to a balance at any one moment immediately yields to a new one without any tendency ever fulfilling itself. In this sense, both domestic and international conflicts of interest and demands are in process of equilibration rather than in equilibrium. The process is steadily striving to achieve a moment of equilibrium, but it is driven on by changing circumstances so that equilibrium is never quite attained.

The use of the idea of an equilibrium to imply a balancing process does considerably enhance its utility as a concept, even though from the implication that all political life consists of moments of equilibrium we leap to a contradictory premise— that all life is a process of disequilibrium. In one sense, it is true, this description of political life gives us no greater informa-

[18] A. F. Bentley, op. cit., p. 274.

tion than the statement that activity is part of an endless process of change. This is undoubtedly a correct insight into all social life, however stagnant life may appear to be on the surface, but it is not very helpful in carrying us beyond the mere statement of the fact of change. If this were the only meaning conveyed by the idea of disequilibrium, it could be considered only as a synonym and a stylistic substitute for the concept of change. It would give us little insight into the functioning of this constant process of change.

Behind this description of political life as a disequilibrium, however, there lurks a deeper theoretical implication. It transforms the concept from a substantive conclusion describing the political system into a tool for the analysis of the system. To speak of political life as being in constant process of disequilibrium suggests that we are in fact contrasting it with a hypothetical condition of equilibrium. Disequilibrium therefore suggests more than change or constant flux, as conveyed by the notion of political process. It hints that tendencies towards equilibrium do exist but that changes take place in the basic circumstances (such as the technology or population, for example) that abort these tendencies. This means that the disequilibrium is quite naturally being contrasted with an equilibrium condition that never materializes, a kind of normal situation which is a pure abstraction. It is as though the research worker held in his mind a model of what the equilibrium would be like if the present tendencies were allowed to work themselves out fully without any change in the basic conditions determining the power of various groups. The disequilibrium is then identified and described in the light of what would have emerged and the reasons for the failure of the equilibrium to come into existence are then sought. In other words, it seems as though the concept of equilibrium is a heuristic, simplifying device to help understand the empirical world. We create in our minds a model of the normal outcome of the process at any period of time, if the identified tendencies could run their course. We then contrast this with what is actually seen to happen and try to explain the difference.

Essentially this is what is done in international relations when students describe the balancing process. They assume that if it were not for certain changes in the resources, technical know-how, population, and so forth, ultimately the conflicting power groups would arrive at a position where, given the relationship of forces, no group would consider it could better itself by changing its position. It might desire to improve its position in relation to the other nations, but given its strength and that of others, no change in its activity could improve its position. At that position, under the given conditions, it is maximizing the returns from the amount of power it holds. But something intervenes to prevent such an equilibrium from being achieved; the given conditions never remain the same for a moment. It has been the task of political science to investigate the reasons for this, that is, for the changing patterns of international power. Such a conception of equilibrium must be present if the notion of the balancing of power is to have any meaning beyond that of constant flux.

This implicit use of equilibrium as a tool for analyzing political life rather than for giving a substantive description of reality, brings it more closely into accord with the way we have seen it to be employed in mechanics and economics. And if it were not for the special problem of quantification, as we shall see, an equilibrium theory might serve quite satisfactorily as the major framework for all political science.

3. General Equilibrium as Theory

Let us look more closely at the possible value of the equilibrium idea as a broad theoretical construct to aid in simplifying and understanding political reality. As we saw, in mechanics the idea of a frictionless world helps to simplify data for analytical purposes. In actual research, on examining the empirical world deviations from the results which the theory of the frictionless system predicts can be accounted for by variables in the empirical system not present in the hypothetical system.

Similarly in economics, the value of constructing a theoretical model of an equilibrium condition under perfect competition is not that it then enables us to identify this condition in an empirical economic system. It is rather a point of reference to help us interpret the real world; it is so important a heuristic device that it has been called the *magna carta* of economists.[19] The hypothesis is that at certain times the empirical system tends towards equilibrium. It has been found helpful to try to identify the reasons for the failure of the equilibrium to materialize, just how far a given condition is from equilibrium, and what paths must be taken in order to reach this point. Through this device it has been possible to obtain considerable insight into such problems as inflation, unemployment, and overproduction.

The question here is whether the equilibrium theory could be used as a heuristic tool in political science, thus emulating its use in mechanics and economics. Could we raise to the level of conscious and deliberate analysis what lies hidden in the frequent use of the idea of equilibrium in political research?

At the present level of development in political science, and for that matter in all social science with the exception of economics, the possibilities seem very slim indeed. To employ a model of a political equilibrium for the purposes of helping us to understand the complicated political system, it would be necessary to reduce the important political elements or variables to measurable terms. This need for quantifiable magnitudes is a substantial barrier in the way of equilibrium analysis of the political system. It is conceivable that in some distant future quantification may be much more successfully applied to political data than at the present and in that case, the utility of equilibrium analysis will immediately change. For the present and foreseeable

[19] J. A. Schumpeter, op. cit., esp. pp. 69-71.

future, however, wanting readily measurable data, we must recognize its limits.

Quantification is a prerequisite for equilibrium analysis because of the kinds of questions we must ask. Let us recall for a moment what we would be trying to do in such an analysis. We would be seeking to trace the way in which the various groups possessing power use it to shape policy: the way in which the power of one group influences the position of all other power groups, the reciprocal effects of the latter's power, and the ensuing authoritative allocation of values. We would be identifying all the power elements in a situation, showing how they interact with one another to produce a particular policy; this we would call the state of the political system at any one time. Hypothetically, as the result of this interaction, a policy would be reached with regard to which no element in the political system would find it worth while to change its position, that is, to seek to change the authoritative allocation of values, because at this point it would have maximized the returns from the exercise of its power. This point would be designated the equilibrium policy. It would be a point of reference with which the actual state of the concrete political system could be compared and explained. The importance of identifying this position is that the equilibrium would immediately reveal the determinants of policy; we would know exactly how much each of the elements influenced the given authoritative allocation of values.

In thus using equilibrium analysis, we would be engaging in two separate kinds of mental operations. First, there is the need to construct at the theoretical level a model of the possible relations among the interdependent political variables. At this stage actual quantities are not required; the relationships can be stated in the form of mathematical equations. Presumably, since we would be searching for reciprocal effects, our model would consist of a series of simultaneous equations. But to demonstrate the empirical validity of the theoretical system so created, it is obviously essential to displace some of the mathematical symbols with actual data. This is therefore the second kind of mental operation. By filling in the actual quantitative data for some of the unknowns, the others could be discovered. Theory here would therefore fulfill its major task of permitting the solution of problems with a minimum of actual observation of data. The limitations inherent in the lack of quantifiable data with regard to power applies to this validating operation. Let us look at this conclusion more closely.

It is clear that at the theoretical level, with no direct reference to empirical data, a political model, emulating the economic model of perfect competition when novelty is stabilized, could be worked out through some form of symbolic mathematical representation. Here no quantification of any of the variables would be required. The task would be to isolate the important elements in a total political situation and then trace out in symbolic terms the way in which simultaneous changes, under specified hypothetical conditions, would affect each of the variables and the ultimate positions of equilibrium for the whole system of variables under the given conditions. It is not inconceivable that a sophisticate in the use of mathematical tools might be able to work out some elaborate logical relations between political variables and policy to indicate points of equilibrium. The reason for this is that he would be tracing out relationships in hypothetical terms only. This kind of logical analysis would be the first stage in developing a framework for simplifying reality.

While such a theoretical model is satisfactory and indeed necessary for working out the possible relations among political variables when approaching the problem in equilibrium terms, the real difficulty comes in testing, when we try to apply the analytic framework to the concrete political system. This is why although a symbolic analysis may be possible, at present and for the distant future it has limited utility in practice and therefore must be characterized as inadequate theory. When we try to fill in the logical terms of the various mathematical equations with empirical data, we find that we have devised very few satisfactory indices with which to measure the power of the interacting political elements.

It is true, we can measure voting, content of communications, numerical strength of various groups such as armies, parties, and interests, the physical resources of nations and of lesser groups within limits, and financial reserves. Preliminary techniques are even available for measuring such intangibles as social status, which plays such an important role in power relations. Even if we were to put all these and other measurable dimensions together, however, we would still not have even the beginning of an adequate composite index to measure the amount of power held by competing groups. For this reason, it would be difficult to discover just what would be a possible empirical position of equilibrium. We would not be able to find out how much power any of the elements possessed, how much each influenced the other, and how much of a particular kind of policy was influenced in a measurable degree by these elements. Lacking measurable terms with regard to power, we could not calculate just what empirical condition we could characterize as an empirical equilibrium, even though we did not expect the concrete political situation ever to work itself out to this point of equilibrium. In terms of the mathematics involved, we could not provide the quantified data to fill in enough of the unknowns in our simultaneous equations to make a solution possible.

In economics for example, the theoretical model is useful to help understand problems in the real world because the magnitudes of demand and supply can be determined quantitatively. If we had similar data for the important political variables, it would be possible to discover the amount of power being exerted in a situation. Presumably, we would then be able to determine how far we were from an equilibrium position. We could tell whether we were tending towards equilibrium or away from it and what path must be followed to arrive there. This would give us a good idea as to what to expect in the way of future politica!

288 / The Political System

activity. We would be in a position to establish how much power each of the participating elements would need to exercise in order to achieve this condition of equilibrium or to abort it. Lacking appropriate indices for the measurement of power, however, much of the usefulness of the point of equilibrium as a theoretical norm disappears.

A little work by L. J. Henderson, the physiologist, entitled *Pareto's General Sociology*,[20] confirms the existence of such limitations, not only for political science, but for all the social disciplines in which measurable magnitudes are scarce. Caught up in the popularity of Pareto during the thirties, Henderson espouses the utility of Pareto's equilibrium analysis for the social sciences as a whole. To that end he undertakes to expound the minimum prerequisites for the satisfactory application of this analysis. His incisive logic, however, overcomes his optimistic over-identification with Pareto. Although the whole work bears the message that equilibrium analysis is the golden key to the social sciences, tucked away in an appendix is a word of caution that turns the gold to lead.[21] He admits there the limited use of this kind of analysis for the present because of the lack of suitable quantitative methods. "But the greatest restriction upon the use of the social system [equilibrium analysis] depends upon the impossibility, at least for the present, of the use of suitable quantitative methods. . . ."[22] In the face of this admission, his conviction about its applicability to the social sciences stands in sharp contradiction to the resources he himself feels are available.

At the present stage in the development of the social sciences, therefore, speculation about the various logical models that might be worked out for politics is only a pleasant intellectual game. To be useful empirically, equilibrium theory must put great store on measurement, and therefore political science would have to concentrate on the discovery of units of measurement for

---

[20] See footnote 1 of this chapter.
[21] L. J. Henderson, op. cit., Appendix, note 6.
[22] Ibid., p. 95.

its major variables. To the extent that political science has failed to do this, it has been remiss in its obligation to equilibrium analysis, the only visible approximation to a systematic theory. As yet political science has not been able to reduce the complex power relations of society to the necessary numerical quantities, and there is little prospect that in the foreseeable future it will be in a position to do so.

The very fact that the equilibrium concept compels us to give such weight to measurement is itself a handicap in the use of this theory. Measurement is, of course, useful since it gives one form of precision to data. It is, however, not the only form. Qualitative description can in its own way be just as precise. In normal communication, for instance, little difficulty is found in conveying precise ideas without a high degree of quantification. The description of the leadership qualities or character traits of a political boss or the structure of a political machine can achieve a high level of precision without the introduction of quantitative terms that go beyond elementary arithmetic. The adoption of equilibrium analysis as the central framework, as has been implied in a large segment of political research, if treated seriously, would lead political science to devote excessive attention to problems of quantification. This is not to say that it ought to neglect measurement entirely; obviously there is and will always continue to be great room and need for improvement here. To the extent that this improvement does take place, the utility of the equilibrium concept will grow. But barring the sudden discovery of satisfactory devices for transforming present qualitative data, the prerequisites for faithful equilibrium analysis would threaten to direct the energies of research workers away from such qualitative data as a most valuable raw material at the present time.[23]

[23] "For it is not to be denied that the carrying over of the methods of natural science to the social sciences gradually leads to a situation where one no longer asks what one would like to know and what will be of decisive significance for the next step in social development, but attempts only to deal with those complexes of facts which are measurable according to a certain already existent method. Instead of attempting to discover what is

Those in political science who would adopt the notion of equilibrium have not entirely neglected these quantitative prerequisites. Catlin, for example, is well aware of the need for this measurement and makes a slight gesture towards it. "An economics without measurement," he writes, "would approach more closely to a philosophy than a science, and would be of small significance in coping with the details of practical problems. Similarly, it is important to recognize the high significance for politics of introducing into its study not only statistics, but a system of measurement of political transactions as such." [24] His own optimism about the early possibilities of such measurement was, however, an expression of the youthful exhilaration with scientific method in his day, and it bordered on scientism, instead of being a sober estimate of the current realities.

There is a further difficulty inherent in the data of political science which distinguishes it from economics. In the latter, for special reasons, it has been possible in the first stages to reduce the significant variables to three: price, demand, and supply. Considerable mathematical difficulty is encountered even in treating the interdependent relations of these three. There is little prospect that political variables could be limited to so few a number. The multiplicity of variables, even if they could be satisfactorily quantified, would still place formidable barriers in the way of a rewarding equilibrium analysis.

In spite of the extreme limitation that the lack of quantifiable variables and their very numbers impose on the explication of an equilibrium theory, we cannot say that the concept has no value at all. Its merit, however, lies at the level of insight rather than of potentially usable theory. It is valuable as an image to

---

most significant with the highest degree of precision possible under the existing circumstances, one tends to be content to attribute importance to what is measurable merely because it happens to be measurable." K. Mannheim, *Ideology and Utopia,* p. 46.

[24] G. E. G. Catlin, *A Study of the Principles of Politics,* p. 275.

strike certain analogies between the political process and a genuine equilibrium condition. As such an analogical image, it conveys important ideas about the relations among the elements in the political process.

In the first place, the description of this process as an equilibrium suggests that the process takes place in a political system. As we have seen earlier,[25] the idea of system is vital for purposes of general orientation to the subject matter of political science and lies at the heart of any attempt to formulate general theory. The suggestion that the parts of political activity are related in a system implies two things. On the one hand, it implies that the parts of the process are mutually dependent and therefore any change in one part will influence the rest of the system. The resulting changes so occurring will in turn react back on the element stimulating the initial change. It insists on plural rather than on single factor causation.

On the other hand, the equilibrium idea implies that the interrelated parts tend to cohere. This is the fundamental meaning of system. To stress again a point made earlier, the idea of coherence is an inescapable premise if one seeks to construct a conceptual framework for any area of knowledge. We must be prepared to make the assumption, in the initial stages, that the elements under inspection are not only functionally interdependent, but that for purposes of analysis it is realistic to consider these elements in isolation from the rest of the world. They form a system of themselves. If the variables were not temporarily isolated, it would be impossible to discover how they influenced one another. We would have to trace the effect of every conceivable factor. An unisolated system would be subject to so many influences that it would be impossible to discover the relation of the most important variables. By isolating the most significant elements and considering them a system separate and apart from the rest of the world for the moment, we are able to simplify

[25] Chapters 2 and 4.

reality. We can then try to work out their relations. At a later stage it would, of course, become necessary to trace the effect of variables from outside the system, in this way gradually approximating the real conditions under which the system functions.

Concretely, the notion of equilibrium suggests, therefore, that the elements of the political process have a real tendency to hang together, because they all bear a more important relation than any other set of elements to the distribution of power and authoritative allocation of values. By perpetuating this idea, the equilibrium concept has retained the necessary foundation for any conceptual framework. Its only difficulty has been that the framework implicit within itself would require for fruition a degree of quantification unattainable today.

In the second place, the idea of a moving equilibrium, or a world in flux constantly striving towards equilibrium but never achieving it, maintains at the forefront of political inquiry the problem of political change. Because the term bears this essential insight, it is understandable why Merriam felt impelled to return to it so frequently. As I noted earlier, most research today still tends to devote itself to an analysis of stationary relations rather than of historical change. Although change as brought about through revolutions—the emergence of new political movements or changing personality types[26]—has drawn the attention of some political scientists, normally the dynamics under investigation have concerned the processes of relatively stationary conditions in the political system. Historical change, which was a problem of paramount importance to the theorists of the nineteenth century, has fallen into disrepute, undoubtedly in part because of its decline by the turn of the century into remote, uninspired philosophies of history. For this reason, the identification of this image of a moving equilibrium or of aborted tendencies to equilibrium should serve to keep alive the importance of studying political change.

[26] See, for example, D. Riesman, *The Lonely Crowd* (New Haven: Yale University Press, 1950).

4. The Constitutional Equilibrium

In political research the equilibrium concept does not only imply a mode of analysis for understanding the general conditions of the political process. Quite often it occurs in a special sense to mean a constitutional equilibrium, the second major meaning mentioned at the outset. A glance at the meaning of equilibrium when it is associated with the idea of a constitutional order will serve to throw into sharper relief the theoretical implications of the notion of general equilibrium. It will at least show that in rejecting the idea of a general equilibrium as a major framework for research this need not deny the utility of the concept in other contexts.

In describing a constitutional order as one of equilibrium among contending forces political scientists have not intended to signify that this order is in a condition of equilibrium in the general sense already described. Nor for that matter do they imply even a state of disequilibrium. The fact that the system is at rest or in restless motion is not a point of primary interest. Instead, used in this sense equilibrium describes those necessary conditions for the existence of a constitutional order within a nation and of peaceful relations among nations. These conditions consist of the existence of a relatively equal distribution of power so that no one group or nation, or combination of them, can dominate over the others. Such a distribution, since it leads to mutual restraint on the part of the power groups, becomes the basis of the rule of law and freedom, both domestically and internationally. Freedom is said to depend upon the existence of an equilibrium among groups contending for power, an idea that has persistently reappeared since the days of Aristotle. In describing this condition as an equilibrium, therefore, the stress falls not on the position of rest but on the absence of a preponderance of influence over policy in the hands of any one of the participants.

Over the course of the history of political thought, the

idea of an equilibrium as the condition of a constitutional order has presented itself in many forms. At times it has appeared as the judgment that only a balance or equilibrium among social classes will permit the rule of law. Perhaps a foremost work in living memory, which received widespread recognition in the United States, was Gaetano Mosca's *The Ruling Class.*[27] In it the role of classes in maintaining a constitutional and a democratic balance is a major theme.[28] At times the proposition has been broadened to include a balance, not only among classes, but among all social groups. This kind of analysis is intimately linked with the prevalence of ethical and empirical pluralism. Where all groups are in balance, the abuse of power by any one group is thereby restrained. Furthermore, as crystallized in the classic statement in *The Federalist,* the point has been made that a social equilibrium is insufficient. A legal order rests upon a political structure in which the major organs are separated and pitted against each other in a nice balance. The procedural restraint of the separation of powers was designed to introduce an equilibrium within the legal structure.[29]

The broadest application of the notion occurs in the field of international relations. Peace, opinion often holds, depends upon an appropriate balance of power, one in which the distribution approaches the point of equality among the major combinations of nations. This differs from the proposition that all nations are in a perpetual condition of balance or process of balancing their power. We met this sense earlier. According to the earlier use, any distribution of power, if allowed to run its course without change in the power held by any nation, would tend towards a point of rest. In the present context, however, balance or international equilibrium constitutes only that distribution of power among

[27] (New York: McGraw-Hill, 1939). Edited and revised by A. Livingston.
[28] See also C. J. Friedrich, op. cit., p. 33.
[29] Ibid., p. 183; and C. E. Merriam, *Systematic Politics* (Chicago: University of Chicago Press, 1945), pp. 173-5.

nations that prevents "any one of them from becoming sufficiently strong to enforce its will upon the others." [30]

When the concept of equilibrium is used in any of these illustrated contexts it may convey two possible meanings, the first of which will be dealt with here, and the second just below. In the first sense it may mean that of all the possible equilibrium positions towards which a political system might tend, there is one that can be called the constitutional. In this state of the system, power would be distributed among the political elements in some rough degree of equality. We could argue that only in this state of the system could political freedom prevail. In this sense, therefore, the constitutional equilibrium would be a special case of the general equilibrium.

We must therefore bear in mind that even though we should conclude at the end of this discussion that something different is meant when speaking of a constitutional equilibrium than when talking of a general equilibrium, it is nonetheless possible to characterize a constitutional system as a point of equilibrium. The reason for this is that when we speak of any political interaction as displaying a tendency towards equilibrium, we mean that each element competes with all others and ultimately, if no changes in the external conditions take place, each would reach a point at which it had the most it could get under the given circumstances. Therefore, any distribution of power may have a tendency towards an equilibrium position. Ultimately some point could be reached at which no element would seek to change its relationship to other elements. In this sense, it would be possible to say that a constitutional system consists of that equilibrium which is achieved when we find power distributed in roughly equal proportions among the major elements in the system.

What brings a constitutional system into equilibrium here, however, is not the equal distribution of power but the tend-

[30] S. B. Fay, "Balance of Power," *Encyclopaedia of the Social Sciences,* Vol. 2, pp. 395-9, on p. 395.

ency of the interacting elements of the system to settle down to some sort of adjustment in which each maximizes the returns from the exercise of the power that it does hold. If power were distributed quite disproportionately this would in itself not prevent an equilibrating tendency. We might call the equilibrium arising where power is equally distributed a constitutional equilibrium, because we suspect that only under the conditions of relatively equal dispersion of power can freedom prevail. The constitutional aspect of the equilibrium refers to the way in which power is distributed at a particular moment; the equilibrium aspect refers to the tendency for movement to cease.

As an illustration, we can look at the way in which various writers who are consciously committed to describing the political system as a moment of or tendency towards equilibrium deal with the question of democracy. In most current conceptions of democracy, constitutional order is usually an important element; accordingly what is said about democracy applies as well to a constitutional system. The converse, of course, would not necessarily be true, since not all constitutional orders need be democratic.

In a logically consistent analysis of the general political equilibrium, constitutional democracy would be just a particular kind of equilibrium. In a state of equilibrium, the theoretical model could take the form of a democracy, a dictatorship, or any other variety of political system. Given the necessary pattern of power relations to begin with, the political process in the system might work itself out in such a way that once a dictatorship was achieved, none of the elements would find any inducement to alter its position. The same result holds true for a democracy.

Thus, for Catlin[31] a democracy is not distinguished by the restraint it imposes on men, although this is a factor in the process of interaction of willing individuals. Democracy is rather the most stable equilibrium of power groups. Its durability derives from the widespread diffusion of power. The point for

[31] G. E. G. Catlin, op. cit., chapters 6 and 7, and esp. pp. 206 and 262.

Catlin is that a certain kind of diffusion leads to a very stable equilibrium and this he calls democracy. Similarly, for Bentley democracy is a variety of balancing tendency, since normally he did not view the political system as being in a condition of equilibrium. Democracy for him is the kind of equilibration that leads to the predominance of "large, united weak interests upon less numerous, but relatively to the number of adherents, more intense interests." [32] With each author, democracy is only a special case of the general equilibrium or equilibrating tendency.

The work of Charles Merriam, especially, is an excellent illustration of why it is quite consistent to associate the idea of general equilibrium with the description of the ethical political system we call constitutional democracy. It is particularly appropriate to turn to his writing because, through his many years as teacher, author, and academic impressario, he has left a deep impression on political terminology and analysis. A diffusion table tracing the spread of the equilibrium concept in American political research would probably reveal him as one of its main recent sources.

His writings show a strong commitment to the idea of a general equilibrium and to the interpretation of constitutional democracy as a moment in a moving general equilibrium. His special concern for democracy exists despite the fact that during one period he was wont to say that he "was not a propagandist for a particular power pattern." [33] In fact, even though he hoped his research was always universally applicable, more frequently than not it was so shaped by his adherence to the democratic ethic that it imposed a limit to the scope of his conclusions.

Merriam interpreted the "political association," [34] or as we would say, the political process, as a mechanism for the attainment of what he variously calls an equilibrium, adjustment, harmony, accommodation, reconciliation, cohesion, *modus vivendi*,

---

[32] A. F. Bentley, op. cit., p. 454.
[33] C. E. Merriam, *Political Power*, p. 325.
[34] *Systematic Politics*, p. 8.

298 / *The Political System*

and resolution of interests. Sometimes, as earlier examples have shown, and as a reading of works by Bentley or Merriam amply illustrates, these terms are freely used as synonyms to avoid literary monotony. And yet, very often there is a slight but important difference in meaning. The difference often indicates that the author is less concerned with any kind of general equilibrium than with the conditions of equilibrium in a political system dominated by ethical rules of conduct normally associated with democracy. This interest in the equilibrium under special norms of conduct must not be permitted to mislead us into assuming at once that the author must be talking about a constitutional equilibrium as such, rather than a constitutional order as a special case of a general equilibrium.

Merriam's work is a good example. He writes as though his remarks apply to all political systems. In fact they usually refer only to systems in which democratic rules of conduct prevail, however much his illustrative material may be drawn from other ethical orders. "Significant as are the group accommodations just discussed," he writes, "the adjustments of personalities in the general framework of the social milieu are of equal meaning. If one looks objectively at government he may observe a mass of personality reconciliations which must somehow be effected. . . ."[35] Or "government arises from the necessity of adjusting the needs and desires of human beings struggling for forms of association through which human personalities may be adjusted, aided, or advanced toward higher levels of attainment."[36] Lurking between the lines of such remarks are two ideas: first, that a condition does occur when the various elements are adjusted, balanced, or in equilibrium; and second, that the balance is a product of some form of give-and-take or proportional use of capacities on the part of the participants. The second idea interests us here. It carries a concealed ethical premise. It suggests that in the political systems

[35] *Political Power,* p. 24.
[36] *Systematic Politics,* p. 1. See also his *New Aspects of Politics,* pp. vii–viii and 240.

he has in mind an ethical rule prevails which induces the various participants to yield something in order to make an equilibrium or adjustment possible.

The ethical rule of compromise is implicit in the use of such terms as reconciliation or accommodation. Each implies that the participants work out a *modus vivendi* on the basis of reciprocal concessions. To attribute the use of these synonyms to the desire for novelty in expression is too superficial a reason. Their use conceals rather that moral imperative under which the author thinks the equilibrium is achieved. It usually reflects the democratic ethos out of which the author's work arises, for Merriam is quite clear that this accommodation not only occurs but that it is desirable for it to occur.[37] A conception of equilibrium devoid of moral content to the maximum degree would suggest that whatever the moral rules governing in a political system, the elements would ultimately end in equilibrium, assuming that basic change was stabilized. The use of the alternative terms already noted suggests that the author is interested rather in the special case in which democratic moral rules govern the behavior of the members of the political system. It is an ethical order in which no member is so intransigeant as to refuse to make some concessions and to compromise for the sake of elementary peace and order.

Quite unwittingly, Merriam and others are in this way concerned with the equilibrium under the ethical rules of compromise normally associated with the democratic character. This is not inconsistent with their use of the notion of a general equilibrium, nor does it convert their thinking to a purely normative level. It is quite within the bounds of systematic causal theory to examine the way an equilibrium would be achieved, assuming that certain ethical rules sway the members of the system. The conditions of equilibrium here would be somewhat different

[37] *Prologue to Politics* (Chicago: University of Chicago Press, 1939), p. 88. Here the author adopts as his ideal what he elsewhere says political systems actually do: "States must set up and maintain a working balance between personalities, interests, and ideologies, in calm and in storm."

from those of the system in which other rules of conduct prevail. Presumably, where a political system contained authoritarian personalities in large numbers, if such persons were absolutely inflexible and unyielding in their demands, the same distribution of power as prevailed in a system governed with democratic ethical rules would nevertheless lead to a different point of equilibrium. The relative merits of the two equilibriums is of course another matter.

The work of Charles Merriam, in particular, makes it clear, therefore, that the kind of constitutional order associated with democracy, and by implication, any other kind, can be analyzed as a special case of a general equilibrium. The usefulness of such an analysis is of course circumscribed by all the handicaps associated with any kind of equilibrium research at the present juncture in political science. If the idea of constitutional equilibrium implied only a special case of equilibrium analysis, there would be little reason to devote special attention to it here. What has been said earlier would automatically apply to it too.

When political scientists refer to a constitutional order, however, they often use the idea of equilibrium in a second sense, as I have intimated.[38] Usually they do not intend to imply that the system is at or tends to a point of rest. What they usually seek to bring out is the fact that freedom is possible only where power is not concentrated in one or a few of the political elements in a system. They are not necessarily implying a framework for analyzing the relationship among the elements of the system. They are not asserting that authoritative policy takes its shape from the fact that the elements are mutually dependent and tend to act and react on each other until a position of rest is achieved, assuming that the system could work itself out. Rather, they are describing certain factual conditions: where the elements of the system are pitted against one another so neatly that no one element is able to act solely in the light of its own interpretation

[38] See p. 295.

of what is desirable under the circumstances, there freedom is possible.

It is for this reason that democracy, being viewed as a type of constitutional order, is often depicted as a political system in which the various elements exercise a mutual restraint, designated also as an equilibrium. A student of the balance of power in general, in referring implicitly to his own idea of democracy, writes: "It follows that the great desideratum is the achievement of an approximate, even if ever-changing, equilibrium among the conflicting institutions. Strife is accepted as normal . . . as a social good. It denies to any institution the power completely to destroy other institutions, therefore putting a limit upon its ambitions to secure the absolute dominion and absolute peace, which is here identified with tyranny." [39] Similarly, in his search for the characteristics of the political process, Childs identifies the political problem, obviously meaning the democratic problem, as the discovery of the way "to preserve an equitable balance among the numerous organized forces" [40] and "to harmonize group desires fairly." [41] The assumption is that all people and groups do or should count equally or proportionately, depending on one's view of justice, in forming policy and that a device for limiting the power of any one group in the process will achieve this goal or is the basis upon which the goal has already been achieved. Equilibrium refers here to the equitable (usually conceived of as roughly equal) distribution of power which makes democracy possible.

Logically, there would be nothing to prevent a research worker from collecting the data to show that any existing democracy does consist of a constitutional equilibrium, that is, of an equal distribution of power. In practice a few do. By far the

[39] F. Tannenbaum, "Balance of Power in Society," 61 *Political Science Quarterly* (1946), 481-504, on p. 500.

[40] H. L. Childs, *Labor and Capital in National Politics*, p. 178.

[41] Ibid., p. 181. See also E. E. Schattschneider, *Politics, Pressures and the Tariff*, p. 288, where he speaks of the need, in the face of unbalanced interest groups "to preserve an equilibrium in many cases."

vast majority, however, associate the notion of constitutional democracy with democracy as a goal imperfectly achieved in practice. We hear more about the conditions of mutual restraint on
power which theorists would like to see prevail than about an unambiguously factual description of democracy in these terms.
Schattschneider, in his *Politics, Pressures and the Tariff,* shows
how social scientists often let their values crowd out the facts.
Here he indicates in a minute way, seldom duplicated since, how
the actual power exerted on governmental agencies is unequally
distributed to the disadvantage of the broader mass of the people.
On the other hand, if the conditions of a mutual restraint among
equally powerful combinations of groups actually did prevail in
any political system, the concept of constitutional equilibrium
would, of course, validly describe such a condition. However,
since the practices of most democracies in history have only imperfectly fitted this description, the notion more often expresses
an ideal than a fact.

It is clear, therefore, that to describe either an ideal or an
existing democracy as a constitutional equilibrium, something
quite different may be and often is meant from a moment of
equilibrium in the earlier sense of the word. This is why the idea
of constitutional equilibrium has been chosen for special attention. It conveys the notion that only under conditions where
power is spread throughout the system so that each element is restrained by other elements can an equilibrium be achieved. Equilibrium here means not a state of rest but a condition where
power is so widely dispersed that each element must vie with
the others to influence policy, and in the process the restraint
exercised by each upon the others permits the existence of political freedom. In this context, a political system is said to be in
equilibrium when there is some kind of equality in the distribution of power, either among social classes, groups, or nations, or
in the political structure, so that no one group can use its power
without inhibition or limitation. In the light of our discussion
of the general equilibrium, as I have said, the equal balance

might conceivably be the point of general equilibrium in the whole system, but this is not necessarily nor customarily implied when the concept is used to depict a condition of constitutional order. Sometimes, however, the concept is used in such a way that it lends itself to both interpretations simultaneously.

The constitutional sense of the equilibrium concept has few theoretical implications. It raises, rather, certain empirical questions about the truth or falsity of the following narrow-gauge generalization: there is an invariant relation between constitutional order and freedom on the one hand, and the mutual restraint and limitation flowing from a relatively equal distribution of power, on the other.

This insight of numerous profound political theorists over the centuries is not, of course, free from doubt. The data are so indecisive that as valid a case might be made for a contrary generalization. Where strong combinations of groups, relatively equal in strength, have each been poised against the other, this has usually been a sign of the threatened disintegration of the going political system with its conversion into a new order or with its complete disappearance. The fact that in Athens during the fifth century B.C., classes were relatively equally weighted, for instance, ultimately helped, because of irreconcilable internal dissension, to lead to the collapse of the city. Similarly, in the international order today we have ample proof that the more closely combinations of nations approach equality in power, the less likely a constitutional or a peaceful order will obtain.

In contrast to what is now the almost axiomatic proposition that equality in power generates restraint, it might be suggested that equality leads rather to fear, semiparalysis in the resolution of important inter-group differences, and ultimately to the appeal to violence to settle an impossible situation. The experience within nations might even be cited in evidence. In the contemporary American political system, there has been considerable fear expressed, temporarily allayed by the Second World War and now to a lesser extent by the cold war, that the growth of powerful interest groups might so divide society and so restrain each group in the desire to take action that the continuation of the very community might as a result be at stake.

It helps little to add Montesquieu's often-forgotten qualification that the balance in the governmental structure called the separation of powers and presumably the substantive balance among social groups can be successfully maintained only under conditions of agreement on fundamentals in the community. Indeed, if we argue that agreement on fundamentals is a prerequisite for division about lesser problems, we destroy the very notion that a true relation exists between roughly equal dispersion of power as a restraining mechanism and constitutional order. Where there is unity on fundamentals, this is evidence of the existence of the united effective power of the bulk of the community behind these fundamentals, whatever they may be. It is conceivable that a constitutional order may depend as much on the united power behind one set of fundamentals as on divided powers each tilting against the other. Competition among social groups may be tolerable only because the power of all groups is unitedly behind constitutional processes; constitutional order may be a function of unified power, not of equilibrium among groups.

I am not concluding that freedom necessarily depends on the preponderance of power in the hands of a combination of social groups so great that it will not fear to tolerate dissenters. The suggestion only is that on the basis of the available data this hypothesis is as plausible as that of constitutional equilibrium through power equality. It is a conclusion that serves to bring out the fact that because the conception of constitutional equilibrium raises essentially factual questions, it applies to a range of problems separate and distinct from the idea of a general equilibrium as a mode of analysis. While the latter may have limited value in political research today, we must bear in mind the suggestive hypothesis associated with the substantially different function of the same term in the idea of a constitutional equilibrium. For this reason it is important to distinguish clearly the sense in which the term is being used.

It is not always easy to determine the meaning. It is obvious, however, that although the word may remain the same, its intention differs markedly depending upon the context. The similarity of expression ought not to mislead us. If it is necessary at present to discard the idea of a general equilibrium as a conceptual framework because of the lack of sufficient measurable data, we must be careful not to destroy at the same time the unassociated idea of mutual power limitation also implicit in the same word. In this sense the concept of equilibrium can be used without raising the problem of quantification; it can remain as a goal or standard against which the achievement of any existing democracy in limiting power can be tested or as a description of the conditions necessary for one possible interpretation of democracy.

In conclusion it may be said that because of the apparent limitations of the general equilibrium as a concept, we are compelled to the opinion that its ultimate value can lie only in the very fact of its inadequacy for a systematic political theory. We would, of course, be in a much stronger position if, in the shadows of empirical research, we could find concealed the outlines of a viable conceptual framework. But lacking that, the next best thing is at least the discovery of some sort of theory, whatever its inadequacies. This may sound like a deliberate and perverse invitation to error. But the truth is that, like all other learning, theoretical development takes place through trial and error. A poor theory is better than none at all, first, because it at least shows us the paths that ought not to be taken. This is no mean accomplishment. Indirectly the underlying equilibrium theory suggests that political science ought to search in other directions for a satisfactory framework in which analysis would rest primarily on qualitative rather than quantitative description. Second, no theory is so inadequate that it does not leave some positive, helpful residue for subsequent research. The idea of a general equilibrium implicit in so much empirical work in political science, as I have already suggested, can help to perpetuate the notion that political activity is part of an empirical system and of a process of change through time. These are insights which future attempts at theory construction can scarcely neglect.

Chapter 12

The Rejuvenation of Political Theory

> *. . . an attempt to fashion a tool.*
> Arthur F. Bentley

PERHAPS the most surprising feature about the equilibrium concept is not the inadequacies of the general theory that it suggests; it is rather the fact that political scientists have shown little awareness of the presence of such a theory in the recesses of their work. If political science had entirely shunned theoretical inquiry, this neglect of the equilibrium idea would have been understandable. But even though in practice the development of a conceptual framework has received very little attention, one field of political research, political theory, is devoted exclusively to theoretical research. The existence of such a field more than justifies our asking why political theory as we know it today has contributed so little to the development of systematic theory.

From what I have already said, it is clear that contemporary political theory is not particularly concerned with empirically oriented theory. Indeed, if anything, it conceives of itself as primarily a moral enterprise, interested particularly in the history of moral ideals. While it is not considered improper to pass judgment on the validity of statements of facts, nevertheless this is secondary and incidental to the historical interpretation of moral views.

Because of this heavy emphasis on the history of moral views, a strange relation has developed between political theory and the empirical part of political science. Nominally they appear to be part of the same discipline; in practice they have become almost entirely independent. Nominally, most students who are committed to empirical research are willing to accept in a very general way the need to consider the alternative moral purposes for which their research might be used; and most political theorists today are equally ready to recognize the need to know how people act in actual situations. In practice, however, neither the empirical nor the moral research worker will go far beyond mere tolerance of the other. Each is equally imperialistic in seeking to convert almost the whole of political science to his own interests. The result is that empirical and moral research workers find difficulty in understanding each other and, what is even more disastrous, find little use for each other's research. Although they are members of the same discipline, their work, in practice, has little relationship.

In spite of this uneasy and tenuous connection between empirical research and moral inquiry, however, many political scientists continue to support the claim that political theory is the central subject matter of political science, the one field, if any, that can give it a sense of unity. This feeling is reflected in the curricula of many universities, for example, where in graduate training political theory is the one field, among a possible six or seven in political science, that is required of all students. In face of the manifest remote connection between current theory and the rest of political science, the feeling has strangely managed to persist that the study of theory helps to provide a common core of knowledge and a unifying framework for all political research.

In part, this feeling is the child of a wish rather than an inference from facts. Acutely aware of the lack of a common frame of reference, political scientists tend to fall back on political theory as a last resort, with the hope that the unity of their discipline might be found there. Historicism has continued to thwart this hope. In part, however, this feeling stems from a sound instinct about the potentialities within traditional theory which even historicism cannot entirely conceal or destroy. The great political theories of the past reveal these inherent potentialities. If we examine the general characteristics of these theories we shall be able to appreciate why the contemporary ineradicable instinct about the place of political theory in research is well founded. Furthermore, an analysis of the general nature of the great theories should help to show how modern theory can once again be securely linked to the main body of political research.

1. The Task of Political Theory

If we divest ourselves of historicist preconceptions about the appropriate way to study the great theories, we shall be in a position to appreciate why political theory is central for the development of reliable political knowledge. A non-historicist approach reveals that in earlier times political theory did not confine itself exclusively or even primarily to moral inquiry or historical interpretation. On the contrary, the great theories sought to embrace the whole of political life. The conception of political theory as a predominantly moral enterprise is of very recent vintage. In the past such theory dealt with all the fundamental problems of political life: with questions about the nature and determinants of political activity, about the goals towards which people ought to act and about the method and techniques for conducting political research. The most cursory examination of political inquiry as early as that of Aristotle or as late as that of John Stuart Mill would indicate that problems such as these fall within the ambit of the great theories.

Thus, although it is true that these theories have always shown a strong concern for the goals of political life, we would be seriously misled about the characteristics of a political theory if we did not recognize that in practice it offered insights into actual political relations. Indeed, there are few political theories which do not go considerably further and offer at least a latent, empirically oriented theory of major proportions. The reason for this is that, as we saw, a theory cannot deal only with values even if the theorist so desired. Values can be explored only in relation to factual conditions. And where profound minds have been directed to things as they exist, it is almost inevitable that in their search for reliable propositions about such things, they should seek to phrase their thought at the most abstract level. In this sense, every theory includes some insights about a possible conceptual framework for the study of the political system.

If we examine closely the components of a political theory, the presence not only of value theory but also of insights with regard to empirically oriented theory becomes quite evident.[1] A political theory consists of four major kinds of propositions: factual, moral, applied, and theoretical. Strictly speaking, we ought to say that these are several logical aspects of propositions since no statement can ever refer exclusively to facts, values, or theories. Each aspect of a proposition is usually involved with one or more of the others. But since this is incidental to our main purpose, we can speak as though what is separable in logic is also separable in practice.

If we look at the most obvious and general characteristic of a political theory, we see that the latter refers not solely to what is but to the state of affairs men would like to see

[1] The relation of political theory to political research has periodically drawn the attention of political theorists; see, for example, W. W. Willoughby, "The Value of Political Philosophy"; G. H. Sabine, "What Is a Political Theory"; and J. R. Pennock, "Political Science and Political Philosophy," 45 *American Political Science Review* (1951), 1081-5.

come into existence. Every theory is consciously oriented to values. Even if pure moral discourse were possible, however, it is clear that a political theory is never an exercise in pure axiology. In the first place, at the base of each theory there are certain propositions describing factual circumstances, either contemporary or historical. The presence of such factual propositions need not detain us long, for no one would deny their existence in a theory. They allege that certain events occurred at stated times and places or that given political circumstances have existed. Facts such as these can be verified in the same way as any other historical facts.

In the second place, each theory implies the choice of a constellation of values which the political theorist uses as criteria to appraise the structure and practices through which social policy is made. Today there is such a disproportionate emphasis on this aspect that we need not dwell on it any longer. In the third place, these value-oriented propositions of a theory also imply that the means advocated by the theorist for realizing his values will be adequate for the attainment of the kind of political system he prefers. These propositions deal with the application of knowledge for the realization of ends. In order to demonstrate that a selected means will be hospitable to given ends, however, the theorist must assume that he can show a universal, that is, highly probable, connection between the means he would use and the ends he desires. As we saw earlier, in order to prove that the use of means B will achieve the goal A, there must be an assumption that, under the given conditions, whenever B occurs, it is more probable rather than less that A will follow. Otherwise there would be no reasonable assurance that the advocacy of the given means would produce the desired results. In effect, then, the theorist must be assuming the existence and validity of still another kind of proposition, namely, some generalized or causal statement about the relations of facts. Only on the basis of this causal theory is he able to specify with some assurance how his goals can be achieved.

To illustrate concretely that a political theory is composed of this variety of propositions we can turn for a moment to Locke in his second treatise *Of Civil Government*. There can be no question that Locke makes observations of political facts that rest on his knowledge of history and of his own time, and, therefore, we do not need to dwell on the factual statements. Similarly, the presence of a value theory is beyond question. The very concept of natural law and derivative natural rights in which Locke's reasoning, like that of his age is imbedded, indicates the existence in this treatise of moral theory. But what is not always so clearly discerned or understood is that if Locke was to show the best way of organizing a political system for the pursuit of a moral life, he was compelled to make certain implicit assumptions in the realm of causal theory. Having claimed to show that a given means would produce a specified result, such as the preservation of one's natural rights, he could have proved this, if called upon, only by asserting a universal connection between relevant facts.

At one point, for example, he says that to obtain a political system that will secure men in their natural rights the legislative must be separated from the executive power. But to have any reliability for this applied principle, Locke must be assuming that, if called upon, he could prove that such a minimum "separation" of powers does prevent the abuse of authority. Presumably, he might turn to the whole constitutional history of England, culminating in the Whig revolution, as evidence for the validity of this assumption. But the assumption that there is an invariant relation between the division of powers and the impartial formulation and execution of the laws is nothing less than a narrow-gauge causal theory.[2] This implicit theory stands out sharply in Locke's own words, even though the statement is cast in the form of an application of knowledge. "And because it may be too great temptation to human frailty, apt to grasp at power, for the same persons who have the power of mak-

[2] For this term see again chapter 2.

ing laws to have also in their hands the power to execute them, whereby they may exempt themselves from obedience to the laws they make, and suit the law, both in its making and execution, on their own private advantage, and thereby come to have a distinct interest from the rest of the community, contrary to the end of society and government." [3] This is clearly a seventeenth-century way of saying that there is an invariant relation between constitutionalism and the structure of political institutions. Although the analysis would take us too far astray from our main purposes, it could be shown that underlying the applied and empirical aspects of Locke's treatise there are certain theoretical assumptions about the nature of the political system as a whole. There are insights in the work that could be tapped as an aid to inquiry into systematic theory. And what is true of Locke's work applies equally to any political theory. Every such theory consists of this variety of propositions: factual, moral, applied, and theoretical.

When properly viewed, therefore, the great political theories of the past are not simply inquiries into desirable political conditions of living. They correspond, at the level of knowledge and skill then available, to what we know today as political science. The thoughtful, so-called political theorists were in fact total social scientists who, knowing no division of labor, felt free to explore every aspect of political life. In narrowing the study of the political thoughts of these earlier social philosophers to a reporting of their moral wisdom, contemporary political theory has helped to conceal from the rest of political science valuable resources for an understanding of causal theory, particularly of alternative conceptual frameworks. Clearly, the wisdom of the great social theorists needs to be scrutinized for its insights about general political theories. In neglecting this task almost entirely, contemporary political theory has thereby contributed directly to the negligible role that constructive theoretical inquiry, in its causal as well as its moral aspects, has played in American political science.

[3] John Locke, (Second Essay) *Of Civil Government*, chapter 12.

The study of political theory today, therefore, has at its hand the subject matter for an inquiry into systematic theory. If it is to exploit fully the potentialities within its subject matter and if it is to carry out the promise implicit in its designation as the theoretical field within political science, I am suggesting that it ought to devote itself to analyzing and constructively formulating causal as well as moral theory. In this way political theory would once again be central to an understanding of political life; it would become a meaningful instrument of research for all political scientists.

2. The Autonomy of Theoretical Research

Inquiry into moral theory cannot be assigned to a separate compartment for research. It invariably requires knowledge about the facts of political life. Accordingly in engaging in constructive theoretical research a political theorist would be compelled to devote attention to causal as well as moral theory. As far as the empirically oriented aspect of theoretical research is concerned, however, a word of caution must be introduced at this point.

The complaint is sometimes heard that where highly general social theory is discussed, as in sociology, the results have usually been too abstract for immediate application to the facts.[4] We sometimes hear that theoretical formulations tend to become so generalized that it is difficult, if not impossible, to reduce the theoretical statements to propositions that can be tested by early reference to the facts. The apparently strange part about this

---

[4] See, for example, R. K. Merton, *Social Theory and Social Structure,* chapters 2 and 3. For the relation between theory and empirical research see as well S. A. Stouffer, "Some Afterthoughts of a Contributor to 'The American Soldier' "; and D. Riesman, "Some Observations on Social Science Research," 11 *Antioch Review* (1951), 259-78; and A. de Grazia, "The Process of Theory-Research Interaction," 13 *Journal of Politics* (1951), 88-99.

accusation is not only that it is perfectly true but that if it were otherwise theory would not be offering itself enough latitude for development. Once theoretical inquiry is undertaken, it may well become caught up in a logical momentum of its own, in which initially the main effort centers in obtaining theoretical insights that some day may be reformulated in verifiable terms. Theoretical insight would be too narrowly inhibited if it had to direct its attention at the outset towards immediately verifiable generalization.

I do not mean to maintain, of course, that the ultimate usefulness of a general theory rests upon anything other than its correspondence with political facts. But we must be perfectly aware of what this paramount need for empirical verification does or does not imply for theoretical inquiry. It does not mean that at every stage in theoretical work we must be able to test our generalizations immediately or to cast them into operational form. On the contrary, at a high level of abstraction, theory needs to be free to develop unhampered by excessive worries of verification; in much the same way mathematical physics, for example, may so far outstrip the realm of possibility that no visible connection between the theory and the facts may at once be apparent. There is an area and a time, in other words, when we may wish to pursue the logic of a theory and its postulates for their own sake. To demand that a theory be actually verifiable at each stage of its development would impose on it an unnecessarily severe burden. All that we need demand of theoretical research is that in *principle* we are able to test it by reference to sensory data. It would be a separable and continuing task to translate theoretical propositions into verifiable form. Of course, to the extent that we could never reduce a theory to terms of research it would thereby have proved itself inadequate.

Thus, while it is true that we ought to be able to state a theory in operational terms, this is the ultimate goal, not the starting point. As a consequence, we ought not to expect that any attempt to formulate analytic tools for an understanding of the political system need immediately lend itself to verification. In some attempts it might be a separate and difficult task to remold any emerging theory so that it could be verified; in the process the theory itself, unless it were miraculously valid for all time, would undergo necessary modifications.

This is the experience, for example, not only in the physical sciences, such as chemistry and physics, but in economics. For over a century economics has dealt with economic activity in systemic terms. The idea of an economic *system* has even become part of lay vocabulary. For the most part, economic theory has followed an autonomous pattern, without being unduly concerned with rigorous empirical verification.

By a chain of logical deductions from a few assumptions, economists have arrived at a body of principles which constitutes the bulk of theoretical economics. Important among these postulates are two: that men are governed by monetary rewards and punishments and that such resources as labor and capital are mobile enough to shift readily from one employment or investment to another.[5] These postulates are not devoid of empirical relevance, but it is clear they can at most only approximate economic reality. From these and other postulates, introduced as the occasion has seemed to require, a body of general economic theory has developed. For the most part economists have been able to weight these theories with obvious empirical implications. But few really persistent attempts have been made to subject the theories to rigorous comparison with the facts. Indeed, within the last quarter of a century, the realization has emerged that ultimately general theory must be anchored more securely in the fact of economic activity. It has led to the plea for empirical studies to test, for example, just how businessmen and consumers do arrive at decisions to save and spend, or to discover whether

---

[5] See R. T. Bye, "The Inductive Testing of an Economic Deduction," in Social Science Research Council, Committee on Scientific Method in the Social Sciences, *Methods in the Social Sciences* (ed. S. A. Rice) (Chicago: University of Chicago Press, 1931).

the concepts of marginal producer and representative firm do represent factual cases.[6]

We could argue that economic theory has strayed too far and for too long from efforts to test its own propositions against actual economic processes. Whatever the truth might be, it would not amount to an argument against the autonomy, for certain purposes, of theoretical speculation in economics. It would simply indicate that the economists had tended to neglect unduly the separate, although equally vital, task of translating their propositions into verifiable form. In political science this problem has not yet emerged, of course, since there is little consciousness of the need to develop theory. We could expect, however, that if political theory as an area of research should measure up to its tasks, any initial attempts at systematic theory, while empirically relevant, would nonetheless not necessarily be readily reducible to verifiable propositions.

3. Conclusion

In drawing this discussion to a close, the burden of the argument can be stated very simply. The attainment of reliable knowledge about political life, I have suggested, depends upon the development of the kind of analytical tool we call a conceptual framework. This is forced upon us not by any emotional attachment to a dogma called scientific method but only because good reasoning demands it. Every factual investigation of political activity turns to a few out of a variety of possible variables or kinds of political relations. Rational research requires that we set up criteria by which to judge the importance of any particular variable for understanding political life. Otherwise, there would be no device for determining why a person should engage in one kind of research rather than another.

A general theory provides just such a set of criteria. It seeks to identify the major variables significant for an understanding of

[6] Ibid.

political life and to show their most important relations. It thereby provides some test for determining the significance of any piece of empirical research towards an understanding of the whole of political life; the empirical investigation, in turn, contributes to the continuing task of improving the correspondence to reality of any existing theory.

It has been my purpose to adumbrate some of the problems which political science must face in undertaking the development of systematic theory. The construction of such theory is obviously not the work of a day or even of a generation of political scientists; it is the continuing obligation of all political research. But some of the problems are vividly apparent at this stage and of these I have examined a few.

I have suggested that the development of theory depends upon the way in which we approach political activity viewed as a body of related phenomena. If we deny the possibility of abstracting from the whole of concrete interrelated social activity an aspect which we can identify as political, then clearly there would be no basis for probing further into a general political theory. Inquiry did reveal, however, that we can isolate a part of social reality for separate analytic treatment and that this is an aspect of social life for which political scientists have in fact traditionally assumed special responsibility. At the minimum, political scientists have implicitly developed a common interest through the fact that they have been exploring the way in which values are authoritatively allocated for a society. Concretely, this means that it is possible to identify a broad variety of structures and practices which are closely associated with the authoritative allocation of values for a society. Collectively these activities can be called the empirical political system. Corresponding to the latter, for purposes of research it is desirable to construct an analytic framework composed of concepts identifying the major political variables and their possible relations. This would constitute the analytic or theoretical system.

Whatever form such a systematic theory should take, two

aspects of it have seemed exceedingly clear at this stage. In the first place, such a theory would be compelled to specify the varieties of data involved in the analysis of any political relations. At the broadest level we would wish to know what varieties of data contribute to an exhaustive description of the determinants and the functioning of social policy. Such knowledge would provide some sure clue to inform the investigator when his research had exploited all relevant types of data. And in the second place, as we saw, a general theory would be compelled to provide categories for examining the moral premises out of which the theory itself emerged. In this way, it could introduce a self-correcting mechanism to reduce error caused by the limitations imposed by the research worker's moral outlook.

Other questions critical for the development of a conceptual framework might have been examined. Since the political system consists of all those interacting elements which contribute to the authoritative allocation of values, we might have inquired into the minimum tasks which any political system must fulfill if it is to function at all. We might have begun with the hypothesis that the very existence of any concrete political system demands that certain basic needs or functions be met. If we could have identified these functions, we might then have proceeded to discuss the various kinds of regularized patterns of activity that have emerged, at any time and place, as mechanisms to fulfill these tasks.

The fruitfulness of this approach is suggested by its implications for the comparative study of political institutions. Given the discovery of similar or identical tasks in every political system, contemporary or historical, it would be possible to examine comparatively the way in which these institutions fulfill the same tasks under the differing conditions of each political system. Political science would then be in a position to draw generalizations that pass beyond the experience of any one political system or of the systems in any one culture or civilization.

This would lead, for example, to two immediately visible

consequences in the study of political phenomena. In the first place, comparative government would find itself in need of drastic re-examination. As comparative government is known today in political science, it seldom passes far beyond the level of pure description of the institutions and practices of individual political systems. The comparisons remain largely at the descriptive level. The approach suggested here could lead to comparisons with theoretical significance. And in the second place, the serious bias in contemporary political research towards the study of stationary conditions could be remedied. The development of analytic tools of the character intimated here would make it possible to contrast the same political systems over periods of time, thereby illuminating the determinants of political change.

It is clear, however, that had we undertaken to speak about these problems we would have been carried far beyond the avowed limits of this work. We would have been compelled to engage in what is undoubtedly the supremely engrossing task of actually undertaking to formulate a tentative theory. It has seemed wiser, however, to express first the ground for thinking that the development of any theory is an urgent task confronting political science today, rather than to undertake here the logical outgrowth of such a belief. My remarks consequently have been largely hortative and exploratory. Some suggestions with regard to the substance of a theory do of course emerge; without descending into totally abstract and arid analysis, it is impossible to discuss the method of research without supporting the inquiry by reference to substance. But for purposes of the discussion here, such references are incidental, however contentious they may be with regard to a possible theoretical framework. They do indicate, however, that without some thought about the nature of such a framework and indeed a preliminary image of it in mind, the present discussion of the need for political science to devote a share of its resources to this matter could and would not have been undertaken. A preliminary formulation of such a theory is, however, the task for a separate study.

Epilogue to Second Edition

The New Revolution in

Political Science

A NEW revolution is under way in American political science. The last revolution—behavioralism—has scarcely been completed before it has been overtaken by the increasing social and political crises of our time. The weight of these crises is being felt within our discipline in the form of a new conflict in the throes of which we now find ourselves. This new and latest challenge is directed against a developing behavioral orthodoxy. This challenge I shall call the post-behavioral revolution.

The initial impulse of this revolution is just being felt. Its battle cries are *relevance* and *action*. Its objects of criticism are the disciplines, the professions, and the universities. It is still too young to be described definitively. Yet we cannot treat it as a passing phenomenon, as a kind of accident of history that will somehow fade away and leave us very much as we were before. Rather it appears to be a specific and important episode in the history of our discipline, if not in all of the social sciences. It behooves us to examine this revolution closely for its possible place in the continu-

Presidential Address delivered to the 65th Annual Meeting of the American Political Science Association, September 2–6, 1969. New York City. Reprinted by permission from THE AMERICAN POLITICAL SCIENCE REVIEW, Vol. LXIII, No. 4, December, 1969.

ing evolution of political science. Does it represent a threat to the discipline, one that will divert us from our long history in the search for reliable understanding of politics? Or is it just one more change that will enhance our capacity to find such knowledge?

1. *Nature of the Post-Behavioral Revolution*

The essence of the post-behavioral revolution is not hard to identify. It consists of a deep dissatisfaction with political research and teaching, especially of the kind that is striving to convert the study of politics into a more rigorously scientific discipline modelled on the methodology of the natural sciences. Although the post-behavioral revolution may have all the appearances of just another reaction to behavioralism, it is in fact notably different. Hitherto resistance to the incorporation of scientific method has come in the form of an appeal to the past—to classical political science, such as natural law, or to the more loosely conceived non-methodology of traditional research. Behavioralism was viewed as a threat to the status quo; classicism and traditionalism were responses calculated to preserve some part of what had been, by denying the very possibility of a science of politics.

The post-behavioral revolution is, however, future oriented. It does not especially seek to return to some golden age of political research or to conserve or even to destroy a particular methodological approach. It does not require an adherent to deny the possibility of discovering testable generalizations about human behavior. It seeks rather to propel political science in new directions. In much the same way, behavioralism in the 50s, by adopting a new technology, sought to add to rather than to deny our heritage. This new development is then a genuine revolution, not a reaction, a becoming, not a preservation, a reform, not a counter-reformation.

Post-behavioralism is both a movement, that is, an aggregate of people, and an intellectual tendency. As a movement it has many of the diffuse, unstable, even prickly qualities that the behavioral revolution itself once had in its own youth. It would be a serious mistake, indeed, a grave injustice, to confuse this broad, inchoate movement with any organized group either inside or outside the profession. Nor ought we to attribute any special political color to post-behavioralists in the aggregate. They range widely, from conservatism to the active left. Nor has this movement any particular methodological commitments. It embraces rigorous scientists as well as dedicated classicists. Neither does it appeal to any one age group alone. Its adherents include all the generations, from young graduate students to older members of the profession. This whole improbable diversity—political, methodological, and generational—is bound together by one sentiment alone, a deep discontent with the direction of contemporary political research.

Even though today the organized cleavages within our profession are writing most of the dramatic scenarios, in the end these cleavages may prove to be the least interesting part of what is happening. What will undoubtedly have far deeper meaning for us is the broader intellectual tendency that provides the environment within which current divisions have taken shape. It is on the purely intellectual components of post-behavioralism, therefore, that I shall focus.

New as post-behavioralism is, the tenets of its faith have already emerged clearly enough to be identifiable. They form what could be called a Credo of Relevance.[1] I would describe the tenets of this post-behavioral credo as follows:

1. Substance must precede technique. If one *must* be sacrificed for the other—and this need not always be so—it is more important to be relevant and meaningful for contemporary urgent social problems than to be sophisticated in the tools of investigation. For the aphorism of science that it is better to be wrong than vague, post-behavioralism would substitute a new dictum, that it is better to be vague than non-relevantly precise.

---

[1] Compare with the Credo of Behavioralism as described in D. Easton, *A Framework for Political Analysis* (Englewood Cliffs, N.J.: Prentice-Hall, 1965), p. 7.

2. Behavioral science conceals an ideology of empirical conservatism. To confine oneself exclusively to the description and analysis of facts is to hamper the understanding of these same facts in their broadest context. As a result empirical political science must lend its support to the maintenance of the very factual conditions it explores. It unwittingly purveys an ideology of social conservatism tempered by modest incremental change.

3. Behavioral research must lose touch with reality. The heart of behavioral inquiry is abstraction and analysis and this serves to conceal the brute realities of politics. The task of postbehavioralism is to break the barriers of silence that behavioral language necessarily has created and to help political science reach out to the real needs of mankind in a time of crisis.

4. Research about and constructive development of values are inextinguishable parts of the study of politics. Science cannot be and never has been evaluatively neutral despite protestations to the contrary. Hence to understand the limits of our knowledge we need to be aware of the value premises on which it stands and the alternatives for which this knowledge could be used.

5. Members of a learned discipline bear the responsibilities of all intellectuals. The intellectuals' historical role has been and must be to protect the humane values of civilization. This is their unique task and obligation. Without this they become mere technicians, mechanics for tinkering with society. They thereby abandon the special privileges they have come to claim for themselves in academia, such as freedom of inquiry and a quasi-extraterritorial protection from the onslaughts of society.

6. To know is to bear the responsibility for acting and to act is to engage in reshaping society. The intellectual as scientist bears the special obligation to put his knowledge to work. Contemplative science was a product of the nineteenth century when a broader moral agreement was shared. Action science of necessity reflects the contemporary conflict in society over ideals and this must permeate and color the whole research enterprise itself.

7. If the intellectual has the obligation to implement his

knowledge, those organizations composed of intellectuals—the professional associations—and the universities themselves, cannot stand apart from the struggles of the day. Politicization of the professions is inescapable as well as desirable.

No one post-behavioralist would share all these views. I have presented only a distillation of the maximal image. It represents perhaps a Weberian ideal type of the challenges to behavioralism. As such the credo brings out most of the salient features of the post-behavioral revolution as it appears to be taking shape today.

2. Shifting Images of Science

What has this developing new image of political science to offer us? In the United States behavioralism has without doubt represented the dominant approach in the last decade. Will post-behavioralism destroy the undeniable gains of the behavioral revolution or is post-behavioralism only a valuable addition that can and should be incorporated into our practices?

One thing is clear. In a rapidly changing world surely political science alone cannot claim to have completed its development. Only on the assumption that behavioral political science has said the last word about what makes for adequate research and an appropriate discipline can we automatically read out of court any proposals for change.

The history of the various theoretical sciences, like physics and chemistry, reveals that every discipline rests on certain fundamental assumptions. It is a captive of what has been described as a research paradigm.[2] Over the years political science has been no less prone to develop models of what constitutes a good discipline or adequate research, and these models have undergone marked transformations.

[2] T. S. Kuhn, *The Structure of Scientific Revolutions* (Chicago: University of Chicago Press, 1962).

The behavioral model of this century has been but the last in a long chain. It has shifted the balance of concern from prescription, ethical inquiry, and action to description, explanation, and verification. Behavioralism has justified this shift on the grounds that without the accumulation of reliable knowledge, the means for the achievement of goals would be so uncertain as to convert action into a futile game. The growing success of the scientific enterprise in political science cannot be denied.

New conditions of the modern world, however, force us to reconsider our image of what we want to be. Scientific progress is slow, and however more reliable our limited knowledge about politics has become in the last fifty years, social crises of unforeseen proportions are upon us. Fear of the nuclear bomb, mounting internal cleavages in the United States in which civil war and authoritarian rule have become frightening possibilities, an undeclared war in Vietnam that violates the moral conscience of the world, these are continuing conditions entirely unpredicted by political science, behavioral or otherwise. The search for an answer as to how we as political scientists have proved so disappointingly ineffectual in anticipating the world of the 1960s has contributed significantly to the birth of the post-behavioral revolution.

In this perspective the legitimacy of raising doubts about the adequacy or relevance of political science in the contemporary world of crises cannot be questioned. We can join the post-behavioral movement at least in asking: Must we be committed eternally to an unchanging image of the discipline, behavioral or otherwise? Is it not incumbent on us to take account of changing conditions and to be ready and willing to reconsider old images and modify them to the extent deemed necessary? Must political science continue to do what it has been doing over the last few decades, in the hope that some "normal" period will one day return in which time will be on the side of those who seek to develop a more reliable understanding of political processes?

The negative answer that many individuals from all generations of political scientists are giving is clear. One of the probable underlying reasons for this answer we can readily understand. Mankind today is working under the pressure of time. Time is no longer on our side. This in itself is a frightening new event in world affairs. An apocalyptic weapon, an equally devastating population explosion, dangerous pollution of the environment, and, in the United States, severe internal dissension of racial and economic origin, all move in the same direction. They move toward increasing social conflict and deepening fears and anxieties about the future, not of a generation or of a nation, but of the human race itself. Confronting this cataclysmic possibility is a knowledge of the enormous wealth and technical resources currently available in a few favored regions of the world, the spectacular rate of increase in man's material inventiveness and technology, and the rich potential just on the horizon for understanding social and political processes. The agony of the present social crisis is this contrast between our desperate condition and our visible promise, if we but had the time.

In the face of a human situation such as this, the postbehavioral movement in political science (and in the other social sciences simultaneously) is presenting us with a new image of our discipline and the obligations of our profession. It pleads for more relevant research. It pleads for an orientation to the world that will encourage political scientists, even in their professional capacity, to prescribe and to act so as to improve political life according to humane criteria.

We can respond by refusing to budge, much as the classicists and traditionalists once did in the face of the onslaught of the behavioralists. Or we can recognize the need for change and explore the best ways of reconstructing our conception of our discipline and of the related professional institutions of which we are part. It is the second course that I propose we consider.

3. The Ideal Commitments of Political Science

A decision to contemplate revising the image of our discipline and profession places the political scientist in a strange and difficult predicament. Fierce pressures are building up for solutions to immediate problems. Yet the nature of basic research is to shift the focus away from current concerns and to delay the application of knowledge until we are more secure about its reliability.

This dilemma of contemporary political science is perhaps best revealed in the ideal commitments of behavioralism. For example, according to the behavioral image of science, those very epistemological characteristics of political research to which the post-behavioralists so strongly object would seem to be unavoidable, indeed, highly desirable. Post-behavioralism deplores what it views as technical excesses in research. Yet no one could possibly deny that technical adequacy is vital. Without it the whole evolution of empirical science in all fields of knowledge in the last two thousand years would have been in vain. Despite some post-behavioral objections to scientific abstractness and remoteness from the world of common sense, by its nature science must deal with abstractions. No science could by itself cope with the whole reality as it is interpreted by the politician. Only by analysis, by chopping the world up into manageable units of inquiry, by precision achieved through measurement wherever possible, can political science meet the continuing need of a complex, post-industrial society for more reliable knowledge. Even to appeal to science to discard abstract theory and models as the test of relevance for research and to put in their place the social urgency of problems, is to ask it to sacrifice those criteria which have proved most successful in developing reliable understanding.

Furthermore, it appears that the use of the methods of behavioral science favors the very kind of sociological position for the political scientist to which post-behavioralism so strenuously objects. These methods help to protect the professional scientist from the pressures of society for quick answers to urgent if complicated problems. The history of the natural sciences shows us how slowly basic research moves. The overshadowing new ideas in the natural sciences—Newtonian mechanics, Darwinian evolution, Einstein's relativity, or modern cybernetics—come infrequently, on a time scale of centuries. But during the intervals between new ideas, great or small, science seeks to work out their implications with a passion for details, even if research seems to lead away from the practical, obvious problems of the day. These seemingly remote, often minute details, about scales, indices, specialized techniques for collecting and analyzing data and the like, these details are the building blocks of the edifice in which more reliable understanding occurs.

What is true about the slow pace of basic research in the natural sciences and about its remoteness we can expect to apply with equal force to the social sciences. Indeed in social research we even have difficulty in agreeing on the great discoveries, so undeveloped are our criteria of adequacy. In addition, even if the political scientist begins with an immediate social problem, as he so often does, in the process of investigation he will be likely to restate the problem in more researchable terms. This reconceptualization usually leads him back to the very kind of fundamentals that appear irrelevant to initial practical concerns.

The ideology of pure or basic research and its success in the better developed sciences in providing a reliable base of knowledge have seemed to justify this research strategy, slow and painstaking as it is. In helping to protect scholarship from the daily pressures of society for quick and ready answers, this ideology has freed science to pursue truth in the best way it knows how.

This same concern for generalized, verifiable understanding has forced social scientists to discriminate with extreme care about what we can and cannot do with our premises and tools. We can describe, explain, and understand but we cannot prescribe ethical goals. The value question is thus set aside, not because we consider it inconsequential, but only because we see it as unresponsive to the tools useful in analyzing and explaining the empirical world.

These then are some of the normal ideal commitments of science: technical proficiency in the search for reliable knowledge, the pursuit of basic understanding with its necessary divorce from practical concerns, and the exclusion of value specification as beyond the competence of science. It is these ideals that behavioral research in political science has sought to import into the discipline.

4. New Strategies for Science

Today these traditional ideals of science are confronted with a set of social conditions which have no historical precedent. This extraordinary circumstance has created the predicament in which behavioral research now finds itself. It derives from the fact that we are confronted with a new and shortened time scale in the course of human events, one in which the future may need to be discounted more heavily than ever before. For many, nuclear war or civil strife, with authoritarianism as a credible outcome, are clear and present dangers, to be counted in decades at the most. For many, without immediate and concentrated attention to the urgent issues of the present day, we may have no future worth contemplating, however uncertain our findings or inadequate our tools. How then can behavioral research, with its acknowledged glacial pace and apparent remoteness, hope to meet the demands now being placed upon our discipline?

For some among post-behavioralists, the fear of physical and political self-destruction has led to the abandonment of science altogether. For them science is simply incapable of measuring up to contemporary needs. Others, who have always considered science to be inherently defective, now feel justified in their convictions. But for those post-behavioralists who continue to place their hopes in modern behavioral science, the current crisis poses the issue about the wisdom of continuing our commitment to a "normal" strategy of scientific research. These kinds of post-behavioralists have been driven to conclude that we have no alternative but to make our research more relevant. For them we can do so only by devoting all our professional energies to research, prescription and action with regard to the immediate issues of the day. In short, we are asked to revise our self-image by postponing the demands of slow-moving basic research and by acting in our professional capacity so as to put whatever knowledge we have to immediate use.

For all of us this plea poses some critical questions. Even in the face of the social crises of our time, do we really need to subordinate the long-run objectives of the scientific enterprise to the undeniably urgent problems of the day? Is there any other way in which we can cope with this transparent need for practical relevance? And if so, can we hope to retain for political science those conditions of theoretical autonomy, precision, and relative insulation so vital if we are to continue to be able to add to our capital stock of basic understanding?

I would argue that we do not need to abandon the historical objectives of basic science. There is a strategy that will enable us to respond to the abnormal urgency of the present crises and yet preserve these traditions. By adopting this course, post-behavioralism need not be considered a threat to behavioral research but only an extension of it necessary for coping with the unusual problems of the present epoch.

To appreciate the strategy implied, we must remember one thing. Even if it *is* arguable that the time scale in terms of which we must think has been greatly shortened, mere projection cannot fully persuade us that the future needs to be counted in decades, not centuries. What little solace we may get from it, we know that our intuitions have been wrong in the past. We may still have centuries rather than only decades ahead of us.

This realistic possibility suggests that we ought to pursue an optimizing strategy in which there is some apportionment of resources for the long run as against the short run, just in case we are not in fact all dead. The cost of devoting our efforts exclusively to short-run crises is far too high. It might easily assure that if we do in fact survive the present crises, the failure to continue to add to our capital accumulation of basic social knowledge will see us tragically unprepared for even greater crises in the more distant future. We will then have lost every chance to prevent the self-annihilation of mankind or the collapse of those political institutions we cherish.

Is there any sensible way in which we can provide for some satisfactory use of our resources without distracting excessively from the attention and altered research orientations that the major issues of the country and the world require? It is to this question that those of us who still have some hope that we may survive the certain and greater crises of the near future ought to be devoting some of our energies. Various courses of action are possible and we need to consider them as they apply to the discipline as well as to the profession.

5. The Discipline

Basic vs. Applied Research. For the discipline, the postbehavioral revolution suggests the appropriateness of revising our ideal image at least as it has been incorporated into behavioralism. It is vital to continue to recognize the part that basic research ought to play. But in the allocation of financial and human resources we must also consciously recognize that a shift in emphasis must occur at once to take into account the critical times in which we live.

In terms of any ideal distribution of our efforts, basic research ought to command a disproportionate share. Although socially useful results from such research are usually a long time in coming, they are in the end more dependable. But under the inescapable pressure of current crises the emphasis needs to be reversed. A far larger part of our resources must be devoted to immediate short-run concerns. We need to accept the validity of addressing ourselves directly to the problems of the day to obtain quick, short-run answers with the tools and generalizations currently available, however inadequate they may be. We can no longer take the ideal scientific stance of behavioralism that because of the limitations of our understanding, application is premature and must await future basic research.[3]

In truth this proposal represents less of a shift in our practices than a change in our ideological posture. The behavioral revolution has never been fully understood or absorbed into the discipline; we are still grappling with its meaning. Any casual inspection of ongoing research would reveal that, regardless of any ideal apportionment, at no time has pure research really consumed more than a very small fraction of the discipline's resources. We have been only too ready to advise federal, state, and local agencies on immediate issues and political parties and candidates about their campaigns. It is just that with the behavioral revolution the ideals of the discipline as incorporated in research ideology were beginning to change. This new image legitimated that kind of basic research, the pay-off of which might not be immediately apparent, but the future promise of which was thought to be considerable. Today we need to temper our behavioral image of the discipline so that in these critical times we no longer see it as commanding us to devote most of our efforts to the discovery of demonstrable basic truths about politics. We will need to obtain more of our satisfactions from seeking immediate answers to immediate problems.

This kind of shift in disciplinary focus will call urgently for the systematic examination of the tasks involved in transforming our limited knowledge today into a form far more consumable for purposes of political action. Certain difficulties stand in the way of applying our knowledge. In the first place, contemporary social problems far outrun the capacity of political science alone or in concert with the other social sciences to solve them. Our basic knowledge is itself limited. What little we have is not necessarily directly applicable to practical issues.

In the second place, like medieval medicine, we may still be

---

[3] See pp. 78 ff. in this book.

at the stage in which we are letting blood in the hope of curing the patient. Because of our low capacity for sorting out the complex causal connections between our advice and its social consequences, we have little assurance that we may not be doing more harm than good. Some efforts are currently under way to correct this situation. In the broadening quest for social indicators we are inventing techniques for isolating the outcomes of policy outputs[4] and for comparing these consequences with the presumed policy goals.[5] Thereby we shall have a measure of the effects of our intervention in the social processes. But the success of these efforts lies some distance in the future.

In the third place, political science alone is unable to propose solutions to social problems; these normally involve matters that call upon the specialized knowledge and skills of other social scientists. Yet seldom do policy makers seek the collective advice of comprehensive teams of social scientists.

These and many other difficulties have stood in the way of the application of our knowledge to specific situations. They have contributed to the low academic esteem of applied science, in comparison at least with basic research. Past efforts at application have experienced too little success to attract the best minds of the day.[6] In temporarily modifying the immediate priorities of the discipline, we will need to devise ways for elevating the self-conscious development of applied knowledge, inappropriately called social engineering, to the respectability that behavioralism has succeeded in acquiring for basic research.

To assign all of our research resources to the present, however, as some post-behavioralists seem to be suggesting, would be

---

[4] For the difference between outcomes and outputs see D. Easton, *A Systems Analysis of Political Life* (New York: Wiley, 1965), p. 351.

[5] For the literature on social indicators see R. A. Bauer (ed.), *Social Indicators* (Cambridge: M.I.T. Press, 1966); "Social Goals and Indicators for American Society," *Annals of the American Academy of Political and Social Sciences,* vols. 371 (May, 1967) and 373 (September, 1967).

[6] See H. W. Riecken, "Social Science and Contemporary Social Problems," 23 *Items* (1969), 1–6.

to discount the future far too heavily. We need to keep alive and active the legitimate long-range interests of all science. Social problem-solving is not totally inconsistent with this objective. The line between pure and applied research is often very fine. Those of us who choose to adopt the long-run point of view, optimistically expecting the survival of mankind, will find much from which to profit in the research undertaken by those concerned with applied problems. Yet this cannot relieve us of the need to continue to devote specific attention to basic problems in the discipline—to the reconceptualization of our significant variables, to the continuing search for adequate units of political analysis, to the exploration of alternative theories and models about the operation of various types of systems, and to our basic methodological assumptions and technical requirements. Admittedly these persisting concerns often lead us far from the practical issues of the day. Yet without attending to these basic problems we cannot hope to add to our store of reliable knowledge, and thereby to prepare ourselves for equally critical political crises in the more distant future.

Value Premises and Research Interests. In addition to suggesting this temporary reallocation of our resources as between basic and applied research, we need to become increasingly aware of the fact that basic research is not without its own substantive deficiencies. This is the message underlying the constant post-behavioral complaint that our research is not relevant. It is argued that excessive preoccupation with techniques and with factual description has distracted us from the significant questions about the operation of the American democratic system in particular. We have learned a great deal about this system but all within a value framework that accepts the ongoing practices as essentially satisfactory and at most subject only to the need for incremental improvements. As a discipline we have proved incapable of escaping a commitment to our own political system. This research myopia, the post-behavioralists argue, has discouraged us from posing the right questions for discovering the basic forces that shape the making and execution of authoritative decisions.

Here the post-behavioralists are alerting us, once again, to what has been repeatedly revealed over the years, by Marx, Weber, and Mannheim, among others, namely, that all research, whether pure or applied, of necessity rests on certain value assumptions. Yet the myth that research can be value-free or neutral dies hard. We have continued to develop our discipline as though the subjects we select for research, the variables we choose to investigate, the data we collect, and the interpretations we generate, have all some extraordinary pristine purity, unsullied by the kinds of value premises to which we subscribe, consciously or otherwise. We do not consistently ask the question, central to the sociology of knowledge: To what extent are our errors, omissions, and interpretations better explained by reference to our normative presuppositions than to ignorance, technical inadequacy, lack of insight, absence of appropriate data, and the like? Behavioralists have indeed failed to insist, with the same fervor we have applied to our technological innovations, that our operating values be brought forward for self-conscious examination and that their impact on research be assessed.

Today the hazards of neglecting our normative presuppositions are all too apparent. There can be little doubt that political science as an enterprise has failed to anticipate the crises that are upon us. One index of this is perhaps that in the decade from 1958 to 1968, *The American Political Science Review* published only 3 articles on the urban crises; 4 on racial conflicts; 1 on poverty; 2 on civil disobedience; and 2 on violence in the United States.[7]

In some considerable measure we have also worn collective blinders that have prevented us from recognizing other major problems facing our discipline. For example, how can we account for the failure of the current pluralist interpretations of democracy to identify, understand, and anticipate the kinds of domestic needs

---

[7] This undoubtedly reflects only the few articles on these subjects submitted for publication rather than any editorial predisposition.

and wants that began to express themselves as political demands during the 1960s? How can we account for our neglect of the way in which the distribution of power within the system prevents measures from being taken in sufficient degree and time to escape the resort to violence in the expression of demands, a condition that threatens to bring about the deepest crisis of political authority that the United States has ever suffered? How can we account for the difficulty that political science as a discipline has in avoiding a commitment to the basic assumptions of national policy, both at home and abroad, so that in the end, collectively we have appeared more as apologists of succeeding governmental interpretations of American interests than as objective analysts of national policy and its consequences? Finally, in even so recent a major research area as political socialization, how can we account for the natural, effortless way in which inquiry has sought to reveal the contributions of preadult political learning to the stability of systems, virtually ignoring the equally significant function of socialization in bringing about political change? [8]

There is no single explanation for the narrow vision of our discipline. We can, however, at least go so far as to offer this hypothesis: Whatever the reasons, the failure to broaden the vision of our basic research may be due in good part to a continuing hesitation to question our normative premises and to examine the extent to which these premises determine the selection of problems and their ultimate interpretations.

Creative Speculation. How are we to make those serious efforts necessary to break out of the bonds imposed on basic research itself by ongoing value frameworks? How are we to create those conditions that will help us to ask fundamental questions about the operation of political systems, that will lead us to pose those "outrageous hypotheses" about which Robert Lynd once

[8] See D. Easton and J. Dennis, *Children in the Political System: Origins of Political Legitimacy* (New York: McGraw-Hill, 1969), chapter 2.

chided us? [9] A new awakening to the part that our value commitments and other social influences play in limiting the range of our basic research may partly correct the errors of our ways. But this moral self-scrutiny may not be enough. If we are to transcend our own cultural and methodological biases, such self-awareness can carry us only part of the way. We may need to take stronger measures and find additional help by returning to an older tradition in political research but in a thoroughly modern way.

Many years ago, in *The Political System* [First Edition], I argued for the urgent need to reconsider our approach to value theory at the same time as we began the equally critical task of constructing empirical theory.[10] The latter task is now under way in our discipline. The first one, creative construction of political alternatives, has yet to begin.

To enrich their own understanding and to give broader meaning to their own social reality, the great political theorists of the past found it useful to construct new and often radically different conceptions of future possible kinds of political relationships. By formulating such broad, speculative alternatives to the here and now we too can begin to understand better the deficiencies of our own political systems and to explore adequate avenues of change that are so desperately needed. This, I would argue, must now be considered part of the task and responsibility of science if it is to retain its relevance for the contemporary world. Those philosophies that seek to revive classical natural law and that reject the possibility of a science of man have thereby forfeited their opportunity and put in question their fitness to undertake this creative task of theory. We require boldly speculative theorizing that is prepared to build upon rather than to reject the findings of contemporary behavioral science itself and that is prepared to contemplate the implications of these findings for political life, in the light of alternative, articulate value frameworks.

[9] R. S. Lynd, *Knowledge for What?* (Princeton: Princeton University Press, 1939).

[10] See chapters 9 and 10 in this book.

The significance for political science of this kind of creative speculation cannot be overestimated. For those who seek to understand how political systems operate, such speculation provides alternative perspectives from which to determine the salience of the problems they choose for research and analysis. If we take seriously the conclusions of the sociologists of knowledge, then our scientific output is very much shaped by the ethical perspectives we hold. In that event, by failing to encourage within the discipline creative speculation about political alternatives in the largest sense, we cannot help but imprison ourselves within the limitations of the ongoing value framework. As that framework begins to lose its relevance for the problems of society, its system-maintenance commitments must blind us to the urgent questions emerging even for the immediate future.

And this is precisely what has happened to political science. Both our philosophers and our scientists have failed to reconstruct our value frameworks in any relevant sense and to test them by creatively contemplating new kinds of political systems that might better meet the needs of a post-industrial, cybernetic society. A new set of ethical perspectives woven around this theme might sensitize us to a whole range of new kinds of basic political problems worth investigating. It might also point up the significance of inquiry into these problems with new or radically modified types of relevant empirical theories. Thereby we could perhaps be freed from that occupational myopia brought about by excessive attention to the facts as they are. We would perhaps be less prone to stumble into the pitfall of "empirical conservatism," [11] or commitment to system-maintenance perspectives, of which political science has with justice been accused [12] by post-behavioralists and others.

In these several ways, then, does our discipline need reordering. Basic research needs to be maintained as an investment for

[11] H. Marcuse, *One-Dimensional Man* (Boston: Beacon Press, 1964), chapter 4.
[12] See C. A. McCoy and J. Playford (eds.), *Apolitical Politics* (New York: Crowell, 1967) and chapters 2 and 11 in this book.

the future. But even *its* priorities need to be rearranged in the light of a better understanding of its own value assumptions. Applied, action-oriented research requires more systematic attention than ever before. We need greater awareness of the limits that our value premises have imposed on our research; and on the solid foundation of knowledge constructed by behavioral research, alternative possible rearrangements of our political relationships need to be seriously contemplated.

6. The Profession and the Use of Knowledge

Not only our discipline, however, but our profession needs restructuring to bring it into harmony with the changing conceptions of social science. Our discipline refers to our intellectual enterprise; our profession, to the trained and expert scholars who participate in the discipline. Post-behavioralism suggests that behavioral commitments create not only a discipline but a profession that shows a declining relevance to the political world around it.

The Behavioral Image of the Profession. Two basic reasons account for this decline, it is in effect argued. First, professionalization of the discipline in behavioral terms has nourished an image of political science in which knowledge and action have been carefully separated and compartmentalized.[13] As scientists possessed of special skills, we see ourselves as purveyors of something called professional expertise. Our task as experts is to offer advice about means only, not about the purposes to which our knowledge might be put. As the well-worn adage puts it, we are on tap, not on top.

In fact, as post-behavioralism correctly asserts, the expert has never lived by this rule. In the discipline, as we have already

---

[13] See especially T. Roszak (ed.), *The Dissenting Academy* (New York: Random House, 1968), Introduction.

noted, behavioral inquiry has not been able to attain any real measure of ethical neutrality. This has had serious consequences for
basic research. In the profession too, the critics point out, ethical
neutrality is no less spurious. In the application of his knowledge
the political scientist explicitly or unwittingly accepts the value
premises of those he serves. His posture of neutrality has the added
consequence of undermining his will or capacity to challenge the
broader purposes to which his knowledge is put.

A second reason accounts for the decline of professional
relevance. Here post-behavioralism breaks sharply with the prevailing professional paradigm about the moral relationship between research and action. In the behavioral interpretation, the possession
of knowledge imposes no special obligation on the political scientist to put his knowledge to use in the service of society. He remains free to choose whether or not he ought to step outside his
scientific role for this purpose. This laissez-faire attitude towards
political engagement has been an accepted moral premise of the
profession. It has permitted if not encouraged withdrawal from political strife. Knowledge is divorced from action.

For post-behavioralism, however, the line between pure research and service begins to fade. Knowledge brings an awareness
of alternatives and their consequences. This opportunity for rational choice imposes special obligations on the knower. The political scientist as a professional is the knower *par excellence*. It is
therefore immoral for him not to act on his knowledge. In holding
that to know is to bear a responsibility for acting, post-behavioralism joins a venerable tradition inherited from such diverse sources
as Greek classical philosophy, Karl Marx, John Dewey, and modern existentialism.

Criteria for the Use of Knowledge. The implications of this
post-behavioral shift in the image of the professional's role in society are considerable. If the political scientist is to evaluate the uses
to which his knowledge is being put and if he is himself to bring his
knowledge to bear on social issues, what criteria are to guide his

choices? Here post-behavioralism returns to the humanist conception of the intellectual as the guardian of those civilized, humane values known to most men. It is incumbent on the professional to see to it that all society, not just a privileged part, benefits from his expertise. His obligations are met only if he takes into account the broadest spectrum of interests in society.

Many post-behavioralists scrutinize the activities of scholars in recent years and conclude that the talents of political scientists have been put in the service largely of the elites in society—in government, business, the military and voluntary organizations. The professional is seen as having little communication and contact with those who characteristically benefit least from the fruits of modern industrial society—the racial and economic minorities, the unrepresented publics at home, and the colonial masses abroad. These are the groups least able to command the resources of expertise for which political science stands. The social responsibility of the political science expert is to rectify the imbalance.

In this post-behavioral view, the application of expert knowledge in the service of social reform becomes competitive with the pursuit of knowledge for its own sake. Reform becomes inseparable from knowledge.

Clearly there is in birth a new image of the professional, one in which science is not necessarily denied its place but in which the scientist is no longer free to divorce the life of the mind from the life of social action. Weber's differentiation between the vocation of the scientist and that of the politician no longer wholly suffices.

This new image leads to the politicization of the profession. If the individual professional is called upon to utilize his knowledge on behalf of society, those collectivities of experts that we call the professional associations are themselves equally culpable if in their corporate capacity they fail to challenge the purposes to which their expertise may be put or if they fail to act when their knowledge warns them of danger. Herein lie the moral and intellectual roots of the constant pressure of the professional associations to take positions on public issues about which their competence may give them special knowledge.

The Politicization of the Profession. This post-behavioral tendency to politicize the professional associations has met with great resistance. Objection arises less from principled argument than from the practical fear that our professional associations will no longer be able to fulfill their normal scientific purposes. Let us grant the plausibility of this practical consideration. Even so, do we need to reject entirely the new moral image being developed by post-behavioralism?

One fact is clear. The crisis of our times spares no group, not even the social sciences. The pressures to utilize all of our resources in critically evaluating goals as well as in providing effective means are too great to be denied. For increasing numbers of us it is no longer practical or morally tolerable to stand on the political sidelines when our expertise alerts us to disaster.

In accepting this new (but ancient) obligation of the intellectual, however, we need to recognize that the professional political scientist may engage in three distinguishable kinds of activity. These are teaching and research on the one hand and practical politics on the other. Somewhere between these the political scientist acts as a consultant and an adviser. Each of these kinds of activity —as a scholar, politician, and consultant—shapes and influences the other. Is it feasible to construct a single organization that will serve the collective purposes of the profession for facilitating all three of these kinds of activities? It seems highly unlikely. Can we provide some sensible division of labor among different organizations that will permit the fullest expression for all those activities into which these critical times are pressing the professional political scientist? This seems possible.

We can conceive of some professional organizations being devoted largely to that kind of action that helps to add to our store of basic knowledge and that eases communication among ourselves and among succeeding generations of political scientists. These we already have in our professional associations. They are designed to aid both teaching and research. We can, however, also conceive of other types of professional organizations that would be concerned with structuring the application of our expertise to ongoing critical social problems. This kind of organization we do not yet have in political science, or, for that matter, in the social sciences as a whole.

But here if we consider the matter only as political scientists we create insurmountable difficulties for ourselves. Social problems do not come neatly packaged as economic, psychological, political and the like. Our crises arise out of troubles that involve all aspects of human behavior. Our professional associations are oriented toward the disciplines, and these are analytic fields. Of necessity they piece up reality into specialties that have meaning largely for the pursuit of fundamental understanding. For purposes of setting goals and determining means for solving social problems, however, we need to draw the disciplines together again into a single organization, one that can mobilize the resources of all the social sciences and bring them to a focus on specific issues.

To this end it is time that we accept our special responsibility as students of politics. We must take the initiative by calling for the establishment of a Federation of Social Scientists, a proposal that has already been advanced by one of our colleagues.[14] The tasks of such a Federation would be to identify the major issues of the day, clarify objectives, evaluate action taken by others, study and propose alternative solutions, and press these vigorously in the political sphere.

Without collectively politicizing ourselves in this way, by the very act of standing by while the problems of the world continue to increase in numbers and intensity, we thereby uncritically acquiesce in prevailing policies. We in fact adopt a political position. By acting collectively in our professional capacities through a Federation of Social Scientists, we will have an opportunity to justify

[14] David Singer of the Mental Health Research Institute, University of Michigan, Ann Arbor, Michigan, in personal correspondence.

our policies intellectually and morally. Thereby we may begin to satisfy our growing sense of political responsibility in an age of crisis. At the same time we shall be able to preserve our historic institutions, the professional associations, for the continuing pursuit of fundamental knowledge.

Such a Federation would fail in its responsibilities, however, if it became merely an echo of national goals, an instrument of official policy, or a bland critic of things as they are. If Mannheim is correct in describing the intellectual as the least rooted of all social groups, the professional social scientist ought to view himself as committed to the broadest of humane values. These need to be the touchstone that he brings to bear on social issues. Yet many barriers block the way. Of these identification with the goals and interests of one's nation is prominent. Political scientists have still to escape the crippling effects for scholarship of unwitting commitment to national goals and perspectives. Just as science as a set of disciplines has pretensions to being international in scope, so the social scientist himself needs to be denationalized. Some day, like the ideal international civil servant, the professional social scientist too may be permitted to achieve maximum freedom from national commitments by being obliged to carry an international passport and to conduct himself accordingly.

For the profession, therefore, the emerging post-behavioral phase is encouraging the development of a new norm of behavior. It sees policy engagement as a social responsibility of the intellectual whatever the institutional form through which this may be expressed. Some day it may also require the release of the social scientist from bondage to the unique needs and objectives of his own national political system.

It is clear that changing times require radical re-thinking of what we are and what we want to be both as a discipline and as a profession. Post-behavioralism is a pervasive intellectual tendency today that reveals a major effort to do just this. Its very pervasiveness prevents it from becoming the possession of any one group or of any one political ideology. It supports and extends behavioral methods and techniques by seeking to make their substantive implications more cogent for the problems of our times. Post-behavioralism stands, therefore, as the most recent contribution to our collective heritage. For that very reason, as an intellectual tendency it is not the threat and danger that some seem to fear. Rather, in the broad historical perspectives of our discipline, the post-behavioral revolution represents an opportunity for necessary change. We may choose to take advantage of it, reject it, or modify it. But to ignore it is impossible. It is a challenge to re-examine fearlessly the premises of our research and the purposes of our calling.

Continuities in Political Analysis:

Behavioralism and Post-Behavioralism

Now that the reader has been exposed to my interpretations of two succeeding revolutions in political science, he may appropriately ask whether, and to what extent, I have modified my point of view or conclusions, especially about scientific method and its relationship to the evolution of political science in the last half century or so. Are there any differences between what I recommended for the 1950s and what I am now proposing for the 1970s? If so, how do I justify them? Can they be construed as revealing, in any sense, dissatisfaction with the rigorous methods of science for the study of politics, that is, with the behavioral revolution?

The personal tone of these questions ought not to be allowed to conceal the broader implications of this inquiry. The questions just represent a convenient way of probing more deeply into the relationship between the post-behavioral changes and the prior behavioral revolution. Thereby we may hope to achieve a better understanding of a new movement that seems to be taking root in American political science.

1. The Place of Applied Science

In one area my point of view has shifted radically. My conception of the priorities of applied science in our discipline and in the social sciences as a whole has been sharply modified to take into account the needs of changing historical conditions. This shift needs to be explained.

As *The Political System* was being written in the years shortly after World War II, the tasks confronting political science were considerably different from those before the discipline today. Political science was immersed in a postwar world in which the tasks of European reconstruction, the emerging colonial revolutions, the Cold War, and domestic, social and economic readjustments all called for better understanding of those social processes that were overwhelming mankind in spite of itself. Man had moved effectively against nature by penetrating to the heart of matter and releasing its violent energies. Yet he had not moved appreciably closer to an explanation of the forces governing his own social order.

Nevertheless, even in the face of the threat of atomic war and the pessimism it had already begun to engender, there did seem to be enough time to work out techniques and theories for research about society. We could hope to understand better the sources of human conflict and the nature of those internal political forces that were dominating our fate. In the United States the rapid economic development of the second Industrial Revolution, after World War II, brought with it a sense of domestic well-being. The colonial revolutions with their high ideals, unlimited ambitions, and growing successes seemed to herald a hopeful age for the mass of peoples abroad as well. In order to channel these forces to benign purposes, the establishment of a richer body of reliable understanding for the social sciences seemed essential. This would provide a solid base from which acceptable resolutions could be sought for the constant dangers of international conflict, enduring political needs at home, and the problems of political development in the new nations abroad.

To be sure, the times, even then, were not free of a sense of urgency. The Korean War, the struggles for independence of the developing nations from colonialism, internal economic recessions, and the ever-present fear of atomic war were deeply disturbing conditions that could not be ignored. For almost a decade McCarthyism spread its chilling effects throughout academic life and the political system,[1] and the social sciences did not appear uniformly courageous in response to this transparent threat to their freedom of inquiry. For most social scientists, however, even these circumstances were not yet so desperate that they could not envision a potentially rewarding future for research as well as for mankind. Only a more pessimistic minority read the signs of the 1950s as pointing unmistakably to an ever deepening world-wide crisis. It has turned out, as we can now see, that this minority displayed the greater wisdom, even though no one at all could foresee the piling up of critical issues that face the world today.

Under the prevailing interpretation of historical conditions, however, time did seem to be available. It was reasonable to conclude that if political science was to make any contribution at all to mankind, it would first need to bend a very large part of its efforts to the search for basic and dependable knowledge. Scientific method had been knocking on the doors of the discipline well before World War II. It seemed imperative now to throw the doors open and welcome the perspectives and technology of science. We might thereby hope to improve the level of reliability of our knowledge.

In *The Political System* I interpreted science as the substitution of empirically oriented theory for intuition and for impressionistically collected unrelated facts. Scientific method also called

[1] See P. Lazarsfeld and W. Thielens, Jr., *The Academic Mind: Social Scientists in a Time of Crisis* (New York: Macmillan, 1958); M. P. Rogin, *The Intellectuals and McCarthy: The Radical Specter* (Cambridge: The M.I.T. Press, 1967).

for recognition of the limits of judgments made in its name. These judgments could deal with the affirmation of facts, but not the assertion of value. The level of development of political research at that time called for this kind of explicit statement about some matters which even today are still not taken for granted. Furthermore, in *The Political System* I interpreted reliability of understanding to be a major goal of science, as a step prior to application. I saw reliability as a product of two equally important factors: Deliberate and intensive attention to the growth of causal theory to give guidance and meaning to rigorous empirical research; and an equally deliberate elaboration of moral theory as a way of clarifying the ethical assumptions underlying this research.

In the 1940s and early 1950s the discipline was sadly lacking in such basic research. It had a surplus of efforts to apply untested, uncertain knowledge to the problems of the day. As critical as the political issues after World War II were for the involved generations of the day, there still seemed to be ample time for us to redirect a greater share of our resources to the accumulation of reliable knowledge. We would then be better able to trust our advice and predictions.

In the 1970s political science is clearly faced with vastly different circumstances, both in the discipline and in society. In the last twenty-five years, a considerable body of more reliable knowledge has been acquired; the behavioral revolution has not been in vain. An appreciable volume of empirically oriented theorizing has emerged. In addition, as my presidential address stresses, the social setting has been fundamentally transformed. Even if we heavily discount the tendency of each age to appraise its difficulties as worse than those of any other age, we can credibly say that crises of magnitudes unimaginable in the past have arisen. The pressures for immediate efforts to resolve these problems now deny us the earlier opportunity to wait until adequate basic knowledge has been accumulated to assure us that the remedies we propose will indeed help meet our needs.

In the face of these new and unforeseen circumstances it

has seemed to me that political science could not stand idly by and hope that somehow mankind would muddle through while we stuck exclusively to our scientific course, basic research. Even with the appearance of empirical theorizing and a considerable body of well established political knowledge, our discipline did not succeed in measuring up to the needs of the times. It had failed to identify the major issues as they emerged in the 1960s. What knowledge we had painstakingly acquired was slow in being put to use, and there is even some question about how useful in fact it has been. What is perhaps worse, we have not seemed to be very agitated either about this slowness or about the doubt over its pertinence for practical major concerns.

In retrospect it now appears that in *The Political System* what I had virtually accepted as an absolute was only an historically conditioned characteristic of science. It had seemed to me that where a science is as underdeveloped as political science was at the time, it would do well to restrain its eagerness to apply its findings and interpretations. To do otherwise would be to mislead policy makers and to defeat the ultimate purposes of the discipline, its search for basic understanding. Even though I recognized that no science can or should seek to avoid the use of its knowledge for current purposes, it did seem appropriate, in light of the needs of the discipline, to argue for the diversion of a greater share of our resources and attention to the improvement of the reliability of our knowledge.

This image of the relationship between pure and applied science seemed justified for that time, at the beginning of the 1950s. For the 1970s, however, as I point out in my presidential address, one vital commodity, time, is in critically short supply. The reader has already discovered that this new and unforeseen circumstance has brought me to revise my conception of the priorities in the tasks of science, including our discipline. I now see it as imperative that, without forsaking pure research as a continuing and major objective, we organize ourselves for the application of whatever knowledge we have, however insecure we may feel about its validity. Fortunately in the last two decades we have added considerably to our store of rigorously derived knowledge. Our advice to policy makers should be somewhat more dependable than in the past.

In conformity with this new emphasis, all the problems associated with the application of knowledge, some of which I touch upon in my address, will now need to receive closer and constant attention. One day, when the world has purchased more time for itself with the modest help of these immediate efforts by political science, we will be able to reallocate a larger share of our efforts to pure science. Those dedicated to basic research will again be able to pursue their calling with full vigor.

For some, this position may be challenged as an unnecessary and undesirable "concession" to what is sometimes described as pressure from a new populist left for the destruction of abstract science. If we accept this interpretation we might be inclined to stand firm and to continue on the path of basic research undeterred, regardless of the immediate consequences. I would prefer, however, to interpret my position as an expression of concern for knowledge that has drifted too far from the complex realities of the present epoch. If we adopt this point of view, we need to consider revising our conception of the apportionment of resources. This is what I have done, secure in the belief that in the future, if and when the present crises pass, a new balance will be restored, one more hospitable to an unrestrained commitment to basic research, regardless of immediate considerations of practical use.

For some, my position may also seem to present dangerous hazards to basic science within the university. In the recent past, at least since the growth of graduate research in Germany during the nineteenth century, the universities have been the primary locus for fundamental science. But in American universities particularly, the applied sciences have grown luxuriantly during the twentieth century culminating in the service oriented multiversity of the present generation. Tension prevails between the professional schools (law, medicine, business, education, engineering, social service administration, librarianship, and the like) and the basic sciences. Would the proposal to increase temporarily the specific importance of applied research today tend to resolve this tension in a direction unfavorable to basic science? Would this strategy ultimately dry up the sources of those fundamental ideas on which applied research itself must thrive? Might the schools of applied science ultimately devour the university? A short run policy of vastly increased attention to applied science problems might set in motion long-run forces in the form of vested academic interests that would later be almost impossible to dislodge.

The strategy I am proposing does indeed carry risks of this kind. Yet these risks need not be as dangerous as they appear. First, there is some evidence, unexpected as it may initially be, that as the resources for applied science grow so do those for basic research. It has been suggested that:

> . . . the widespread uses of science have created a very wide foundation for "pure" research, the aim of which is to increase knowledge without consideration of its potential uses. How the practical uses support science for its own sake can be seen from a comparison of the statistics of research expenditure in different countries. . . . [These show] that entrepreneurial applied science which extended research and training to new and often relatively risky fields did not ultimately diminish the share of basic research relative to the society's total resources, . . . but rather is associated with an increase of this share.[2]

Increased attention to application may alert society to the need for increased resources on behalf of basic research. Indeed the experience of the sciences today shows how difficult it often is to distin-

---

[2] J. Ben-David, "The Universities and the Growth of Science in Germany and the United States," 7 *Minerva* (1968–1969), 1–36, at p. 29.

guish basic from applied problems. In the end, a renewed concern for the use of our knowledge may be the very stimulus for basic research required at a time when criticism of the latter's remoteness is so widespread.

Second, insofar as the emphasis on applied science problems does put basic science in jeopardy, this ought to awaken us to the need to reconsider the structure of the university so that its historical commitment to basic understanding will not be undermined by our manifest short run needs. Such a restructuring is possible, although specifying its nature here would require excessive space. To state the problem briefly and generally, we would need to reorganize the university so that within its walls applied and action oriented educational units could be established with a legitimacy of their own. Structural safeguards would have to be established to prevent these new institutions from endangering those units of the university that would continue to be dedicated to the pursuit of basic science. Permeable walls among these action, applied, and basic research units within the university would need to exist so that each could learn from the other, through both faculty and students, without hampering their separate activities. The budgetary and administrative arrangements would need to be sufficiently flexible to permit the reallocation of resources—human, organizational, and financial—among these units as circumstances change.

It is not enough, therefore, just to argue on behalf of the reordering of our priorities in research so as to meet the justifiable pressures for increased attention from social science to current problems. We need to link our proposals for changes in emphasis to the restructuring of the universities if in the process basic science is not to be eclipsed. On the other hand, if we intransigently resist all efforts to realign our sights under the present crises and refuse to adapt the very structure of the university to these objectives, we could easily find the university irreparably damaged as the historic center of learning. It is not inconceivable that those concerned with basic research would be forced to leave the universities for private or public research institutes, a pattern already well known in continental Europe but hitherto unacceptable in the United States. The universities might even be converted into glorified technical schools.

In short then, my emphasis between pure and applied research has shifted to take into account changing conditions. In general terms, I am now proposing that we need to modify our accepted image of science to recognize that we can give no final weight in advance to the distribution of time and resources between pure and applied research in a discipline. However strongly we may have believed in the past that science ought to reserve judgment until it has something to say that is far more reliable than common sense, it is clear that the pressure from society may not always give us this option. The balance struck at any moment will need to depend on historical circumstances rather than on any absolute or lofty principle that we may seek to legislate for all time. And this realization has vital implications for the structure of the university itself.

2. Values in Science

What emerges inadvertently from the previous discussion is evidence that our conception of the obligations of science and of the distribution of its attention and resources rests in the end on a set of value judgments about what we want science to be and to do. This image of what science should be is also seen to be related to the pressures of time and place.

These implications open up another question in the comparison of my views in *The Political System* and my presidential address. Do any differences in proposals between the two flow from a fundamentally revised image of the nature of science, especially about the place of values? A close reading of my address should reveal that there has been no radical change. But I do extend the application of my position in *The Political System* and this could easily be mistaken for an alteration of principle. Thus it may be instructive to re-examine my conception especially as it touches on the place of values.

This analysis will have some significance other than as a reflection of my personal views. Rather, my long-held image of science offers an unconventional resolution to the "value problem" that continues to trouble social scientists. This discussion will help to explain first, my continued insistence today on the creative role for political science in the construction of images of the good political life; and second, why, even in *The Political System,* I have never been able to accept an interpretation of values in science that has been associated with a radical positivist position.

Under the influence of a strict construction, both of positivism and of Max Weber, it has been taken for granted in the social sciences that neither the classroom nor the university is a place for extensive disputation on behalf of an ethical point of view or set of moral judgments about the world. We are permitted to examine value judgments, account for them, trace their consequences, explain them, clarify them, even assert them so as not to deceive others about where we stand. But since scientific judgments are supported by evidence and moral judgments are warranted only by preferences, these two kinds of propositions and related discourses are logically separate and need to be kept scrupulously apart. The first is intersubjectively determinable on the basis of evidence and is therefore valid within the classroom; the other is an exhortation related to preferences and therefore appropriate only from the pulpit or political platform. So, in effect, run Max Weber's authoritative arguments in his famous essays, "Science as a Vocation," "Politics as a Vocation," and "The Meaning of 'Ethical Neutrality' in Sociology and Economics."

This image of the relationship of moral and empirical propositions to the classroom is of course nothing less than a value statement itself. From the conclusion that facts and values are logically heterogeneous we cannot derive a moral position that value propositions ought not to be formulated from the same platform on which factual judgments are being considered. Max Weber left little doubt in our minds about this. He is the first to acknowledge that his conclusions cannot be defended or denied except on the ground of value preference.

Weber's prescription has created an anomalous situation. If he is to continue to argue for the complete exclusion of value dispute from the university, as he does, he cannot remain consistent and still provide any place within the university for social scientists themselves to debate this very conception of science. Such debates cannot be part of scientific discussion, since, as Weber himself acknowledges, they must rest on varying value judgments, and the latter he places outside the competence of science. We end up in the strange position of having to find some platform outside the university to settle an issue central to the future of science itself—its own conception of itself. It is clear that a philosophy about science and values that prevents the scientist himself from arguing from a university platform for the merits of one as against another conception of science leaves us with a serious problem.

Indeed the conflict this creates is so intolerable that Weber himself could not abide by his own injunctions, a fact that should long ago have alerted us to the difficulties in accepting his image of science insofar as it concerns the place of positive value construction. He constantly debated on behalf of his own position within the walls of the university, thereby engaging in the very kind of ethical controversy that his position sought to rule out as inappropriate except from the pulpit. It was not entirely clear to Weber that his position is logically defensible only under one condition: If it is assumed to apply to all ethical questions with the exception of one, that dealing with the place of ethical disputation itself in the university. But once such an exception is permitted, the logic of the position is undermined. The sluice gates are opened for other kinds of exceptions, and this hampers the acceptance of any general exclusionary rule. Hence Weber's formulation of the appropriateness of ethical debate within the university confronted him with a dilemma from which there was no logical escape.

In *The Political System* I had refrained from meticulously following Weber in this respect and did not support the complete exclusion of value discourse from science. At the time, however, it did not seem to be especially important to draw specific attention to the differences or to recount the reasons for them. Weber was not then an authority figure for American political science; his writings were as yet largely unread. Nonetheless, in *The Political System,* the reader will recall, after explicitly sharing much of Weber's understanding about the relationship of science to values, I argued at length for going beyond the mere assertion of values for purposes of clarification and analysis as permitted by Weber. Indeed, I sought to reconstruct the image of science so as to justify the inclusion of creative moral discourse and dispute within the boundaries of the scientific enterprise itself and not only within the university, while continuing to accept the logical heterogeneity of facts and values.

My grounds for this modification were that I considered constructive inquiry into values necessary if we were to be able to reveal in their fullness the ethical premises underlying all empirical research, including causal theory. Only in this way could we adequately explore the contribution of our value assumptions to error, distortion, omission, and the like in the identification and delineation of research problems as well as in the collection, analysis, and interpretation of data. In the interests of valid research, it seemed imperative that the scientist undertake to contemplate the kind of world to which he was committed, wittingly or otherwise.

This inclusion in the scientific enterprise of a maximal elaboration of world views as an aid to valid research itself did not violate the letter of Weber's position. The latter permitted the clarification of moral premises. It prohibited only the pleading of a cause, the harangue of the politician, or the rhetoric of persuasion of the prophet. My own proposal went no further than to accept the comprehensive presentation of an ethical view as part of scientific discourse; it continued to exclude a hortatory defense of this view.

Yet this proposal could not help but violate the spirit of

Weber's position. Self-clarification for Weber had seemed a much simpler task, one that only called for formal statements about what the scientist believed. It needed to be elaborated only enough to inform the listener of the speaker's values. Nothing said by Weber implied that the social scientist should go so far as to engage in an extended formulation of his moral position, a kind of inquiry that creatively sets forth an image of alternative political arrangements and, implicitly at least, assumes a posture about their desirability. The boundary line between full explication of a value position through creative ethical inquiry, as advocated in *The Political System,* and forthright ethical disputation is maintained. But it has narrowed markedly from the one supported by Weber.

Over the years this aspect of *The Political System* has not commanded too much attention even though it occupied many pages. Nor have I had occasion to elaborate or comment on it frequently in later years. The discipline did not appear to be ready to consider seriously the revision of the place of values in our conception of science, even a revision well within our commitment to positive science. Perhaps, in part, this was a defensive overreaction to those militant advocates of value disputation who have seen the latter as a substitute for a scientific approach in political analysis. Uneasiness about the continued challenges to science, while science was still struggling for legitimacy in political research, tended to suppress a more responsible consideration of the relationship of values to the development of a rigorous science itself. In addition, as I have already suggested, given the circumstances of the 1950s, there seemed to be some reason for placing a higher priority on the development of basic empirical understanding and causal theory.

Today, however, what had been a secondary theme at an earlier time has been elevated by history, if not to a leitmotif, at least to a position of parity with that of empirical theory. Thus, in my presidential address, I took advantage of the new circumstances to revive the plea for moral speculation, on the same grounds already advanced in *The Political System.* By this time, however, I was also prepared to go somewhat further. I have now extended my ethical position to take into account the changed circumstances of the late 1960s as against the early 1950s. Today the need to escape the research limits imposed by the unwitting adoption of prevailing moral-political premises is more urgent than ever before. But, in addition, as I argue in my address, today knowledge brings with it new responsibilities; it leads to a changing image of the role of the professional political scientist. We now see him as being involved more intimately than ever before in the application of knowledge to the urgent problems of the day. If this new conception is accepted, it also carries with it the supplementary obligation to think in the broadest terms about the direction that such social engagement might take.

If applied science is to command our serious attention it is not enough for the social scientist just to seek to leave his impact on specific social policies, such as racial tension, pollution, war, or hunger. His activities will be responsible only if they are linked to broader conceptions of the kinds of political systems that could be, systems in which such policies would be more likely to be accepted or with which they could be consistent. A responsible acceptance of his new role would lead the political scientist to refuse to accept automatically the prevailing political or moral premises about what is desirable or possible. He could question them adequately only by engaging in creative moral speculation that seriously contemplates new kinds of institutional arrangements in political systems, after the style of the great social scientists of old (known to us as social philosophers). This is implicit in the new image of the role of the professional political scientist. And this new obligation reacts back on his intellectual activities. He who has the best understanding of how men behave politically and of how political systems operate is best able to spell out new political arrangements to avoid identifiable problems created by the old.

This expanded image of the responsibilities of political science with respect to involvement in moral discourse can be only too readily misconstrued. We can avoid this danger if we carefully bear in mind what this position does not include. For example, it is not to be interpreted as a prescription for a return to intuitive speculation in the mold of the ancient philosophers. There is no intention here to encourage the anti-methodology of contemporary political classicism with its antagonism to modern science. Scientists can adopt a rational interest in value construction and application without denying the validity of their science or sinking back into impressionistic analysis as a substitute for rigorous research.

Nor am I proposing to convert the classroom into a platform for the pleading of special causes. This would indeed be creating an image of science that would leave it barely distinguishable, if at all, from politics. It would revive those very conditions at the turn of the century which politicized the classroom in the German universities and against which Weber was defending basic science. But between the simple clarification of moral premises (still seldom undertaken by social scientists, unfortunately) and outright political disputation, there is ample room for the creative formulation of new political arrangements, their consideration in the light of what we know about human behavior and potential, and their use as criteria to assess the adequacy of research, basic and applied. As political scientists engage in basic research, we require this in-depth exploration of our value premises in order to probe the relationship of values to the nature of our research. As we engage in applied science we can understand the full implications of specific policies only within the context of our general political philosophy. Adequate science itself would therefore seem to require this involvement in creative moral inquiry.

I am, of course, not proposing that all those scholars who seek fundamental knowledge must at the same time propose alternative conceptions of the good political life or even that all scientists must be prepared to defend a fully developed moral position. The division of labor that contributes to the growth of science is equally applicable here. Some scientists may still consider it their métier to strive solely for basic understanding and explanation of empirical phenomena. But others, interested in the value assumptions of research or in the application of knowledge, must be given room, status, and recognition within science itself to speculate about alternative policies in the broadest contexts, to warrant them in the light of images of new political orders, and to use their knowledge to cast these new orders in terms consistent with our findings about political behavior.

The formulation of new value perspectives as a base for research cannot, and need not be, assigned exclusively to philosophers divorced from the special empirical knowledge of social science, to publicists outside the universities, or to statesmen. Each of these brings a special and therefore important outlook and interest to bear on the creation of new political philosophies. But in addition, the political scientist who is cultivating special and reliable knowledge about the constraints on human behavior develops his own understanding of what is possible and desirable. From this value point of view, he has a special obligation to participate actively in the construction of new political alternatives and to air these for rational analysis within the same pedagogical context in which he fulfills his other commitments as a social scientist. Thereby, social science will be able to meet its obligation to explore fully the value underpinnings of its own research.

In the outcome, although my basic conviction expressed in *The Political System* about the validity of a creative interest in value construction within political science remains firm, it has now been extended to take into account the increased concern that social science must show for the immediate application of its knowledge. In my presidential address I develop a somewhat expanded image of the obligation of the social scientist from what was prevalent during the 1950s and 1960s. Like all other conceptions of science this image itself is based on a set of value assumptions. It seeks to relate our conception of the role of science more intimately to the needs of the times without, however, abandoning the historical character of science as the pursuit of empirically based knowledge.

3. The Obligations of the Profession

Just as we need to reconsider our image of the nature of our discipline as a science, I also suggest in my presidential address that we need to modify our conception of ourselves as a profession. Although this proposal is new, in fact it too represents only an extension of a position on values already adopted in *The Political System*. It also flows logically from my reassessment of the place of applied science in our discipline. It is but a short step from the suggestion that we ought to apply our specialized knowledge to the policy issues of the day, within the classroom, to the idea that we ought to carry this expertise from the university into the political market place itself.

Here I touch on a subject that appeared to require little attention in the early 1950s. As *The Political System* was being written there was little sentiment for, or consideration about, bringing political scientists into an active political role. If anything, the very opposite was the case. The initial frightening reluctance, in the country at large, to combat the clear threat to freedom, academic and otherwise, from McCarthyism, led many scholars, in a nervous state of apprehension, to adopt an intuitive political strategy of retreat into protective quietism.

On the other hand, I would not suggest that political scientists, even those in this state of enforced withdrawal, were necessarily apolitical during the 1950s. In *The Political System* I tried to show that typically political science has tended toward an uncritical acceptance of basic political arrangements as they are. In the United States political scientists have traditionally been socialized in the discipline with a benign set of attitudes towards the existing regime. More than for most of the other disciplines the subject matter of political research, until the recent past, has dealt largely with governmental institutions and offices. It was understandable that political scientists should be prone to interpret political processes from the perspectives of officialdom, with its needs in mind. Consulting services to government were accepted as a natural concomitant of this special relationship. This close connection between government and political science, as a source of data and an object of service, tended to leave the profession as friendly critics of national policy and its assumptions, and often as neutral consultants willing to serve equally any task master. A set of norms compatible with these roles sealed in the critical energies and resources of the profession.

In this way political science was protected from the stress and strain of active political involvement. The profession could devote itself exclusively to the pursuit of new knowledge. Political scientists could fulfill any felt obligation to put their knowledge to practical use by acting as readily available and accommodating advisers to public agencies. This professional norm of behavior continues to be so widely accepted today that most members of the profession might be rather surprised perhaps, if not irritated, to find anyone questioning it. It is a comfortable professional position since it frees us as political scientists to do what we feel we can do best, basic research, and to purvey it on the open market to all would-be buyers. We do not need to question the purposes to which our expertise is being put.

In my presidential address, however, I have been led to cast serious doubt on this conception of our role as professional social scientists. I conclude that we can no longer remain either only consultants—an instrument constantly available to public agencies in the fulfillment of their policies—or as cosy and congenial bedfellows of officialdom. At one time, in the interest of a higher value— the pursuit of basic knowledge—the professional political scientist might have found an easy rationalization for restricting himself to this kind of relationship. Today historical circumstances have changed, and with them our moral image of the responsibilities of the social scientist ought to do likewise.

In my presidential address, in effect, I contend that the present historical situation reveals the illusionary world in which the social scientist must live today if he continues to believe that by refraining either from questioning the use to which his knowledge is put or from using his expertise self-consciously in the public forum, he somehow protects the purity of his skills and calling. On the contrary, it may be that by opting out of the active political process he hastens the day when he will no longer be free even to pursue his basic research, as he defines it, and to continue to fortify his expertise. The threat that current crises pose for the freedom and survival of mankind extends to political science as well.

Atomic fission radically altered the self-image of the natural scientists. After Hiroshima they entered the political fray as a new and militant interest group pressing for the adoption of policies considered essential, given their expert knowledge, for the avoidance of atomic war. For the social sciences, the domestic and international crises of the 1970s serve as the atom bomb for their social conscience. For the first time in the modern epoch these critical conditions have begun to awaken social scientists to a new and broader sense of their political responsibilities. These crises are opening up the question for social scientists as to whether their own expertise does not carry with it an obligation to speak out, not only within the inner circles of officialdom, but from the public platform as well.

My changing conception of the social obligations of the political scientist is, then, a product of the new and urgent times. They have led me to extend my earlier position and to argue, in my presidential address, that the exigencies of the present day require us to revise our ideas about the scholar as an intellectual and to assimilate him to the dominant historical role of the intellectual as the defender of humane values. As these values are decisively threatened by the course of events, some reordering of scholarly values themselves needs to take place. For the professional political scientist this suggests the allocation of part of his time and resources for active and critical involvement in contemporary politics.

4. The Relevance of Basic Research

In *The Political System* I had extolled the virtues of empirically oriented theories as a set of independent guideposts for basic research. In my presidential address I argue the continued need for basic research and point out that by its nature it tends to become increasingly abstract and remote in its details from the practical issues of everyday life. Despite this forthright commitment to basic research, however, I also recognize and share the complaints that basic research itself needs to be more attuned to the crises of our day. Is this a concession to substantive issues as a test of relevance for the selection of research topics? If so, is this view consistent with my previous position in *The Political System*? Will this problem orientation in the end serve to undermine basic research and divert it into the study of contemporary problems? Can basic research retain its responsiveness to purely scientific criteria of relevance and at the same time remain substantively germane to the issues of the day? In short, can basic political research be simultaneously scientifically relevant and socially relevant?

The criticism of basic research may be restated in terms even more forceful than in my presidential address. Concern for technical competence in quantifying phenomena and testing generalizations has, in the minds of many post-behavioralists, led to the evisceration of politics. Quantification, it is argued, all too frequently requires reconceptualization of political events as they appear to common sense. In the search for measurable units of analysis, science has been led to abstractions in which one can only remotely recognize the phenomena normally called political. Confronted in the United States by a disastrous war in Vietnam, slowly starving children, angry blacks, frightened whites, aroused vigilantes, three major political assassinations within a five-year period, student uprisings on campus, and rumors of guerrilla warfare, the behavioral scientist calmly contemplates alternative modes of analysis involving such apparently remote concepts as systems, functions, culture, games, simulation, economic models, and coalition formation. Little wonder, the post-behavioralist complains, that some students look back nostalgically to the pre-behavioral days for some taste of the language and flavor of street corner politics, however much inherited wisdom was more folklore than fact, more guesswork than probability. Science, it is argued, with its emphasis on basic research, has led to measurement, measurement to necessary abstraction, and abstraction to the disappearance of recognizable politics from our discipline.

The relationship of basic research to immediate problems is a complex issue to which there is no simple answer even though here it will be possible only to attempt to answer it simply. However it is this kind of reasoning that underlies the criticism of basic research in my presidential address.

At the outset one quality of basic knowledge is clear. In the long run it provides for the maximum relevance to practical matters. Knowledge developed specifically to solve today's problems may be obsolete tomorrow as the problems change. Generalized basic knowledge is more enduring if only because it is adaptable for understanding broader ranges of specific and changing problems. Since theory is basic knowledge in its most generalized form, this flexibility in application attests to its ultimate relevance for social issues.

This general statement about the function of theory, however, really does not answer the issue that has been raised. In the long run, it might be argued, theory may in fact perform in this way. But today we are still very far from anything that looks like a general theory. All that parades as political theory is in reality only the first small step on the way to the construction of theory. It consists largely of the formulation of theoretical frameworks of analysis and conceptual structures, not broadly integrated statements about the relationships of variables. Not only are we at a very early stage in theory construction but even within these limits no single paradigm has been widely accepted as most useful, however prevalent systems formulations may be. The selection of a theoretical approach is still very much an open matter, a characteristic of an "immature" science.

If the choice of a theoretical approach on the grounds of scientific adequacy alone is still indeterminate, this gives us the opportunity to import other criteria for assessment between alternative modes of analysis. Because of the. urgent requirement for meeting the unusual social crises of our day, it does not seem artificial to inquire into the relative potential of any proposed theoretical approach for assisting in the solution of social problems. Given whatever theoretical analysis we do have in political science, therefore, each can be tested by its immediate and transparent relationship to the practical world of politics. Other things, such as scientific adequacy, being equal, there would be some merit in selecting among alternative theoretical analyses in this way.

Other things are seldom equal, however, so that this may be an unfair test. The only answer to this is that as long as scientific adequacy is itself indeterminate there is little reason for excluding social relevance as a second order or supplementary criterion. In this sense critics of political science who complain about the failure of the discipline to address itself to vital issues of the day have the opportunity, even within the framework of scientific criteria of choice, to select those theoretical efforts that seem most directly and easily related to the crucial issues of the times. Among theoretical approaches, therefore, we may ask whether one or another shows greater promise for application, poses more searching questions about the real world, or draws attention to more problem-related subjects. If so, we have some use-criteria to add to our logically prior scientific criteria for favoring one mode of analysis over another. In this way we may remain faithful to science and yet bend our basic research somewhat to meet the particular needs of the time. Essentially this is what I had in mind in arguing, in my presidential address, for the desirability of making even our basic research more relevant.

There is always the danger that in applying a secondary

criterion of selection in this way, a powerful analytic approach may be overlooked or slighted simply because at the moment, in its early formulations, potential applications may not be apparent or even interesting. This is a true and inescapable risk. Yet the very reason for arguing on behalf of scientifically adequate but socially relevant basic research is the kind of conditions confronting mankind today, not tomorrow. In my presidential address I have assumed some plausibility to the argument that without a sense of urgency today there may not be a distant tomorrow by which time the less relevant theories of the present may be developed to the point of applicability. If one has no sense of this urgency then the gamble is negligible, and we may choose to continue the use of our normal scientific standard alone for evaluating alternative theories. But if we do believe that there is a probability higher than chance that we may be at a decisive point for the continuity of mankind, we may wish to gamble on putting our confidence in those scientifically acceptable approaches to theory that show greater promise for contributing toward the solution of practical problems.

Without attempting to assess various proposed theoretical approaches such as game theory, functional analysis, economic models, or power theory, I can at least briefly illustrate the test of social relevance by reference to a mode of theorizing with which I am most intimately familiar, systems analysis. It is a useful test since in its formal statement it does look forbiddingly remote from reality.

My ideas about a possible systems analytic approach began to take shape in the later 1940s and early 1950s. Some indications of my thinking appeared in *The Political System,* but the first rounded statement was written during 1955 and appeared in print under the title, "An Approach to the Analysis of Political Systems." [3] In this paper, for perhaps the first time in political science, it was possible to provide some simple imagery to help us understand the scope of our interests in most inclusive terms. There I depicted political life in simplistic form as a black box with inputs,

[3] 9 *World Politics* (1957), 383–400.

372 / *The Political System*

outputs, and feedback. Since then, the discipline and scholars from adjacent disciplines have continued to ring the changes on this diagram; it is pleasing to see that systems analytic formulations now abound in one guise or another.

Nothing could appear to be more removed from the rich variety of political life than a box with arrows indicating inputs of demands and support, their conversion into outputs of authoritative decisions, and feedback processes representing the importance of output consequences for the next round of inputs. Yet, despite its clearly abstract and general quality and despite its construction with the needs of scientific adequacy in mind, this type of systems analysis shows direct relevance for understanding major substantive issues of our times. And this is not an accidental outcome. It resides in the very nature of adequate theory. Kant has proclaimed that a thing cannot be true in theory without also being true in practice. We may go further and parody this by saying that a theory cannot be true in science without also being relevant to society (regardless of how we define truth). Tests of scientific and of social relevance are really not that far apart. A theory that cannot ultimately stand up under both tests would have to be viewed with considerable suspicion.

Systems analysis is a theoretical approach that in its general orientation tends to facilitate research about practical social issues. In effect, this mode of analysis interprets a political system as a major social arrangement for engaging in collective action. It must therefore draw attention to the problems that members of a system identify—as demands—or fail to identify, to the decisions that they adopt for specific purposes—the outputs, to the kinds of action taken to implement these goals—the outcomes, and to the support available within the system for undertaking any collective action at all. Because a political system is viewed as a purposefully organized form of behavior, this theoretical approach focuses our attention on why some purposes are selected for action while others are ignored or rejected, why some kinds of action are in fact taken, and what their consequences are for satisfying the wants and needs of various members of the system. In effect, therefore, because the raw material upon which political systems work consists of social problems, systems analysis has had to be problem-oriented in its approach.

For example, this mode of analysis suggests that at the outset we inquire into the presence or absence of demands for the consideration of those matters most directly related to the critical issues of the day.[4] Who, if anyone, has put demands into the system about these issues? What kinds of needs and wants give rise to demands that have been made? Why were the demands so slow in emerging during the last two decades as the present crises were taking shape? Why is it that certain members of the system who might have been expected to make such demands did not in fact do so? For example, why have the poor appeared so apathetic about their own needs and interests? Even when they or others in their name have put in such demands, what circumstances have led to the demands being ignored or sidetracked? This leads directly to a much larger question: What conditions keep vital concerns off the political agenda (demands) of the system even when in retrospect their significance cannot be denied? Who controls what has been designated as the area of non-decision such as, until very recently, ecological pollution, urban blight, hunger amid plenty, and population growth?

In short, a systems analytic approach alerts us to search for an understanding of how it comes about that what later turn out to be critical needs for the society are not, in fact, even formulated as demands, or if they are, they never manage to reach the stage of viable political issues. It opens up the whole vital practical matter of how agenda for discussion are controlled in political systems and the impact of this control on the satisfaction of expressed or unarticulated needs. On the demand-input side, this framework of analysis is as germane as the substantive interests of the political re-

[4] My fullest statement of a systems approach appears in *A Framework for Political Analysis* (Englewood Cliffs, N.J.: Prentice-Hall, 1965) and *A Systems Analysis of Political Life* (New York: Wiley, 1965).

search worker will require it to be. If for historical reasons political scientists were to continue to ask questions that accept the ongoing system, without doubt the substantive questions will have little bite. But if the political scientist observes serious deficiencies in the operation of the system, the concepts suggested by an approach such as systems analysis, as basic as it is in intention, nonetheless provide a direct means for illuminating sources of these defects.

What applies to demand-inputs also applies to outputs. Characteristically, political science has sought to understand how outputs are produced—the contributions of the executive, legislative, and administrative agencies and the relationship of their behavior to organized interest groups, informal public opinion, and the like. In spite of the vast efforts at research in this area, the complexities of the conversion process are still poorly understood. We have an infinity of detail about how participants in the allocative process act but very little overall understanding. Systems analysis suggests that we need to interpret outputs as a gigantic conversion process whereby demands are or are not transformed into issues and the latter in turn are or are not transformed into outputs. Partial theory is called for to identify and show the relationship among the multiplicity of factors contributing to the outputs. Attention is here drawn in a systematic way to a critical control point in determining what it is that a system does with the demands that are presented, that is, how it performs for meeting wants and needs.

In formulating a systems approach I have also suggested that we need to distinguish carefully between outputs and outcomes. Otherwise we shall have great difficulty in understanding the impact of whatever authoritative allocations are in fact made and their reactive effect on the members of the system. By the end of the 1960s it was becoming apparent that decisions need to be separated clearly and systematically from their social effects. The road to social disaster may be paved with the best of intentions. Laws (authoritative allocations) passed to reduce poverty, inhibit pollution, or ease racial tensions may in fact end up by aggravating the very conditions they are designed to alleviate. Recent concern for the generation of social indicators to estimate more reliably the effect of outputs on bringing about changes in society—of crime, poverty, safety, political apathy and involvement, health, and the like—represents a first step toward formally differentiating outputs (laws) from outcomes (social effects). With reliable time series as measures of various social conditions it will be possible to explore the association of changing outputs with states of society in specific areas such as those mentioned. My theoretical emphasis on outcomes as against outputs therefore suggests tools of analysis for understanding some political sources of present discontents and of the accumulating social and political crises of the 1970s.

Furthermore, as political scientists, systems analysis calls upon us to assess the strictly political effects of exclusion of certain demands and their related needs, the failure to meet other demands, or error in estimating the consequences of outputs for satisfying demands or unarticulated wants. As I have formulated the problems here, we may usefully examine these feedback effects with respect to the input of support for various components of a political system; the authorities, regime, and political community. This kind of research focus would reveal many of the sources of the current decline in confidence in political authority in the United States and of the conditions that are creating pressures for fundamental change. As has become so clear by the 1970s, the cumulative effect of indifference to the needs of the poor, the blacks, and other ethnic groups alone has created a tide of discontent that has been keeping the system on the threshold of violent eruptions. Together with outputs in foreign policy, the inadequacy or absence of outputs in the other areas mentioned, has over the years seriously eroded the input of support for the authorities and the regime from such groups as the blacks and other ethnic minorities, the students, the poor, and even large segments of the middle class. A thorough study of the feedback effects of outputs would reveal some of the important sources of this unparalleled political disaffection.

These are but small samplings of the kind of immediate

social problems that are pointed up by a systems analytical approach. They suggest that this kind of analysis of a political system, formal as it has appeared to be, is not inimical to the identification and investigation of what intuitively we recognize as central substantive issues confronting society.

Although the adequacy of a conceptual structure (as a step on the road to a political theory) cannot rest on its social relevance alone, it is not an unhappy circumstance when such a body of concepts does turn out to draw attention to variables that help us to understand the possible sources of urgent current problems. If a theory is scientifically adequate, this is its own reward. Basic research means precisely that: Research without regard for its possible uses. We may hope that in due course its applied utility will emerge. But if the theory in its initial formulation goes beyond this and is clearly applicable to the topics of the day, this is a dividend that we cannot ignore. Indeed, it is a goal toward which we might strive today. We might self-consciously wish to seek those basic theories that conform to criteria of scientific significance and yet which also display a high level of readily available social utility. Systems analysis illustrates the plausibility of seeking to develop theoretical approaches that are significant on both levels, however successful we may choose to adjudge it for either purpose. It was with this possible dual role for theory in mind for the present era that in my presidential address I felt it was realistic to plead for more relevant basic research.

It should be clear that the differences between *The Political System* and "The New Revolution in Political Science" do not lie in basic assumptions either about the utility of scientific method in political research or about the intellectual integrity of political science as a discipline. In both these essays I see modern behavioral science and its methodological commitments as central to the growth of more reliable understanding of political systems. But since the publication of *The Political System* social circumstances have changed dramatically. These changes have demanded a reconsideration of the nature of the immediate tasks confronting our discipline. In 1953 the challenge was the acceptance of a rigorous methodology that could produce knowledge of an intersubjectively valid sort. Today the need for a commitment of this kind is questioned by very few. It has seemed to me that the times now call for dedication in the application of whatever knowledge we may have to transparently critical problems. This does not imply the abandonment of or even a retrenchment in our search for basic understanding. But it does require a reordering of our concerns. It imposes on us the obligation to increase greatly the resources to be devoted to meet the needs of the day.

In broadest perspectives the present tasks confronting our discipline remind us that science can never be allowed to become the dead hand of the past that constricts the present. Science must remain a living, growing set of ideas, adaptable to changing needs by the way it orders its priorities, yet faithful to its purposes for increasing the reliability of our knowledge about man in society. We are faced with the question not of a new science but of an appropriate contemporary strategy for science.

Index

accommodation. *See* theory, equilibrium

action and research, 345–7

adjustment. *See* theory, equilibrium

administration:
politics of, 180 n.
public, generalizations in 33–4; policy-makers and data of, 39; psychological research in, 213–216

aggregates, social, groupings as, 185–191; groups as, 180–5; organizations as, 182–5; types of, 180–91

allocation of values, authoritative, allocation of values, 129–31; as a minimum condition for maintenance of a society, 136–7; as central question of political research, 106, 126–48; authority, 131–3; formal vs. effective, 130–1; international society and, 138–9; legitimacy and, 132–3; need for, 135–41; non-literate society and, 139–41; psychological determinants of, 200–18; situational determinants of, 149–99; society and, 133–41; validity of this orientation, 146–7; *see also* policy

American Political Science Association, attitudes towards research of, 77; Committee on Instruction (1916), 47 n.; Committee on Policy (1930), 47 n.; Committee on Political Research, 75; conceptual interests of, 67; Report of the Committee for the Advancement of Teaching, 38 n.

American Political Science Review, 338

analysis, systems, *see* systems analysis

Anderson, W., 38 n.

Anshen, R., 24 n.

Appleby, P., 47 n.

applied science, 78–89, 334–7, 346, 349–57

Aristotle, 3, 7, 104, 235, 293, 309

Ash, M. A., 268 n.

Austin, J., 157

authority, 129, 131–3; *see also* allocation of values, authoritative

Bacon, F., 8

Bagehot, W., 163–5

Bantu, 140, 141

Barnard, C. I., 268 n.

basic research, 334–7, 349–57; relevance of, 368–77

Bauer, R. A., 336 n.

Beard, C., 68 n., 188–9, 219

behavior, political, consequences of attention to, 206–17; meaning of, 151; political process contrasted to, 203–06; *see also* data, behavioral; motivation; personality; psychology

behavioralism, 324; model of, 328, 330–2; and professional image, 342–3

behaviorism, Bentley and, 177–9; distinguished from political behavior, 151, 202

Ben-David, J., 355 n.

Bendix, R., 24 n.

Bennett, J. W., 135 n., 190 n.

Bentham, Jeremy, 10, 154–5, 202

Bentley, A. F., 94–5 n., 149, 176–9, 180 n., 189–90, 192, 270–2, 277, 280–1, 297 n., 298, 307

Bergson, H., 161

Black, D., 268 n.

Bodin, Jean, 157

Bryce, J., 64, 71–5, 79

DAVID EASTON

received his Ph.D. in 1947 from Harvard University. Since then he has taught at the University of Chicago, where he is Andrew MacLeish Distinguished Service Professor of Political Science. He has been a Fellow at the Center for Advanced Study in the Behavioral Sciences at Stanford, California. In 1960–61 he was Ford Professor of Governmental Affairs at the University of Chicago. He served as President of the American Political Science Association in 1968–69 and as President of the International Committee on Social Science Documentation in 1969–71. He has been elected a Fellow of the American Academy of Arts and Sciences. Currently he is a member of the Board of Editors of *Behavioral Science* and *Youth and Society*. Among his various publications are the well-known books *A Framework for Political Analysis* and *A Systems Analysis of Political Life*.

A NOTE ON THE TYPE

The text of this book was set on the Linotype in a face called TIMES ROMAN, *designed by* STANLEY MORISON *for* The Times (*London*), *and first introduced by that newspaper in the middle nineteen thirties.*

Among typographers and designers of the twentieth century, Stanley Morison has been a strong forming influence, as typographical adviser to the English Monotype Corporation, as a director of two distinguished English publishing houses, and as a writer of sensibility, erudition, and keen practical sense.

In 1930 Morison wrote: "Type design moves at the pace of the most conservative reader. The good type-designer therefore realises that, for a new fount to be successful, it has to be so good that only very few recognize its novelty. If readers do not notice the consummate reticence and rare discipline of a new type, it is probably a good letter." It is now generally recognized that in the creation of Times Roman *Morison successfully met the qualifications of this theoretical doctrine.*

Composed, printed, and bound by H. WOLFF, *New York. Designed by* HARRY FORD.